USING LITERATURE ACTIVITIES TO TEACH CONTENT AREAS TO EMERGENT READERS

MILDRED R. DONOGHUE

California State University—Fullerton

ALLYN AND BACON

Boston ■ London ■ Toronto ■ Sydney ■ Tokyo ■ Singapore

To the loving memory
of my parents, Caroline and James Ransdorf,
who emigrated from Czechoslovakia
to an even better life in the United States

Vice President: *Paul A. Smith*
Senior Editor: *Arnis E. Burvikovs*
Editorial Assistant: *Patrice Mailloux*
Executive Marketing Manager: *Lisa Kimball*
Editorial-Production Service: *Chestnut Hill Enterprises, Inc.*
Manufacturing Buyer: *Julie McNeill*
Cover Administrator: *Brian Gogolin*
Electronic Composition: *Omegatype Typography, Inc.*

Internet: www.abacon.com

Between the time Website information is gathered and published, some sites may have closed. Also, the transcription of URLs can result in typographical errors. The publishers would appreciate notification where these occur so that they may be corrected in subsequent editions.

Library of Congress Cataloging-in-Publication Data

Donoghue, Mildred R.
    Using literature activities to teach content areas to emergent readers / Mildred R. Donoghue.
        p.   cm.
    Includes bibliographical references and index.
    ISBN 0-205-31825-8 (pbk.)
    1. Children's literature—Study and teaching (Early childhood)   2. Reading (Early childhood)   3. Children—Books and reading.   4. Interdisciplinary approach in education.
    I. Title.

LB1139.5.L58 D65   2001
372.64'044—dc21

00-060899

Printed in the United States of America
10 9 8 7 6 5 4   05   04   03

CONTENTS

CHAPTER THREE

Forty Literature Activities Promoting Science Understandings   33

PART C   MATHEMATICS AND EMERGENT LITERACY   59

CHAPTER FOUR

Mathematics for Young Children   61

CHAPTER FIVE

Forty-five Literature Activities Promoting Mathematical Understandings   77

PART D   SOCIAL STUDIES AND EMERGENT LITERACY   105

CHAPTER SIX

Social Studies for Young Children   107

CHAPTER SEVEN

Forty Literature Activities Promoting Social Studies Understandings   121

Low reading scores reported in the 1990s for elementary public school students caused considerable alarm, although the 1998 results among the National Assessment of Educational Progress (NAEP) reading scores published for fourth graders in 39 states (and the District of Columbia) showed some gains. Nevertheless, about half of the country's students are still unable to read at "the most fundamental level," according to the *Los Angeles Times*, which is continuing its Reading by 9 Literacy Project with a full daily page entitled "The Kids' Reading Room."

These low scores have caused increased emphasis on skills development, *chiefly in the lower grades*, which in turn has resulted in:

- Limited coverage of literature in reading sessions due to time constraints and
- Near elimination of content area instruction, especially in science and social studies and to some extent in math, due to the additional time demanded by administrators and parents for literacy instruction of young children.

The latter situation exists despite the acknowledged need for all students entering the intermediate grades to have at least a minimal background in the content areas in order to progress satisfactorily through the challenging and lengthy assignments in social studies, science, and math in grades 4–6.

It is imperative, therefore, that we encourage emergent literacy without sacrificing literature or an introduction to some of the basic concepts in the content areas. The early childhood curriculum provides the foundation for all other school learning, and we must use prudently the time allotted us.

ORGANIZATION

Using Literature Activities to Teach Concept Areas to Emergent Readers is divided into four parts. Part A, Chapter One, Literacy, Learning, and Literature, serves as an introduction to the book, describing emergent literacy, how children learn, and the importance of literature as a critical component of emergent literacy.

Part B consists of two chapters on science and emergent literacy. Chapter Two, Science for Young Children, is a narrative account of the four areas of content for young children: earth and space science, life science, physical science, and health science. It also lists content standards at both the national and state levels, and discusses assessment in early elementary science. Chapter Three, Literature Activities Promoting Science Understandings, is evenly divided among the four content areas and offers coverage of 40 books of literature for early childhood.

Part C, Mathematics and Emergent Literacy, also consists of two chapters. Chapter Four, Mathematics for Young Children, defines the five content standards published in 2000 by the National Council of Teachers of Mathematics: number and operations; algebra; geometry; measurement; and data analysis and probability. It also describes program principles, key vocabulary/symbols, and assessment in early elementary mathematics. Chapter Five, Literature Activities Promoting Mathematical Understandings, provides coverage of 45 literature titles for early childhood divided among the five content area.

Part D, Social Studies and Emergent Literacy, again comprises two chapters. Chapter Six, Social Studies for Young Children, discusses content standards; critical concepts in history, geography and economics; analysis skills for history and social sciences; the important process of attitudes and values; and finally, assessment in early elementary social studies. Chapter Seven, Literature Activities Promoting Social Studies Understandings, details coverage of 40 books of literature for kindergarten through third grade.

All literature activities are planned to meet the developmental levels, interests, and abilities of children in grades K to 3 who are emergent readers in the beginning literacy program. There are more than 500 activities divided among the areas of science, social studies, and math, thereby allowing the teacher the opportunity to select from a series of follow-up assignments those that are best suited for any one particular class.

KEY FEATURES

To support lesson planning of literature and literary activities, the book includes several special features:

1. The 125 book selections for which activities have been planned are literature established by listings in one or more of the following: *Best Books for Children* **(R. R. Bowker);** *The Wonderful World of Mathematics* **(National Council of Teachers of Mathematics);** *The Horn Book Magazine; Literature for Science and Mathematics* **(California Department of Education); or** *Literature for History-Social Science* **(California Department of Education).** At least 90 percent of the titles can be found in the highly regarded Bowker reference. One reference is shown for each selection below the brief biographical entry for the book.

Titles include both fiction and nonfiction genres.

2. A useful supplement for teachers unable to locate some of the titles listed in the regular text (or wishing to enrich or explore further specific content material) can be found at the end of Chapters Three, Five, and Seven. These sections noted as *Recent and Recommended: Related Books for Additional Reading* consist of more than 150 titles published in the last decade and deemed as literature in science, math, and social studies by reputable sources.

3. Each read-aloud selection is followed by an average of four optional activities in an effort to meet diverse student needs and classroom situations. Teachers may thus choose to implement one, two, or all of the suggested assignments.

4. The only reading *required* during each activity is done by the teacher (or classroom aide). Children, of course, are encouraged to examine or "read" an earlier read-aloud book after it has been placed on the library table. Among the activities listed after each selection is often one that allows volunteer students to read briefly some of their own written work or some of the shared writing prepared by the group for a class chart.

5. The limited amount of writing (composition) during some of the activities can again be done by the teacher (or classroom aide) as he or she takes dictation from the children. This proven link from oral to written language piques students' interest and is a step in modeling and thereby encouraging emergent literacy.

6. The limited amount of handwriting completed by the children during some of the activities is often an exercise during which students can *copy and practice* letters, words, and short sentences from the chalkboard or from an overhead transparency.

(A few may even begin by drawing some of the letters.) Studies have shown that a desire to "write" is another important first step in emergent literacy.

7. A bibliography of children's books cited appears twice, once at the end of the appropriate chapters (Two through Seven) and again in the Index of Children's Literature at the end of the book for quick reference.

ACKNOWLEDGMENTS

This book would not have become a reality without the professional interest and practical support of two members of the College of Human Development and Community Service at California State University–Fullerton: Dr. Soraya M. Coley, Dean; and Dr. Tom Savage, chairman of the Department of Elementary, Bilingual, and Reading Education from 1995–1999.

I would also like to express my appreciation to my editors, Virginia Lanigan and Arnis Burvikvos and their editorial assistant, Patrice Mailloux, all of whom were always supportive of my efforts and tolerant of my queries. Thanks, too, to the reviewers of the manuscript for their insights and comments: Professor Kaye W. Anderson, California State University, Long Beach; and Professor Cathy Collins Block, Texas Christian University. Special thanks to Nancy Anderson of the Santa Ana (CA) Unified School District for her artistic talent and photographic skill; and to Kathleen Donoghue Merritt and Virginia White for their assistance in the preparation of the final draft of the manuscript. Finally, I am grateful to my daughter, Kathleen, and my son, James, for their continuing pride in my work.

Mildred R. Donoghue

LITERACY, LEARNING, AND LITERATURE

CHAPTER ONE

LITERATURE AND EMERGENT LITERACY

Literacy is a critically important, multifaceted, and complex process. Events and activities that promote it start as early as infancy as children begin to develop their language skills. The relationship among the communication skills (reading, writing, listening, and speaking) is ongoing and occurs in daily contexts. The more young children know about the functions and nature of language before they start kindergarten, the better their chances are for a successful reading and writing experience in school.

EMERGENT LITERACY

Emergent literacy has been described as the earliest phase of literacy development, the time between birth and the period when children read and write conventionally (Sulzby & Teale, 1991).

How Students Become Literate

There are several assumptions about the ways that young children acquire literacy. *First*, they acquire literacy skills as others read aloud to them. Boys and girls enjoy the emotional interaction between the reader and the audience, and gradually comprehend more about books generally, and specifically, how print is used. They learn how to handle books, and especially appreciate repeated readings of the same story. After a read-aloud, students may complete a wide variety of activities suited to their particular interests and abilities. Still, not every read-aloud session demands further student work; many sessions can end simply with a general feeling of pleasure by the audience and a wish to listen to another book soon. (This assumption of how children learn to read and write will be explored at greater length later in this chapter.)

Second, as boys and girls observe others reading and writing, they imitate this behavior as they participate in meaningful activities that are relevant to them. From "reading and/or writing" grocery lists, telephone numbers, cereal boxes, magazines, and the mail, they become familiar with forms of literacy; they understand their purposes and pretend to use them in dramatic play. They realize that their everyday needs can be met as they read and write.

Third, students interact socially in their reading and writing efforts with peers and adults. Outside of school, family members and friends who reply to them in writing help promote literacy among young children. Inside the classrooms, it is the teachers who respond to the journal writings of boys and girls so that those writings become progressively longer and more detailed. They also encourage students to share their written thoughts with others in small groups.

Fourth, children build on life experiences that they have had prior to starting kindergarten. Many begin school with considerable information about writing and reading gained from reading environmental print (e.g., street signs) and understanding the usefulness of knowing how to read (e.g., a restaurant menu) and write (e.g., a postcard to their grandparents). Young girls and boys can tell the difference between drawing and writing (even if it is illegible scribbles) and associate books with reading. Some even recognize the left-to-right progression of print and the difference between the beginning and the ending of a book, and know how to turn pages and where to start reading. Children's use of oral language gained from past experiences is a necessary component of concepts reinforced in literacy lessons.

Fifth, children learn to read and write through direct instruction. If they have a special interest in the literacy task assigned (e.g., writing invitations to a parent or grandparent to attend a Thanksgiving program in their classroom), they will gain more than by completing a worksheet about the Letter of the Week. Nevertheless, they still need explicit instruction in the many areas involved in the literacy process. Such teaching can occur in whole-class or small group settings, or during individual conferences. Without it, students will not acquire many of the critical skills involved in reading and writing.

Sixth, children realize that, while their own reading and writing efforts differ from those of adults, their ideas about communicating with written language are still important and will eventually conform to adult models as they progress through the grades. Young children need many opportunities to develop and practice their skills in a risk-free setting.

Seventh, children understand that writing and reading are interrelated and difficult to separate from one other. They learn about writing by reading and further their reading skills by writing. They sense that written language is the other major element of communication, and that it is related to oral language, which they use daily.

Emergent Readers: Some Successful, Some at Risk

We know from The National Research Council that the more girls and boys know about literacy and language before starting school, the better prepared they are to be successful readers (Snow, Burns, & Griffin, 1998). Their accomplishments can be summarized as follows: Children possess phonological awareness that language is composed of smaller units (such as words, syllables, and sounds) as well as oral language skills; they are motivated to learn and appreciate literate forms; and they have letter knowledge and print awareness. The Council cautions against confusing phonological awareness with phonics, as the development of such awareness in the preschool period is a critical step toward comprehending the alphabetic principle—and eventually learning to read.

Once the children arrive at school, the necessary—and obvious—agent for reading success is carefully prepared instruction, with formal reading programs focusing on developing mastery in both comprehension and word recognition (Snow, Burns, & Griffin, 1998). Young girls and boys need to be given opportunities at school to: practice and intensify language, vocabulary, and comprehension skills; use writing and reading as learning tools; experience the satisfaction of becoming literate; explore and eventually master the numerous functions of written language; understand the relationships between the sounds of speech and the spellings of words so they can recognize and spell printed words; listen to and discuss literary read-alouds; and be enrolled in intervention or remediation programs as early as possible if they appear to be at risk.

Among students potentially at risk are six distinct groups (Snow, Burns, & Griffin, 1998; Burns, Griffin, & Snow, 1999). The *first* contains children with limited English proficiency, with Hispanic students in the United States targeted as being at particularly high risk. Some language minority students start school with no English proficiency and speak a language for which there are no resource materials and no available proficient instructors. Other language minority students may begin their formal education with no English proficiency, but for them there are instructional guides and locally fluent teachers.

Related to members of the first group are children unfamiliar with standard English dialect, and these comprise the *second* group of students who find learning to read laborious. When the home dialect children speak differs from the dialect presented in the classroom (and in the reading materials used), it becomes critical to stress phonemic awareness. Especially important is an appreciation of the phonemes that are involved in the way that words are spelled (e.g., *sold,* not *sol*).

Another group of young children risking reading difficulties includes boys and girls living in low-income communities, often with uneducated parents who are also unable to provide even adequate nutrition for their families. Kindergartens enrolling many such students of the *third* group who are poorly prepared in literacy skills may offer reading programs especially planned to help bolster the negative effects of community poverty.

Young children assigned to attend an elementary school whose achievement levels are chronically low comprise the *fourth* group of students facing reading difficulties. A *fifth* group is made up of children who suffer from hearing impairments, severe cognitive deficiencies, and/or early language impairments; and a *sixth* group contains boys and girls whose parents have a history of reading problems.

Briefly, however, despite what is known about the prevention of reading difficulties in young children, a recent review of prediction studies (Snow, Burns, & Griffin, 1998) concludes that *no single, individual risk factor is sufficiently valid to be of any practical value for forecasting which students will encounter reading problems in school.*

Reading Aloud to Children

Whether students entering kindergarten are marked as being at-risk or whether they are apt to become fluent readers who use and acquire comprehension strategies and

A young girl reads silently a picture book read aloud earlier by her teacher.

skills in order to obtain meaning from the text and who understand and use the alphabetic principle, both groups of children benefit from listening to books read aloud to them by teachers and other adults. According to a research summary (Jalongo, 2000), such reading aloud has been found to have an overall positive effect on the students' motivation to read, their interest and appreciation of literature, their understanding of different kinds of texts, their knowledge of varied writing abilities and literary styles, their reading competence and strategies, and, finally, their vocabulary growth and listening comprehension.

Since young children beg to hear a book read again and again, there are specifically two major conclusions from considerable research on the value of repeated read-alouds (Jalongo, 2000). The first is that children learn how to discuss a story over time and then initiate additional conversations about it, because the interactions between the reader and the audience change as the same books are read over and over again. Adult readers can promote these enriching discussions by asking questions that require children to predict, compare/contrast, classify, and evaluate.

The second conclusion is that after repeated read-alouds of their special favorites, students show more insight about the story aspects, moving away from superficial traits of characters and plot to questioning the relationships among the characters and the underlying meaning of events. Adult readers can encourage the growth of such insight in young children by facilitating read-alouds and repeated readings through strategies such as: visits to the school library media center and local public library whenever story hours are scheduled; bookpack programs which circulate familiar books, often accompanied by tapes; recordings of beloved stories placed at listening centers; recommended software programs of storybook favorites; and, particularly, frequent opportunities for students to retell treasured stories using impromptu drama or flannel board figures.

The significance of the last-described strategy of the children's reenacting or retelling a story was investigated in a study (Nielsen, 1993) of eighty-seven low-achieving kindergarten students assigned to one of four story reading groups for a total of eighteen sessions over a period of six weeks. They were divided into three literacy achievement levels based on measures of story structure, concepts about print (i.e., an overall understanding of how print can be used), and story comprehension. Those in Group One simply listened to the eighteen books with no follow-up. Those in Group Two had a directed reading format with discussions led by teacher questioning. Read-alouds for Group Three focused on story structure followed by activities that gave repeated experiences with the same story (e.g., retelling with puppets and reenactment). Group Four read-alouds concentrated on concepts of print, and the children had repeated experiences with the book by constructing a chart showing a briefer version of the book, then rereading that chart and, finally, illustrating individual copies of the chart.

Nielsen (1993) found that it was the low-achieving students in Group Three that did significantly better than the low achievers in all other groups. Furthermore, these same girls and boys, who had had repeated opportunities to retell the stories, even outperformed average students in Group One and did as well as the high achievers in Group One. It should be emphasized at this point that many of the achievements of reading aloud as measured in kindergarten have been significantly related to reading achievement results in grades one through three (Snow, Burns, & Griffin, 1998).

Finally, while most read-alouds with young children are fiction, there has been some interest during the recent decade in using nonfiction books, too. Surprisingly, it was found that teachers consistently and spontaneously altered the instructional emphases of the follow-up discussion and activities depending on whether they were asked to read storybooks, informational texts, or easy-to-read picture books (Mason, Peterman, & Kerr, 1989). Both they and the students even changed the complexity of

An emergent reader dictates a new story ending to her teacher.

the language they used, depending on the type of book chosen. Fiction read-alouds followed the usual pattern of prereading, during-reading, and post-reading experiences. Nonfiction read-alouds, on the other hand, had children involved in activities intended to aid them in relating the text to their daily life, to examine and test causes, and to acquire new vocabulary by developing underlying concepts rather than by merely defining the words.

Beginning Readers and Writers

The children with the least experience in reading are generally the youngest in the class. They may or may not be aware that the print on the page corresponds to what the reader says. When they bring a book to share with the class, it is the teacher who does most of the reading. At times with a pattern book, however, the owners will chime in with the refrain because the storyline is easy to predict, (e.g., *Have You Seen My Cat?* by Eric Carle, which has only three sentences: the title, the answer and another statement).

Gradually after "reading" an easy pattern book, the student will master the pattern and recite the text from memory. Nevertheless, the concept of one-to-one correspondence of print to sound is still not completely understood; and, despite finger-pointing, the child can readily lose his or her place on the page. Repeated reading of the same book, however, will slowly develop a student's confidence together with a growing awareness of the word-to-sound correspondence.

The beginning writer also needs to experiment with sounds and letters on unlined paper, lined paper, or a board, using pencils, markers, or a paintbrush. Most of early writing efforts resemble scribbles; still their owners can "read" them and will do so proudly.

A checklist of characteristics of the beginning reader and writer is shown in Figure 1.1.

FIGURE 1.1   Characteristics of the Beginning Reader and Writer

Name _____ Date: _____	YES	NO	SOMETIMES
KNOWLEDGE OF LITERACY The child understands: ■ that reading is meaning-making and expects print to make sense;			
■ that writing is talk written down;			
■ that print holds meaning and conveys information;			
■ that reading is a worthwhile skill to achieve;			
■ that books are enjoyable;			
■ that books will be about something related to the pictures.			
READING BEHAVIOR The child: ■ likes to listen to stories, rhymes, poems;			
■ has favorite stories, can't miss a word of old favorites;			
■ "role plays" self as a reader; likes to look at books, handles books voluntarily;			
■ knows how to hold a book and turn the pages one at a time, front to back;			
■ reads pictures and knows you can predict meaning from them; draws on prior knowledge to "read";			
■ understands print directionality. Words in English start on the left and move to the right, and go from top to bottom;			
■ can show you words;			
■ knows where to find title and author's name;			
■ knows where a story begins and ends;			
■ tries to read environmental print, knows some words by sight such as own name and names of family members;			
■ reads pattern books, memorizes them holistically;			
■ relies heavily on picture clues and on language patterns to aid memorization of text;			
■ can hear rhyme;			
■ matches beginning and final sounds accurately;			
■ does not read word for word;			
■ can retell the main events of the story;			
■ reads at a literal level;			
■ borrows materials to read to others.			

(continued)

FIGURE 1.1 *Continued*

	YES	NO	SOMETIMES
WRITING BEHAVIOR These descriptors are shown as a continuum. Children move from random scribbling to representing words with letters.			
The child: ■ scribbles and plays with paper and pencil;			
■ uses arbitrary symbols to represent sounds or words;			
■ uses letters to represent sounds and words but without sound–letter accuracy;			
■ writes without spacing;			
■ hears only one major sound in a word;			
■ hears more than one sound in a word;			
■ knows names of letters in sequence;			
■ recognizes individual letters and can say their names;			
■ has beginnings of accurate sound–letter accuracy, knows some letters by sound and by name.			

From *Better Books! Better Readers!* By L. Hart—Hewins and Jan Wells. © 1999. Reprinted with permission of Stenhouse Publishers, a division of Pembroke Publishers Limited. FAX 905-477-3691.

HOW CHILDREN LEARN

What is known today about literacy learning and how young children acquire and develop language is based on the support from theories from the past; these supply explanations of how language and thought are developmentally interwoven. Two major theories are those formulated by Jean Piaget of Switzerland and Lev Vygotsky of Russia. Educators of young children also understand the interactive process known as learning and teaching and are familiar with the learning styles or multiple intelligences identified by Howard Gardner of the United States.

One Theorist of Concept Development: Piaget

Piaget identified four periods of mental or cognitive development and growth: The sensorimotor period (from birth to about age two); the preoperational period (extending from ages two to seven); the concrete operations period (generally from ages seven to eleven); and the formal operations period (from age eleven through adulthood). Educators involved in emergent literacy are concerned with the second period and the early stages of the third.

During the preoperational period, young children develop preconcepts (which are incomplete or immature concepts compared to those reached in later periods) and use speech increasingly to express their knowledge of concepts. Words are tied to activities and the children's ability to use language is deemed one of the symbolic behaviors of this period. They use these behaviors in their representational play, and their later understanding of letters, written words, and numerals is founded on this earlier understanding of symbolic functions or behaviors. These children are completely self-centered; everything is based on what they see.

Important characteristics of preoperational students are *centration* (or the ability to focus on only the most obvious aspects of what is seen), and an *inability to conserve* (or reverse physical change mentally). Children work with precursors of conservation when they count, compare, and do one-to-one correspondence. During this period, students work on *classification* (or grouping items logically on the basis of some commonality such as shape or color), and *seriation* (or placing items in a logical sequence such as large to small).

Between ages five and seven, the preoperational children transition to the period of concrete operations, at their own individual rates. During this time some are still preoperational while other students are conservers, and this continues to be an important concern for kindergarten and primary teachers as they plan.

Piaget believed that children acquire knowledge by constructing it as they interact with their environment and try to make sense out of everything that they encounter. They must be able to connect something new with something they already know. He divided knowledge into three areas: social (or conventional), logico-mathematical, and physical. *Social-conventional knowledge* is the sort that is created and agreed on by people, e.g., the names of the days of the week. The other two areas are learned simultaneously and depend on each other. *Logico-mathematical knowledge* (whose source is the relationships mentally constructed inside each child) covers connections that students make individually in order to organize information, e.g., classifying the various species at the zoo. *Physical knowledge* (whose source is external observable reality) covers learning about objects in the environment and their traits, e.g., what happens when a ball rolls down an incline.

Four factors facilitate the construction of physical knowledge among young learners (Kamii & De Vries, 1993). First, the child must be able to try things out in different ways. Then there must be a connection between what the young child does and how that substance or object reacts. Third, the more the child sees how that substance or object responds, the better. Finally, the faster the reaction time of the substance or object, the more the child learns.

Another Theorist of Concept Development: Vygotsky

Vygotsky accepted only Piaget's sensorimotor period, which covered birth to approximately the age of two years. He believed that, after that period, culture and cultural signs are needed to produce and expand new thoughts. *Signs* was the term he used to describe the mental tools that people develop to help them master their own behavior. External speech is the most important sign system because it allows children to interact socially and represents the first step in internalized thinking. Writing and numbering are also vital sign systems.

Unlike Piaget, who believed that children should construct knowledge independently, Vygotsky advocated the concept of the zone of proximal development (ZPD), which is the area between where the child is operating independently in his or her mental growth and where the child can go with assistance from a parent, teacher, or other adult or even a more mature peer. He believed that, while language acquisition is partly biological, teachers must identify each child's ZPD and plan developmentally appropriate instruction because language stimulates conceptual learning. That learning in turn will depend on interactions with people and objects in the environment. The development of higher order mental functions begins in social interaction and later is internalized psychologically. According to Vygotsky, it is adults who constitute the major force for motivating children to extend their language.

Both Vygotsky and Piaget believed that thinking processes are developmental and that they grow from within each child's system. And, while the work of the two theorists fails to explain everything that educators should know about learning (Bredekamp & Rosegrant, 1992), it is helpful in overcoming the man-made dichotomies that too frequently arise in early childhood education.

Learning/Teaching as an Interactive Process

Several assumptions about the interactive process known as learning and teaching are accepted by educators of young children (Bredekamp & Rosegrant, 1992). First, boys and girls learn best when they feel safe psychologically and their physical needs are being met; school programs must, therefore, support children's emotional and social development and respect their biological needs. Second, students construct their own knowledge through interactions between themselves and their social and physical environments; their emergent literacy demonstrates that children even construct their understanding of written language.

Third, children learn through social interaction with other human being; such interaction is necessary for the development of social competence, self-esteem, and, most importantly, the intellect (Vygotsky, 1978). Fourth, children learn through play, which contributes to the growth of representational thought and offers opportunities to practice newly acquired skills or deepen conceptual understandings. Fifth, children's interests and "need to know" stimulate learning; intrinsic motivation for learning is found in activities based on student interests as well as individual abilities.

Sixth, human development and learning are marked by a wide range of individual and normal variation; patterns and timing of growth and development, cultural backgrounds, family experiences, and learning styles vary from adult to adult and from child to child. Seventh, young children's learning is made up of a cycle of four repeating processes; every time that a new experience occurs or a new concept is met, six-, seven- and eight-year-olds will move through all four levels (Rosegrant, 1989). (Preschoolers and kindergarteners only reach the third level.) The first process is *awareness*, which develops from experience and involves recognition of people, objects, events, or concepts. The second is *exploration* as the child determines the components of what is being learned by using the various senses with people, objects, events, or concepts. At this level direct, hands-on experiences with the content are needed so that it becomes personally meaningful to that child. *Inquiry* is the third process whereby children compare their own concepts or behaviors with those observed in the society and then modify their generalizations to cultural conventions. Finally, when students are able to apply their learning to new situations and settings and employ it for a variety of different purposes, they have reached the fourth process, *utilization.*

Educators of young children realize that the learning cycle is not hierarchical (with one process being valued over another) nor is it linear, as some children may be exploring and inquiring at the same time. The cycle does agree with the theories of Piaget and Vygotsky in that they both believed that learning starts with awareness and exploration and that concept development moves from the naturalistic to the informal and then to structured experiences.

Learning Styles or Capacities for Learning: Multiple Intelligences

Eight learning styles have been identified by Gardner (1993), who calls them multiple intelligences or capacities for learning: linguistic, logical–mathematical, spatial, bodily–kinesthetic, musical, interpersonal, intrapersonal, and naturalistic.

Linguistic intelligence deals with word sense and the capacity to use words well in spoken and written language; students who are strongly linguistic use language to express themselves and to understand other people. *Logical–mathematical* intelligence, sometimes termed scientific thinking, is the ability to recognize important problems and resolve them through both inductive and deductive thinking; students who are strongly logical–mathematical think by reasoning. *Spatial* intelligence is the ability to visualize, create, and recreate accurate mental images of the visual world; students who are strongly spatial think in pictures and images. *Bodily–kinesthetic* intelligence relates to physical movement and the ability to use one's whole body or body parts (e.g., fingers and hands) in highly skilled ways to express ideas and solve problems; students who are strongly bodily–kinesthetic think through physical sensations and movement.

Musical intelligence is the ability to hear and use musical sounds, to recognize tonal patterns, and to remember them and transform them; students who are strongly musical think through melodies and rhythms. *Interpersonal* intelligence is the ability to handle person-to-person relationships, to interpret accurately the verbal and nonverbal behavior of others, and to display sensitivity to their feelings and moods; students who are strongly interpersonal think by discussing ideas with other people and planning with them. *Intrapersonal* intelligence is the ability to know one's self, to recognize one's strengths and limitations and act accordingly, and to understand one's moods and motivations; students who are strongly intrapersonal think deeply within themselves, and confidently work alone. *Naturalistic* intelligence is the ability to exhibit sensitivity to one's natural surroundings and discriminate among living things; students who are strongly naturalistic think by using sensory input from nature (Gardner, 1995).

Gardner believes that all human beings possess all the intelligences, although, the strength in each intelligence will vary from one individual to another (Checkley, 1997). Readers, for example, will demonstrate all of the intelligences when they finally learn to read successfully, but they may have relied more on some intelligences than on others in order to accomplish their goal (Carreiro, 1998). Furthermore, teachers should not attempt to include all eight intelligences or learning styles in every lesson but, instead, use their understanding of the eight areas to help them identify and respond to student needs. (Lastly, Gardner is considering adding a ninth intelligence to his list, i.e., *existential intelligence,* which would refer to the inclination of humans to question their existence as they ask, Who are we?, Where did we come from?, and Why do we die?)

LITERATURE: A CRUCIAL COMPONENT OF EMERGENT LITERACY

Children's literature has been defined as nonfiction and fiction writing that relates to the developmental levels, activities, and literary interests of the intended audience, offers intellectual stimulation and/or insights, expresses imaginatively and authentically emotions, experiences, and information about the human condition, includes the literary conventions of all nonfiction and fiction, and possesses high literary quality (Goforth, 1998). It specifically excludes instructional materials with controlled vocabulary and prescribed content (i.e., textbooks) as well as newspapers.

The difference between nonfiction and fiction is determined by the content, and there are more nonfiction books than any other type of writing for children (Glazer, 1997). Nonfiction includes informational books and biographies which present concepts, generalizations, and facts about a specific topic or biographee rather than telling a story, although some books do both. Fiction books, on the other hand, are created from the imagination of the author, whether they are based on actual happenings and termed realistic fiction or whether they are pure fancy and defined as fantasy.

Boys and girls listen to and/or read the different genres of literature for a variety of reasons (Stewig, 1988). First, for sheer enjoyment; second, to escape from present situations; third and fourth, to gain understanding of themselves and of others; fifth, to stimulate their imagination; sixth, to gain an understanding of the nature of language; seventh, to learn about other places and times; and, lastly, to gain information.

It has been asserted that literature makes a difference in the lives of children. Those who learn to read early, for instance, are the same students who have been read to by parents, teachers, siblings, or other caring adults. Their later educational achievement is related to early experiences of listening to books. Children's linguistic development is also enriched by exposure to literature; the more advanced the stage of that development, the greater the exposure has been. Girls and boys build their language background from their communicative experiences, with the form and content of their language and stories reflecting the literature they have heard or read (Cullinan, 1989).

Guidelines for Classroom Reading to Young Children: Fiction

Before the reading, teachers may display the cover of the book and invite the class to make predictions about the content. They may discuss the author and illustrator, especially if one or both are already familiar to the children (e.g., Mercer Mayer). They may ask some of the students to describe their own experiences that are related to the probable content of the book, and also discuss the type of book the class will be hearing (e.g., a folktale). They may introduce the boys and girls to the main characters and the setting of the story, as well as stating a purpose for the class to listen to the reading.

During the reading, teachers may encourage each listener to react to the story and possibly make comments about it. Then, in order to help the children comprehend the style and written language used in that story, teachers may explain the text, targeting the important story components, and even rephrase it when necessary. To monitor comprehension, they may also pose occasional questions or have the class make predictions at certain points in the book. They can have some of the children discuss their own interpretations of what is happening in the story.

After the reading, teachers may help students link the experiences that occurred to the main character(s) to similar experiences in their own lives. They may briefly review some of the text components such as setting, problem, and solution. Finally, they should involve the class in one or more follow-up activities that demand reflection about the story.

Guidelines for Classroom Reading to Young Children: Nonfiction Informational Books and Biographies

Before the reading, teachers must assess the children's current understanding of the topic or person presented in the book by leading a discussion about the title, the illustration on the book cover, and student experiences (if any) with the topic. They may introduce specialized vocabulary and briefly demonstrate difficult concepts. They should establish a bridge between what the children already know about the topic or biographee and what they will be learning, so that there is a specific purpose for their listening to the book.

During the reading, teachers should periodically check class comprehension of the text and expand understanding of unfamiliar concepts by providing pictures or demonstrations. These visual representations will promote comments from the children so they can talk more freely about the new concepts. Suggestions can also be made about activities in which the class can participate later to further explore the topic or biography.

After the reading, teachers should allow additional questioning of the text by the students and help them see how informational books and biographies can help them learn more about specific places, people, and things as well as the world in general. Lastly, teachers should involve the class in one or more follow-up activities that will connect the concepts introduced in the text to the everyday experiences of the children.

Evaluating Fiction and Nonfiction Literature for Young Children

Teachers are aware of the criteria for judging the elements of *fiction* written expressly for young boys and girls (Salinger, 1993). First, the plot is well-organized and original, plausible (in realistic fiction), and consistent within the story framework (in fantasy fiction); there is a distinct problem that must be solved, and culminating action that resolves that problem satisfactorily. Second, the characters are clearly developed with personal traits that are apparent and believable; they are free from stereotypes and evolve during actions that are credible in terms of the story.

The third element of fiction, the theme, is clearly recognizable and interwoven throughout the story; it presents positive values without being didactic. Fourth, the content is developmentally appropriate for this age-group and tells a worthwhile story; it is presented accurately (in realistic fiction) and plausibly (in fantasy fiction). And fifth, the style is appropriate for the intended audience and for the subject, and includes an enriched vocabulary that students understand and enjoy. In summary, the book of fiction for young children is well-written, generally with illustrations that broaden and enhance the story, and meets the designated level of student maturity, literacy, and experiential background.

Nonfiction or informational books and biographies are preferred over fiction by many boys and girls, and, therefore, their teachers should recall the four important elements of quality nonfiction. Accuracy is first, with correct and current facts shown in context to support generalizations; theories and opinions are separated from knowledge and there is documentation of information sources. The second element is organization, with a format that is readily understood and logically arranged; there are tables of contents and indices to further help the reader locate specific information. Writing style is the third element: The authors' writing is interesting and clear and its tone reveals their viewpoint on the topic. There is no teleology (or belief that there is an overall plan in nature) and no anthropomorphism or what is known in fiction as *personification* (Glazer, 1997). The fourth and final element is accurate illustrations that not only have artistic excellence but also increase the listeners'/readers' understanding of the text.

Benefits of Using Informational Books to Support Student Learning

Standards recently adopted in science, mathematics, and social studies stress an integrated strategy for acquiring the content and processes of the three curricular areas (Freeman & Person, 1998). These new standards propose decreased emphasis on memorization and drill exercises and greater emphasis on developing concepts and critical thinking in children. As educators become less dependent on textbooks, there is an increased need for literature that promotes meaningful learning experiences in the content areas.

Happily, informational books and biographies offer specific benefits to support integrated learning across the curriculum (Freeman & Person, 1998). Young children can satisfy their innate curiosity and explore topics of special interest to them—that may or may not match those of curriculum developers. Children are able to see inter-relationships and bridges among concepts and content. As they compare and contrast books on the same topic or biographee, they foster their problem-solving skills and critical thinking abilities; they note differences and similarities among data that are included and among the viewpoints of various authors. Through nonfiction books, students can learn about concepts and ideas of today as well as those of other times and places; they broaden their knowledge and excite their imagination. Hearing and reading such books lead children to question and even investigate, thereby aiding in the development of inquiry and problem solving.

Additional reasons for sharing informational books in particular in the primary-grade classroom include: building background knowledge, contributing to a better understanding of the processes and purposes of reading, serving as a catalyst to literacy, and exposing students to a variety of text features and structures (Yopp & Yopp, 1999). The last is especially significant because authors of informational books write in an expository style markedly different from the narrative style of fiction writers since the chief function of an expository text is to communicate information.

A recent study of twenty preliterate kindergarteners in a multicultural setting in a large urban area examined children's knowledge of informational book language in a classroom where read-aloud time had been prolonged to include expository as well as narrative texts (Duke & Kays, 1998). Students were asked to pretend-read an unfamiliar informational book when school started and then again after three months of listening to expository texts during read-aloud periods. The study concluded that young children can gain substantially in their knowledge of strong features of information book language and also generalize that language to reading unfamiliar books in the same genre. These features included standard verb construction, generic noun

Informational picture books help young readers write simple reports.

construction, repetition of topical theme, usage of technical vocabulary, relational/existential verbs (forms of *be* and *have*), general statements at the opening and the closing, and comparative/contrastive statements.

Two other results of the aforementioned study (Duke and Kays, 1998) suggested that young children not only can interact with informational books but also enjoy doing so, and that reading aloud may effectively expose these students to expository books in early childhood classrooms.

REFERENCES

Bredekamp, S. & Rosegrant, T. (Eds.) (1992). *Reaching Potentials: Appropriate Curriculum and Assessment for Young Children, Volume 1.* Washington, DC: National Association for the Education of Young Children.

Burns, M., Griffin, P., & Snow, C. (Eds.) (1999). *Starting Out Right* Washington, DC: National Academy Press.

Carriero, P. (1998). *Tales of Thinking.* York, ME: Stenhouse.

Checkley, K. (1997). The first seven...and the eighth: A conversation with Howard Gardner. *Educational Leadership, 55*(1), 8–13.

Cullinan, B. (1989). Literature for young children. In D. Strickland & L. Morrow (Eds.), *Emerging Literacy: Young Children Learn to Read and Write,* (pp. 35–51). Newark, DE: International Reading Association.

Duke, N. & Kays, J. (1998). "Can I say, 'Once upon a time'?": Kindergarten children developing knowledge of information book language. *Early Childhood Research Quarterly, 13,* 295–318.

Freeman, E. & Person, D. (1998). *Connecting Informational Children's Books with Content Area Learning.* Boston, MA: Allyn and Bacon.

Gardner, H. (1993). *Multiple Intelligences: The Theory in Practice.* New York: Basic Books.

Gardner, H. (1995). Reflections on multiple intelligences. *Phi Delta Kappan, 77,* 200–209.

Glazer, J. (1997). *Introduction to Children's Literature,* 2nd ed. Upper Saddle River, NJ: Merrill/Prentice-Hall.

Goforth, F. (1998). *Literature and the Learner.* Belmont, CA: Wadsworth.

Jalongo, M. (2000). *Early Childhood Language Arts,* 2nd ed. Boston, MA: Allyn and Bacon.

Kamii, C. & DeVries, R. (1993). *Physical Knowledge in Preschool Education: Implications of Piaget's Theory.* Englewood Cliffs, NJ: Prentice-Hall.

Mason, J., Peterman, C., & Kerr, B. (1989). Reading to kindergarten children. In D. Strickland & L. Morrow (Eds.), *Emerging Literacy: Young Children Learn to Read and Write,* (pp. 52–62). Newark, DE: International Reading Association.

Nielsen, D. (1993). The effects of four models of group interaction with storybooks on the literacy growth of low achieving kindergarten children. In D. Leu & C. Kinzer (Eds.), *Examining Central Issues in Literacy Research, Theory and Practice* (pp. 279–287). Chicago: National Reading Conference.

Rosegrant, T. (1989) *The Developmental Characteristics of Three-and-a-Half to Five-and-a-Half Year Olds and Implications for Learning.* Unpublished paper.

Salinger, T. (1993). *Models of Literacy Instruction.* New York: Macmillan/Merrill.

Snow, C., Burns, M., & Griffin, P. (Eds.) (1998). *Preventing Reading Difficulties in Young Children.* Washington, D. C.: National Research Council.

Stewig, J. (1988). *Children and Literature,* 2nd ed. Boston: Houghton Mifflin.

Sulzby, E. & Teale, W. (1991). Emergent literacy. In R. Barr, M. Kamil, P. Mosenthal, & P. Pearson (Eds.), *Handbook of Reading Research, Volume II,* (pp. 727–757). New York: Longman.

Vygotsky, L. (1978). *Mind to Society.* Cambridge, MA: Harvard University Press.

Yopp, H. & Yopp, R. (1999, November). *Primary Grade Students' Exposure to Informational Text.* Paper presented at the 33rd annual conference of the California Reading Association, Long Beach, CA.

SCIENCE AND
EMERGENT LITERACY

CHAPTER TWO

SCIENCE FOR YOUNG CHILDREN

Beginning in the early grades, an appreciation of scientific methods and an understanding of the nature of science are essential components of education. How the natural world operates is important to all of us. However, in order to be effective, science education should be enjoyable (California State Board of Education, 1990), and that enjoyment and appreciation increase as students become more knowledgeable about what science is and how it works.

NATIONAL SCIENCE EDUCATION STANDARDS: PRINCIPLES, PROGRAM, AND CONTENT

In order to establish a foundation for fully integrated and developmentally appropriate science activities and experiences in their classrooms, early childhood educators should carefully review the National Science Education Standards (Rakow & Bell, 1998).

The National Science Education Standards were developed on the basis of four *principles* (National Research Council [NRC], 1996). First, science is for all students, regardless of ethnicity or cultural background, gender, age, disabilities, interest and motivation in science, or personal aspirations. Second, learning science is an active process, concerned with both mental and physical activity, and, therefore, involving "minds-on" as well as "hands-on" experiences. Third, school science reflects the cultural and intellectual traditions embodied in the practice of contemporary science, so that even young students should begin to understand what science is and is not, what it can and cannot do, and how it has contributed to culture both past and present. Finally, reforming science education is a component of improved national, state, and local education.

Quality science education requires six *program* standards. The first three are addressed to individuals and groups that design and implement science programs, asking that these be consistent with other content area standards and across grade levels, that these programs be coordinated with mathematics education, and that they be interesting, developmentally appropriate, inquiry-oriented, and relevant to children's lives. The last three standards state that all students can equitably learn science, provided that there are enough proper resources and that communities encourage and support the teachers (NRC, 1996).

Among the *content* standards for grades K–4 are earth and space science, life science, physical science, and science in personal and social perspectives (NRC, 1996). In the area of Earth and Space Science, students should begin to understand the properties of earth materials, objects in the sky, and changes in the earth and sky. In the field of Life Science, boys and girls should begin to understand the characteristics and life cycles of organisms, and learn about organisms and their environments. In the area of Physical Science, children should begin to study the properties of materials and objects, the motion and position of objects, and light, heat, magnetism, and electricity. A major aspect in the field of science in personal and social perspectives is Personal Health.

Basic to all science education is *the standard of science as inquiry.* As a result of activities planned for grades K–4, children will develop: (1) an understanding of scientific inquiry; and (2) the intellectual and physical abilities needed to do such inquiry. They must study a few fundamental science concepts while teachers integrate all aspects of science content and implement inquiry as instructional abilities, strategies, and ideas to be acquired. Scientific concepts must be understood and abilities of inquiry developed.

Briefly, young students learn science content by using the processes of science inquiry, which allow them to acquire new information through concrete experiences that are progressive (Charlesworth & Lind, 1999). There are five skills that are the most appropriate for young learners: observing, comparing, classifying, measuring, and communicating. The first demands that the children involve their senses in order to collect data about events or objects. The second encourages the students to contrast and compare concepts, ideas, and objects. The third requires the children to sort and group according to such properties as color and shape. The fourth allows the observers to make quantitative descriptions directly through observation or indirectly by using units of measure. The fifth skill promotes the children's ability to communicate directions, descriptions, and ideas either in written form (e.g., in journals) or orally so that someone else can understand what they mean.

The last-named skill of communication indicates that at times science lessons are language lessons because some processes of communication are basically the same as the processes of science (Owens, 1999). Both look for patterns among infor-

Girls listen intently as classmates share the science journals they are keeping.

The school library media center is a useful place for a young student to begin her research project.

mation pieces and later inform others of the developing ideas. If oral language is used to indicate relationships, it can bolster science learning for speakers and listeners alike. For this learning to take place, however, children need: experiences to discuss; new ways to express their thoughts; assurance that their ideas are valuable; trust in others when expressing incomplete scientific reactions; and, finally, tools and time for making observations as well as the freedom to ponder about science as another way to regard the world.

One of the communication tools that can assist in extending and supporting scientific investigations is a classroom library of children's literature that teachers can use to promote emergent literacy abilities and interests (Barclay, Benelli, & Schoon, 1999). It is important to stress, however, that the information in both the nonfiction and fiction books must be accurate.

CALIFORNIA SCIENCE CONTENT STANDARDS (K–3)

Content for the National Science Education Standards outlined earlier can be also found in many state frameworks of science education, such as the one published recently by the California Academic Standards Commission (1998):

Kindergarten

PHYSICAL SCIENCES OR OBSERVING THE PHYSICAL WORLD
1. Students state common properties of materials, such as shape.
2. Students know how to sort and compare common materials based on one physical characteristic, such as color or relative size and weight.

LIFE SCIENCES OR EXPLORING THE WORLD AROUND US

1. Students identify their five senses and use them to investigate and learn about living and nonliving things.
2. Students compare and describe the characteristics of living and nonliving things in simple terms such as breathing and eating.

EARTH SCIENCES OR OBSERVING THE EARTH AND SKY

1. Students compare the properties of Earth materials and sort them.
2. Students observe and compare the appearance of objects in the sky at different times—including the moon and clouds.
3. Students recognize changes in weather from day to day and over the seasons; and relate their daily activities to weather conditions.

INVESTIGATION AND EXPERIMENTATION

1. Students will participate in various investigations during which they can demonstrate their ability to: describe the properties of common objects and the relative position of objects using one reference (e.g., *above*); to compare and sort common objects based on one physical attribute; and communicate their observations verbally and in drawings.

Grade 1

PHYSICAL SCIENCES OR FUNDAMENTALS OF FORCES

1. Students know that forces are pushes or pulls, and can identify a variety of forces such as magnetism and friction.
2. Students know there is a force called gravity that pulls things down so they fall unless some other force holds them up.
3. Students know that changes in motion are caused by forces.

LIFE SCIENCES OR BASIC NEEDS OF LIVING THINGS

1. Students identify the basic needs of organisms and realize that organisms survive only in environments where needs are met.
2. Students can describe environmental factors that affect the health of organisms and know that animals and plants respond to changes in these factors.
3. Students compare animals and plants that inhabit different environments, and recognize that living things interact both with each other and with their physical environment.
4. Students can describe how organisms sometimes live together in groups because the environment is favorable or there is a need for social or mutual support.

EARTH SCIENCES OR CHANGES IN THE ATMOSPHERE AND SKY

1. Students know that the atmosphere surrounding Earth changes.
2. Students identify routine changes in the sky and length of these changes or cycles, including day and night.

INVESTIGATION AND EXPERIMENTATION

1. Students will conduct various investigations in which they demonstrate the ability to: perform previous investigative skills; make predictions; record observations on a bar graph or with drawings, numbers, and written work; label parts of a diagram of an observed object; and describe the relative position of objects using two references (e.g., *below* and *left of*).

Grade 2

PHYSICAL SCIENCES OR PROPERTIES OF MATTER

1. Students know that liquids, gases, and solids are different states of matter.
2. Students know how to describe observable properties of common liquid and solid materials, using standard and nonstandard units.

3. Students know that changes in temperature, color, and state of properties can occur with physical and chemical changes.

LIFE SCIENCES OR LIFE CYCLES

1. Students analyze the differences and similarities of offspring and parents of common animals and plants. They identify variations between organisms of one sort.
2. Students compare sequential stages of a life cycle and know that living things come only from other living things.
3. Students compare the life cycles of organisms that generally resemble their parents throughout the life cycle with those organisms that do not, such as butterflies and frogs.
4. Students know that as organisms progress through their life cycles their needs (such as food intake and habitat) may change.
5. Students know that light, gravity, touch, or environmental stress can affect the growth and development of plants.

EARTH SCIENCES OR EARTH STRUCTURE AND MATERIALS

1. Students know that the Earth is made of different sorts of materials which have distinct properties and that these materials help us learn the story of the Earth's past.
2. Students know that Earth materials (air, water, rock, and soil) provide numerous resources, including fuel, food, and building resources which people use.
3. Students know that Earth's surface changes over time.

INVESTIGATION AND EXPERIMENTATION

1. Students will participate in various investigations during which they demonstrate the ability to: perform all previous investigative skills; follow verbal instructions for a scientific investigation; make predictions based on patterns of observation; measure with appropriate tools and express measurements in standard and/or nonstandard units; compare and sort common objects based on two or more physical attributes (including shape, size, and weight); compare measurements; construct bar graphs to record data using numbered axes; and draw or write descriptions of a sequence of events, observations, or steps.

Grade 3

PHYSICAL SCIENCES OR REACTIONS

1. Students know that condensation, evaporation, melting, and freezing are physical changes that depend on the temperature of the substance.
2. Students know that substances soluble in water dissolve faster and in greater quantity as the water temperature increases.
3. Students know that many common dissolved substances can be recovered from solutions through evaporation and concentration.
4. Students know that all substances are made of very small particles called atoms and molecules.
5. Students observe or know the outcome of simple chemical reactions.

LIFE SCIENCES OR UNITY AND DIVERSITY OF LIFE

1. Students know how environmental factors may greatly affect the ways in which the basic needs of organisms are met.
2. Students can analyze the roles of specialized structures (e.g., lungs, brains, and teeth) in helping animals meet their needs for air, food, and water.
3. Students know examples of diverse life forms in various environments, such as oceans and deserts, and can identify examples of how adaptations in physical structure or behavior may improve the survival of life forms.

The teacher demonstrates the concept of condensation to a group of third graders.

4. Students analyze how changes in the environment may affect the survival, re-production, or relocation of animals and plants.
5. Students can compare living species and their ecosystems to groups of extinct animals or plants and their ecosystems.

EARTH SCIENCES OR WATER, WEATHERING AND SOIL
1. Students know that water on Earth moves between land and oceans.
2. Students explain the interactions of air and water with rocks, and know these interactions change the Earth's surface.
3. Students describe the processes which create soil, and the importance of soil to life on Earth.

INVESTIGATION AND EXPERIMENTATION
1. Students will participate in a variety of investigations during which they demonstrate their ability to: perform all previous investigative skills; differentiate observation from opinion; construct and interpret a simple scale map; repeat observations to improve accuracy; predict the outcome of a simple investigation and compare the result to the prediction; and measure length, temperature, volume, and mass to the nearest centimeter, degree Celsius, milliliter and gram, respectively.

CONTENT FOR YOUNG CHILDREN: EARTH AND SPACE SCIENCE

Included in earth and space science for grades K–4 are eight concepts (NRC, 1996) concerned with basic astronomy, geology, and meteorology. Many of these concepts can be promoted by carefully chosen literature that teachers share with the class.

Properties of Earth Materials

- The earth is made up of solid rocks and soils, atmospheric gases, and water. This variety has different chemical and physical properties that make them valuable in different ways, such as fuel sources or as building materials. Many of the resources that people use come from earth materials.
- Fossils tell us about animals and plants that lived many years ago and about the environment in which they lived.
- Soils have properties of texture and color, and the capacity to retain water. They can support the growth of many types of plants, including those that provide food for people.

(**Sample read-aloud literature** for this section includes: *Everybody Needs a Rock* by Byrd Baylor and *Fossils Tell of Long Ago* by Aliki.)

Objects in the Sky

- The sun furnishes the heat and light needed to preserve the temperature of the earth.
- The sun, stars, moon, clouds, birds, and airplanes all possess locations, movements, and properties that can be observed and noted.

(**Sample read-aloud literature** for this section includes *Sun Up, Sun Down* and *Stargazers*, both by Gail Gibbons, and *The Cloud Book* by Tomie dePaola.)

Changes in the Earth and Sky

- Weather changes from day to day and over the seasons throughout the year. It can be described in measurable quantities, including temperature, precipitation (e.g., rain or snow), and wind speed and direction.
- The earth's surface changes, sometimes due to rapid processes (e.g., landslides) and sometimes due to slow processes (e.g., erosion).
- Objects in the sky have movement patterns. While the sun appears to move daily in the same way, its path changes slowly over the year. The shape of the moon that we can see, however, changes daily during a near-monthly cycle.

(**Sample read-aloud literature** for this section includes: *Earthquakes* by Franklin Branley, *So That's How the Moon Changes Shape!* by Allan Fowler, and *The Sun, the Wind, and the Rain* by Lisa Peters.)

CONTENT FOR YOUNG CHILDREN: LIFE SCIENCE

Included in life science for grades K–4 are concepts in biology which can be grouped under three major headings (NRC, 1996). Many of the concepts can be promoted by carefully selected literature that teachers share with the class.

Characteristics of Organisms

- Organisms have basic needs and can only survive in environments where those needs are met. Since there exist many varied environments in the world, each can support the life of different kinds of plants and animals.
- How individual organisms behave is influenced by external cues (e.g., environmental changes) and internal cues (e.g., thirst).
- Each animal or plant has different structures for different functions in growth, reproduction, and survival.

A second grader reads her classmates' reports about the pumpkin plant.

(**Sample read-aloud literature** for this section includes: *Bugs* by Nancy Parker and Joan Wright, *Linnea's Windowsill Garden* by Christina Bjork, and *Birds of Prey* by Lynn Stone.)

Life Cycles of Organisms

- Animals and plants have life cycles whose details differ for different organisms.
- Animals and plants closely resemble their parents.
- Numerous characteristics of an organism are inherited from the parent animal or plant (e.g., the number of feet on an animal or the height of a plant); however, other traits result from interactions with the environment and cannot be inherited (e.g., the human ability to read).

(**Sample read-aloud literature** for this section includes: *The Tiny Seed* by Eric Carle and *Creepy, Crawly Caterpillars* by Margery Facklam.)

Organisms and Their Environment

- All organisms create changes in the environment where they live. Some changes are beneficial to the organism or other organisms while other changes are harmful.

- People depend on both their natural and their constructed environments, and can change them in ways that are either beneficial or harmful to themselves and other organisms.
- All animals depend upon plants directly or indirectly. Some eat them for food while others eat the animals that have eaten the plants.
- The behavior pattern of an organism is related to its type of environment.
- When the environment changes, some animals and plants survive and reproduce but others move to another environment or die.

(**Sample read-aloud literature** for this section includes: *The Lorax* by Dr. Seuss, *My Visit to the Zoo* by Aliki, and *How to Be a Nature Detective* by Millicent Selsam.)

CONTENT FOR YOUNG CHILDREN: PHYSICAL SCIENCE

Included in physical science for grades K–4 are concepts which can be grouped under three major headings (NRC, 1996). Many of the concepts can be promoted by carefully selected literature that teachers share with the class.

Properties of Materials and Objects

- Objects are made of one or more materials (e.g., wood) and can be described by the properties of those materials. In turn, those properties can be used to classify or separate a group of objects or materials.
- Materials can exist in different states, i.e., liquid, gas, and solid. Some common materials can be changed from one state to another by heating or cooling.
- Objects possess many observable properties (e.g., size and temperature) which can be measured with tools (e.g., rulers and thermometers). The properties can react with other substances.

(**Sample read-aloud literature** for this section includes: *How Is a Crayon Made?* by Oz Charles and *Fire! Fire!* by Gail Gibbons.)

Motion and Position of Objects

- The motion of an object can be explained by measuring and tracing its position over a period of time.
- The position of an object can be depicted by locating it relative to another object or to the background.
- The motion and position of objects can be changed by pushing or pulling. How much of a change occurs will depend upon the strength of that push or pull.
- Vibrating objects produce sound whose pitch can be varied by changing the rate of vibration.

(**Sample read-aloud literature** for this section includes: *Katy and the Big Snow* by Virginia Burton and *Sound* by Angela Webb.)

Light, Heat, Electricity, and Magnetism

- Light travels in a straight line until it reaches an object. It can be then absorbed by that object, refracted (by a lens), or reflected (by a mirror).
- Heat is produced in various ways (e.g., rubbing). By conduction it can move from one object to another object.

- Electricity in circuits produces light, sound, heat, and magnetic effects. However, electric circuits demand a complete loop through which the electrical current can travel.
- Magnets attract and repel each other and also certain types of other materials.

(**Sample read-aloud literature** for this section includes: *What Makes a Magnet?* by Franklin Branley and *Me and My Shadow* by Arthur Dorros.)

CONTENT FOR YOUNG CHILDREN: HEALTH SCIENCE

Included in the standard of science in personal and social perspectives for grades K–4 are four concepts in the area of personal health science (NRC, 1996). These can be promoted by carefully chosen literature that teachers share with the class and then discuss now:

1. Good nutrition is essential to good health, and recommendations include eating a balanced and varied diet with less sugar and fat.
2. Substances such as tobacco, alcohol, and drugs can damage the body and how it functions.
3. Students bear some responsibility for their own personal care and good health, especially in the areas of cleanliness, exercise, and dental hygiene.
4. Security and safety are fundamental needs of people. The first involves a lack of fear and a feeling of confidence; the second concerns freedom from injury, risk, or danger. Students must learn to follow safety rules at home and school; understand whom to ask for help and when and how to say "no"; and acquire ways to prevent neglect and abuse.

(**Sample read-aloud literature** for this section includes: *What Food Is This?* by Rosemarie Hausherr and *Human Body* by Steve Parker.)

ASSESSMENT IN EARLY ELEMENTARY SCIENCE

Assessment has been defined as the process of documenting the work that children do and how they do it as a foundation for many educational decisions that affect those children (Bredekamp & Rosegrant, 1992). Some of that documentation can be in the form of observing and recording because evaluation comprises many steps of data collection. Young children have several roles in assessment, according to the National Association for the Education of Young Children: They are its subjects, its sources of assessment information, and the beneficiaries of the ways in which that information is used. They are also critics of their personal progress and thinking skills.

Each teacher must be aware that certain characteristics of young children affect their assessment in science and other curricular areas. First, they are extremely sensitive to their surroundings and are easily distracted, and their emotional reactions to assessment procedures readily skew the results. Consequently, those procedures must take place in a variety of familiar situations in which the students feel comfortable. Second, they must be assessed often, due to their rapid changes in emotional and social development. Finally, they have only limited interest in being assessed at all, particularly when the evaluative procedures interfere with activities that meet their own desires and needs (Bredekamp & Rosegrant, 1992). These three basic characteristics of early learners are clearly revealed in the experiences of one engineering student (Hagerott, 1997) who voluntarily and successfully taught everyday physics to twenty-four first graders weekly for an entire term, often using only playground equipment such as the slide, the monkey bars, the merry-go-round, and the swings.

Assessment standards are changing in their emphasis of science knowledge, learning, and teaching (NRC, 1996). Greater emphasis is being placed on what is most highly valued, not on what is readily measured. Well-structured knowledge, together with scientific reasoning and understanding, is being assessed over simply discrete and scientific knowledge. Less stress is being placed on achievement alone, and greater emphasis on achievement coupled with the opportunity to learn. Assessing what students understand, rather than what they do not, is receiving greater attention. Students are being more involved in their own ongoing assessment and that of their peers (e.g., during cooperative group projects), and less in being evaluated at

FIGURE 2.1   Sample Practical Process Skill Assessment for Early Elementary Children

---

STATION 1: THREE OR FOUR DIFFERENT VEGETABLES
Activity: Describe the characteristics of each vegetable. Tell what senses you used.
Process skill assessed. Observing

STATION 2: A COLLECTION OF 10–15 SEEDS
Activity: Group the seeds into two groups and name each group.
Process skill assessed. Classifying

STATION 3: AN OBJECT IN A PAPER BAG
Activity: Describe the object to a partner, without naming it, such that the partner can identify it correctly.
Process skill assessed: Communicating

STATION 4: A WOODEN BLOCK AND A RULER
Activity: Measure the length of the block.
Process skill assessed: Measuring

STATION 5: A TUB OF WATER WITH SEVERAL OBJECTS BESIDE IT
Activity: Predict whether each object will sink or float.
Process skill assessed: Predicting

STATION 6: THREE OPAQUE CANISTERS WITH DIFFERENT THINGS IN THEM
Activity: Tell what's in the canisters.
Process skill assessed: Inferring

STATION 7: TWO CLEAR SODA BOTTLES, EACH FILLED TO A DIFFERENT LEVEL WITH WATER; A WOODEN STICK
Activity: Tell which will make the higher sound when hit with the stick.
Process skill assessed. Predicting

STATION 8: THREE DIFFERENT ROCKS
Activity: Describe the characteristics of each rock. Tell the similarities and differences among them.
Process skill assessed: Observing

STATION 9: A COLLECTION OF 10–12 SHELLS
Activity: Group the shells and name each group.
Process skill assessed: Classifying

STATION 10: TWO WOODEN BLOCKS AND A SIMPLE TWO-PAN BALANCE
Activity: Tell which is heavier; tell how you know.
Process skill assessed: Measuring

STATION 11: PICTURE OF AN OUTDOOR SCENE WITH LONG SHADOWS
Activity: Tell where the sun is.
Process skill assessed. Inferring

From *Elementary Science Methods*, 2nd ed., by D. Martin © 2000, reprinted with permission of Wadsworth Publishing, a division of Thompson Learning. FAX 800–730–2215.

FIGURE 2.2 Scoring System for Practical Process Skills Assessment Shown in Figure 2.1

SCORE	CRITERION
1	Not seen
2	Performed satisfactorily
3	Performed well
4	Performed in an outstanding and advanced manner

STATION	PROCESS SKILL	SCORE
1	Observing	_____
2	Classifying	_____
3	Communicating	_____
4	Measuring	_____
5	Predicting	_____
6	Inferring	_____
7	Predicting	_____
8	Observing	_____
9	Classifying	_____
10	Measuring	_____
11	Inferring	_____

TOTAL

Divided by maximum total of 44

PERCENTAGE

From *Elementary Science Methods,* 2nd ed., by D. Martin © 2000, reprinted with permission of Wadsworth Publishing, a division of Thompson Learning. FAX 800-730-2215.

the conclusion of each semester by their teachers alone. Finally, teachers have a greater role in the development of external assessments, with less emphasis being placed on work done by experts in the field of educational measurement.

General strategies for assessing children's achievement in science include evaluating what is said and done and what is written (Kellough, Carin, Seefeldt, Barbour, & Souviney, 1996). The first involves the teacher's listening to the students' queries, replies, and interactions with peers as well as observing their involvement in class activities. Some guidelines that the teacher must follow for this evaluation procedure include: keeping an anecdotal record book as well as a checklist of specific instructional objectives, and recording all observations as soon as possible (with the aid of tapes or computer software programs when these are available).

Students' proficiency in the process skills discussed earlier in the chapter can be evaluated by performance-based or hands-on activities (Ostlund, 1992). A teacher can set up stations around the classroom, each requiring the completion of some activity that shows proficiency in a process skill; then the children rotate from station to station, individually or in groups, and perform the assignment (Martin, 2000). Figure 2.1 on page 29 is a sample practical process skill assessment for early elementary children, involving eleven stations; Figure 2.2 is the scoring system for that assessment, and Figure 2.3 is a sample of using the scoring system with one child (who earned a percentage score of 73 percent).

The second general strategy for assessing student achievement in science involves evaluating what the child writes (Kellough et al., 1996). This can include journal entries, student portfolios, worksheets, written homework, and tests. Portfolios are col-

FIGURE 2.3   Sample of Scoring for a Child Doing Practical Process Skill Assessment Shown in Figure 2.1

STATION	PROCESS	SCORE	REASON FOR SCORE
1	Observing	2	Child did not use sense of smell.
2	Classifying	4	Child formed two mutually exclusive groups.
3	Communicating	1	Child was able only to identify object, not describe it.
4	Measuring	3	Child measured whole units; did not round increments to nearest whole.
5	Predicting	4	Child made accurate predictions and tested each.
6	Inferring	2	Child used limited investigation.
7	Predicting	4	Child made accurate predictions and tested each.
8	Observing	3	Child described properties; did not tell similarities and differences.
9	Classifying	3	Child formed only two groups, but they were mutually exclusive.
10	Measuring	4	Child operated balance properly.
11	Inferring	2	Child said "sun is in the sky"; did not give location.
	Total Score	32	
	Percentage	$32 \div 44 = 73\%$	

From *Elementary Science Methods,* 2nd ed., by D. Martin © 2000, reprinted with permission of Wadsworth Publishing, a division of Thompson Learning. FAX 800-730-2215.

lections of dated samples of student work over a period of time, such as drawings, paintings, tapes or video recordings, logs of books read by or to the child, and self-adhesive notes from interviews or conversations. In evaluating the written efforts of the young students, the teacher should: provide positive comments about the work (either orally or in writing); discuss student journals and portfolios individually with their owners; and recall the instructional objectives of the assigned work, especially in designing and administering tests. Short, frequent tests are less stressful for the children and more informative for the teacher, insofar as planning future lessons.

REFERENCES

Barclay, K., Benelli, D., & Schoon, S. (1999). Making the connection: Science & literacy. *Childhood Education, 75,* 146–149

Bredekamp, S. & Rosegrant, T. (Eds.) (1992). *Reaching Potentials: Appropriate Curriculum and Assessment for Young Children,* Volume 1. Washington, DC: National Association for the Education of Young Children.

California Academic Standards Commission. (1998). *Science Content Standards: Grades K–12,* First Draft. Sacramento: Author.

California State Board of Education. (1990). *Science Framework for California Public Schools: Kindergarten through Grade Twelve.* Sacramento: California Department of Education.

Charlesworth, R. & Lind, K. (1999). *Math and Science for Young Children,* 3rd ed. Albany, NY: Delmar.

Hagerott, S. (1997). Physics for first graders. *Phi Delta Kappan, 79,* 717–720.

Kellough, R., Carin, A., Seefeldt, C., Barbour, N., & Souviney, R. (1996). *Integrating Mathematics and Science for Kindergarten and Primary Children.* Englewood Cliffs, NJ: Merrill/Prentice-Hall.

Martin, D. (2000). *Elementary Science Methods,* 2nd ed. Belmont, CA: Wadsworth.

National Research Council. (1996). *National Science Education Standards.* Washington, DC: National Academy Press.

Ostlund, K. (1992). *Science Process Skills: Assessing Hands-On Student Performance.* Menlo Park, CA: Addison-Wesley.

Owens, C. (1999). Conversational science 101A: Talking it up! *Young Children, 37,* 4–9.

Rakow, S. & Bell, M. (1998). Science and young children: The message from the National Science Education Standards. *Childhood Education, 75,* 164–167.

CHILDREN'S LITERATURE CITED

Aliki. *Fossils Tell of Long Ago* (HarperCollins, 1990).

Aliki. *My Visit to the Zoo* (HarperCollins, 1997).

Baylor, B. *Everybody Needs a Rock* (Macmillan, 1985).

Bjork, C. *Linnea's Windowsill Garden* (Farrar, 1988).

Branley, F. *Earthquakes* (HarperCollins, 1990).

Branley, F. *What Makes a Magnet?* (HarperCollins, 1996).

Burton, V. *Katy and the Big Snow* (Houghton Mifflin, 1973).

Carle, E. *The Tiny Seed* (Picture Book, 1991).

Charles, O. *How Is a Crayon Made?* (Simon & Schuster, 1988).

dePaola, T. *The Cloud Book* (Holiday, 1975).

Dorros, A. *Me and My Shadow* (Scholastic, 1990).

Facklam, M. *Creepy, Crawly Caterpillars* (Little, Brown, 1996).

Fowler, A. *So That's How the Moon Changes Shape!* (Children's Press, 1991).

Gibbons, G. *Fire! Fire!* (HarperCollins, 1984).

Gibbons, G. *Stargazers* (Holiday, 1992).

Gibbons, G. *Sun Up, Sun Down* (Harcourt, 1983).

Hausherr, R. *What Food Is This?* (Scholastic, 1994).

Parker, N. & Wright, J. *Bugs* (Greenwillow, 1987).

Parker, S. *Human Body* (Dorling Kindersley, 1994).

Peters, L. *The Sun, the Wind, and the Rain* (Holt, 1988).

Selsam, M. *How to Be a Nature Detective* (Harper, 1966).

Seuss, Dr. *The Lorax* (Random House, 1971).

Stone, L. *Birds of Prey* (Children's Press, 1983).

Webb, A. *Sound* (Watts, 1988).

CHAPTER THREE

FORTY LITERATURE ACTIVITIES PROMOTING SCIENCE UNDERSTANDINGS

CONTENT STANDARD: EARTH AND SPACE SCIENCES
(with students keeping science journals)

■ ■ ■ (1) CONCEPT: Fossils are prints of animals and plants that lived millions of years ago.

Literature: *Fossils Tell of Long Ago* by Aliki (HarperCollins, 1990), 32 pp.

Listed in: *Best Books for Children* (R. R. Bowker, 1998).

Synopsis: A non-fiction book, it is an introduction to fossils and tells how they are formed, what they can tell about the past, and where they might be located.

Activities After Read-Aloud:

1. Have students collect various types of leaves and bring them to school. Then have the students make impressions by pressing the leaves firmly into flattened clay. They must carefully remove the leaves and let the clay dry. Later they can display their fossillike prints.
2. Take the clay fossils from Activity One and bury them in sand. Let students go on a "fossil hunt." Show them how to use brushes to clean the fossils. Take the "fossils" back to the classroom and let the students identify their own.
3. Make copies for each student of several of the colorful illustrations from the book. Have the children cut out each fossil and arrange the illustrations into categories of different types of fossils.
4. Have the students imagine that, while participating in a fossil dig, each has uncovered a skeleton of a brand-new animal. Have them tell or write where they found their skeleton, what they named it, and how long ago they think it lived.
5. Help the class make a one-minute-old fossil: Each student takes some soft clay, flattens it out, presses his/her hand in it, and then lifts the hand away. When the handprint is dry, its owner has a fossil. _____

■ ■ ■ (2) CONCEPT: Rocks come in various shapes, sizes, and colors.

Literature: *Everybody Needs a Rock* by B. Baylor (Macmillan, 1985), unpaged.

Listed in: *Literature for Science and Mathematics* (California Department of Education, 1993).

Synopsis: Through free verse poetry, the author offers ten rules for finding the rock that is perfect for its owner.

Activities After Read-Aloud:

1. Have students each find and bring a rock to school. Ask them to write three sentences that describe their rock to make it different from other rocks. Next, put all rocks together on a table, and have each student read his/her sentences to see if a classmate can find the rock being described.

2. Bring in a medium-sized, smooth rock for each child in the class. Tell the children to write their names on the rocks, using any color marker they wish. Have students suggest different ways of classifying rocks into categories. Discuss whether some rocks fit more than one category.
3. Baylor offers ten rules for finding and keeping a rock. Have students each write their own rules for finding a perfect rock, and share some of these with the class.
4. Compile a class list of adjectives that can be used to describe the physical characteristics of rocks.
5. Rocks serve many purposes for animals and people. Help the class make a chart listing and illustrating the uses of rocks.
6. Have students glue together rocks in order to make their own "pet rock," and later paint features on it. Some may wish to name their "Creature." _____

■ ■ ■ **(3) CONCEPT:** The movement of large sections of the earth's crust causes earthquakes.

Literature: *Earthquakes* by F. Branley (HarperCollins, 1990), 32 pp.

Listed in: *Best Books for Children* (R. R. Bowker, 1994).

Synopsis: A nonfiction book, it discusses basic information about earthquakes, including causes and effects, and also tells how people can safeguard themselves during earthquakes.

Activities After Read-Aloud:
1. Have a student hold one end of a yardstick close to his/her ear while another student taps on the other end. The first student should hear the tapping sound. Discuss with the class how earthquake waves travel through rock in the same way that sound travels through wood.
2. Bring in toothpicks and marshmallows. Have students each build a structure out of them on a piece of construction paper. Explain to the students that when the earth's crust moves, buildings are often damaged. Next, have them move their papers back and forth to simulate an earthquake. Examine and discuss the results of the shaking. Finally, list with the class some ways that buildings could be made more earthquake-proof.
3. Explain that a major fault in this country is the San Andreas Fault in California where two large sections of the earth's crust scrape alongside each other and cause earthquakes. Give children each a map of California and have them color it green. Then tell them to draw a red line going north to south to highlight the San Andreas Fault, as shown on page 18 in the book.
4. Divide students into groups of three and give each group a map of the world. Have groups cut out the seven labeled continents and try to arrange the pieces into one large shape. Then ask each child to write if he/she thinks that the coasts of Europe and Africa fit into North and South America much like the pieces of a puzzle and why.
5. Have students in cooperative groups research the two main earthquake belts in the world: the Ring of Fire or Circum-Pacific belt and the Alpide belt. Each group can use red markers to indicate its chosen area on a small world map. The groups can later point out the same area on a large wall map. _____

■ ■ ■ **(4) CONCEPT:** Clouds can be used to predict changes in the weather.

Literature: **The Cloud Book** by T. dePaola (Holiday, 1975), 32 pp.

Listed in: *Best Books for Children* (R. R. Bowker, 1994).

Synopsis: A nonfiction book introduces the ten most common clouds and some related myths and sayings.

Activities After Read-Aloud:
1. Have the children each fold a piece of blue construction paper into three sections, labeling each *cirrus, cumulus,* and *stratus,* the major types of clouds. Then

have them use cotton to make a sample cloud for each section and glue it in place. Ask each child to choose his/her favorite kind of cloud and write briefly the reason for the selection. Discuss.

2. On a day with clouds divide the students into groups of four and send them out to observe the sky. Have each group draw and tell the types of cloud(s) it observed.

3. Give each pair of children two sheets of construction paper, one white and one blue, and have them cut out several cloud shapes from the white paper. Explain that, because people often see pictures in cumulus clouds, each pair can use their cutouts to create pictures (of animals, castles, planes, etc.). Then they are to glue the cutout to the blue paper. Finally, each pair will write about their creations and share their stories or pictures with the class.

4. Because there are many other types of clouds that resemble a mixture of cirrus, cumulus, and stratus clouds, tell the children to draw some of these clouds and tell which two types of clouds they come from.

5. Fog is a kind of cloud. Ask the students to write what fog looks like and feels like. Some may wish to share their descriptions. _____

■ ■ ■ **(5) CONCEPT:**   The moon reflects the light from the sun and seems to change its shape throughout each month.

Literature: *So That's How the Moon Changes Shape!* by A. Fowler (Children's Press, 1991), 32 pp.

Listed in: *Best Books for Children* (R. R. Bowker, 1998).

Synopsis: A nonfiction book with color photographs, it introduces the phases of the moon with minimal text in large print.

Activities After Read-Aloud:

1. Since there is no atmosphere on the moon, sound cannot travel. Ask the children to think of ten different ways that they could communicate with others on the moon without using sound, e.g., hand signals or flags.

2. In a darkened room, shine a flashlight on a large ball. One side will be illuminated like a full moon. As children move to the side of the ball, less of the light will be seen and the moon will appear to become a crescent. By moving from one side of the ball, across the front of it to the other side, it is possible to observe the phases of the moon. Discuss.

3. Ask the students to observe the moon each night for seven days, and sketch how it looks. Explain why some nights they may not be able to see the moon. Have them share their drawings and impressions of the moon's shape and surface as seen by the naked eye.

4. Have the children draw three major phases of the moon on white paper and label each phase.

5. Have the class ask family members if they recall watching on television on July 20, 1969, the landing of the first person on the moon: astronaut Neil Armstrong of the United States. He and astronaut E. Aldrin explored the lunar surface. Have the class research what Armstrong said. _____

■ ■ ■ **(6) CONCEPT:**   Stars are huge balls of gas.

Literature: *Stargazers* by G. Gibbons (Holiday, 1992), unpaged.

Listed in: *Best Books for Children* (R. R. Bowker, 1998).

Synopsis: A nonfiction book explains what stars are, how groups (or constellations) of them were named, and how telescopes are used by astronomers or other stargazers.

Activities After Read-Aloud:

1. Have the children each draw a copy of the Little Dipper constellation with the North Star, as shown in the middle of the unpaged book. Then have them demonstrate in the classroom how they could find the North Star. Later, at home on

a clear night, they should move in a northerly direction toward the Star and then note what things in their immediate surroundings are to their north, e.g., a neighbor's garage. Finally, ask them to share in class what they observed at home.

2. Prepare with the class a bulletin board of some of the more familiar and major constellations such as Orion (the Hunter), the Greater Dog (or Canis Major), and the Great Bear (or Ursa Major). The students can draw them with white chalk on dark blue paper, and then label them.

3. Help the students each make a constellation gazer using an empty shoe box. With a pin, they must poke holes in the form of a constellation in a sheet of black paper. Then they can cut a rectangular slot in one end of the box to hold the constellation. In the opposite end of the box, a hole for a flashlight can be cut. With classroom lights off, each student can project an image on a light-colored wall.

4. Have students in pairs create their own constellation by drawing an outline of some stars, naming the constellation, and writing a story about the people, animals, or things their outline suggests. _____

■ ■ ■ **(7) CONCEPT:** The sun provides many benefits and regulates life on Earth.

Literature: *Sun Up, Sun Down* by G. Gibbons (Harcourt, 1983), unpaged.

Listed in: *Best Books for Children* (R. R. Bowker, 1998).

Synopsis: A nonfiction book, it concerns one day in the life of a little girl who wakes up when the sun lights up her room. Later she goes to sleep when it gets dark because the sun is now shining on the other side of our planet.

Activities After Read-Aloud:

1. Explain to the students on a sunny day that the position of the sun in the sky determines the lengths of shadows. Have them work in pairs to measure their shadows in the morning and again in the afternoon. Make a bar graph with the class comparing the two measurements of all the students.

2. Since the sun's light is make up of many different colors, use a prism to separate the sun's light into the colors of a rainbow. Explain how the sun's shining through small drops of water forms a rainbow in the sky. Then have the students draw and color a rainbow, using the proper colors in the correct order (as shown toward the end of the unpaged book).

3. Compile with the class a word wheel on the Sun, brainstorming associated vocabulary, e.g., *ray, energy, eclipse*. Ask students to read and explain the new words, and write them in their journals.

4. On a sunny day, show how to make "sun tea" by putting four bags of tea and one quart of water in a clear, closed container and placing it outdoors for several hours. Serve over ice to volunteers who wish to sample it. _____

■ ■ ■ **(8) CONCEPT:** Comets are found in outer space and travel around the sun in long elliptical orbits.

Literature: *The Comet and You* by R. Krupp (Macmillan, 1985), 48 pp.

Listed in: *Best Books for Children* (R. R. Bowker, 1990).

Synopsis: An nonfiction book about comets, it offers basic facts and clever illustrations about their composition, orbits, speeds, and histories. It focuses especially on Halley's Comet.

Activities After Read-Aloud:

1. Have students each draw a picture of the solar system (as shown on page 13) with the sun and the nine planets. Then have them include several comets traveling around the sun in long elliptical orbits.

2. Since comets resemble a moving star that has a tail, help the children each to make their own model of a comet. Provide each child with a cotton ball for the head of the comet and yarn and glitter for its tail. Display the comets on the bulletin board.

3. Develop with the class a timeline of the orbits of Halley's Comet, beginning in 1682 as the Comet passes the earth every seventy-six years. Have the children calculate what their age will be the next time Halley's Comet passes the earth.

4. To help students understand the meaning of the word *ellipses* or loops (which describe most comet orbits), draw two large ellipses on the playground. Make one follow the path of the earth, and the other elongated to represent the path that comets take. Have students walk around each path several times. _____

■ ■ ■ **(9) CONCEPT:** Mountains can be eroded or transformed by the effects of the sun, the wind, and the rain.

Literature: *The Sun, the Wind, and the Rain* by L. Peters (Holt, 1988), 48 pp.

Listed in: *Best Books for Children* (R. R. Bowker, 1998).

Synopsis: A little girl named Elizabeth builds a small sand mountain on the beach that is affected by the sun, wind, and rain just like a huge earth mountain. Elizabeth's activities are small-scale compared to the centuries-old geological process, but the transformations involved are the same.

Activities After Read-Aloud:
1. On a warm, sunny day fill several large trays each with sand and a small amount of water. Have children work outside, in groups of three, to build sand mountains. Have them observe the effects of erosion by using small spray bottles to simulate rain. Then let the sun dry their mountains and have students observe how the sun and rain changed the shape of their mountains.

2. Have students draw pictures on construction paper of new mountains including several peaks and valleys. Then, on another sheet of construction paper, have them each draw the same earth mountains millions of years later, showing the rounded tops typical of older mountain ranges. They must explain the reasons for the difference between the two pictures.

3. Since the illustrations in the book were done in consultation with a geologist/professor concerned with the Chuckanut Formation in the state of Washington, have the children examine carefully the technical details in those illustrations and list simple but basic geological facts.

4. Tell the students that they are investigators hired by Elizabeth. They must prepare a written report that tells her why her mountain changed and make a prediction as to the future of her mountain of sand. _____

■ ■ ■ **(10) CONCEPT:** The four types of volcanoes are composite or strato-volcanoes (which are the most common), shield, cinder cone, and dome (like Mount St. Helens in Washington).

Literature: *Volcanoes* by S. Simon (Morrow, 1988), unpaged.

Listed in: *Best Books for Children* (R. R. Bowker, 1998).

Synopsis: A nonfiction book with color photographs, it is an introduction to the formation and eruption of volcanoes around the world.

Activities After Read-Aloud:
1. Divide the class into four research teams who must each investigate a different type of volcano. Each team must explain and give examples of its type. Later, a compare-and-contrast chart can be developed using the data presented by the research teams.

2. Share some pictures of Mount St. Helens, which had the most destructive volcanic eruption in the United States some twenty years ago. (Before and after photos appear early in the unpaged book.) Locate the area on a map of the United States, and discuss with the class what effects the eruption had on families living in the area.

3. Demonstrate the gas pressure that builds up inside of volcanoes by shaking a bottle of warm soda and then taking the cap off, cautiously. Invite children to compare what happened to the soda with the eruption of Mount St. Helens and then write their observations.

4. Bring in samples of volcanic ash and/or lava and show them to students. Discuss the substances and have the class create a story about Effects on the Environment after a Volcanic Eruption. (Samples can be obtained from science supply companies like Scott Resources, P.O. Box 2121F, Fort Collins, CO, 800-1289-9299 or Hubbard Scientific, P.O. Box 104, Northbrook, IL, 800-323-8368.) _____

CONTENT STANDARD: LIFE SCIENCES
(with students keeping science journals)

■ ■ ■ **(1) CONCEPT:** Zoos can help save endangered animals from extinction.

Literature: *My Visit to the Zoo* by Aliki (HarperCollins, 1997), 33 pp.

Listed in: *Best Books for Children* (R. R. Bowker, 1998).

Synopsis: Two cousins visit a modern zoo and are relieved to find that the animals are not all caged. They describe the animals, tell where they came from, and whether or not the animals are endangered

Activities After Read-Aloud:

1. Collect many small pictures of animals, from house pets to endangered species. Divide the class into groups and give each group a stack of cards, and ask that the children sort the cards into two piles, house pets and zoo animals, or into several piles by classes, e.g., birds, reptiles, and so on.
2. Using the postcards from Activity One that show endangered species (e.g., pandas), have each child draw a card from that pile, describe the animal shown, and then write (or tell) where it came from, what it eats, and how the zoo environment helps protect it.
3. Distribute to each student one square of red, yellow, brown, or black construction paper. Have students with yellow paper (for healthy animals) come to the front. Repeat with red paper (for vulnerable or threatened animals), with brown paper (for endangered animals), and with black paper (for extinct ones). Discuss what is happening as each group comes up. Pass out circle graphs for students to fill in with names of some (a) healthy, (b) vulnerable, (c) endangered, and (d) extinct animals.
4. Divide the entire classroom into fourths, using string and marking each quadrant 1 through 4. Have the class measure the room size. As the day goes on, the students will be restricted to three-fourths of the room, then one-half, and finally one-fourth. Have them write what it is like to have their environment restricted to smaller and smaller areas. Ask them to relate their experience to what happens to endangered animals. _____

■ ■ ■ **(2) CONCEPT:** Animals use camouflage to hide safely in their habitats.

Literature: *I See Animals Hiding* by J. Arnosky (Scholastic, 1995), 32 pp.

Listed in: *Best Books for Children* (R. R. Bowker, 1998).

Synopsis: A nonfiction book with watercolor paintings and a large-print text, it explores all kinds of camouflage in animals, including seasonal changes.

Activities After Read-Aloud:

1. Have the children each choose their favorite animal from the book. Help them use encyclopedias to find out four important facts about their animal, and make a poster which is entitled "Now You See It!" Have them share their facts and posters with the class. Prepare a display.
2. Ask the students how they think an animal could camouflage itself in the classroom. Ask them to pair off with a partner to create a fictional animal of their own, using a variety of art materials, and then write a paragraph describing how that animal uses camouflage, e.g., a bug that is rectangular could blend in with the classroom library collection, especially if it had markings on its back. Encourage students to name their animals.

3. Ask the children to think of different ways that wild animals can protect themselves. List these defense mechanisms on a class chart for reading and discussion.

4. Have the students divide into groups of four to make a class mural of various environments (i.e., the desert) depicting animals (e.g., the horned toad) hiding from danger. Distribute colored pencils and butcher paper and ask the groups to label their chosen environments and animals.

5. Scatter a box of colored toothpicks (including white ones) over square yards of cloth or paper (of various colors). Ask a child to pick up as many toothpicks as possible, one at a time, in ten seconds. Count the number of toothpicks of each color that are retrieved. Continue the challenge, changing backgrounds and students. Finally, rank the colors that are retrieved most often from each background. Discuss protective coloration/camouflage. _____

■ ■ ■ **(3) CONCEPT:** Plants need four things in order to grow: water, air, nutrients from the soil, and, most importantly, sunlight.

Literature: *Linneas's Windowsill Garden* by C. Bjork (Farrar, 1988), 59 pp.

Listed in: *Best Books for Children* (R. R. Bowker, 1998).

Synopsis: Linnea is a city girl who loves plants and grows them all over her apartment in flowerpots, boxes, and cans. She takes the reader on a tour of her indoor garden and explains her activities with birds, seeds, bulbs, bugs, and so on.

Activities After Read-Aloud:
1. Create a pictorial class chart of what plants need to survive, patterning it after the drawing on page 32.

2. Divide the class into eight groups and give each group some zinnia or nasturtium seeds. Help the children plant their seeds and watch them sprout; then do the following four activities simultaneously. (Have weekly discussions regarding changes in each group's plants, suggesting reasons behind the changes.) Groups One and Two test for water needed by plants (both put plants in the sun but only Two waters its plants); Groups Three and Four test for sunlight needed by plants (both water plants when they are dry but only Four keeps its plants in a sunny place); Groups Five and Six test for air needed by plants (both place plants in a sunny place but only Six encloses its plants in a large airtight plastic bag); and Groups Seven and Eight test for soil needed by plants (both keep their plants moist but only Eight puts its plants in a pot with moistened soil *after* they sprout). All groups record results.

3. Bring in a variety of bulbs to share with the class. First, cut one in half to show its contents. Then, identify each of the bulbs (e.g., tulip) and distribute a different bulb to each group to plant in a pot with moist soil. Little green shoots should sprout in about two weeks. Each group will need to choose a vigilant water monitor.

4. Linnea is named after a flower. Have the class learn more about the flower linnea and also about the botanist who named it. _____

■ ■ ■ **(4) CONCEPT:** Plants, including flowers, come from seeds.

Literature: *The Tiny Seed* by E. Carle (Picture Book, 1991), 32 pp.

Listed in: *Best Books for Children* (R. R. Bowker, 1998).

Synopsis: Describing a flowering plant's life cycle through the seasons, the book relates how various seeds survive wind, weather, and animals before taking root and growing.

Activities After Read-Aloud:
1. Have the children each observe a different kind of seed under a hand lens or microscope. The seeds may come from packaged flower or vegetable seeds. Students then write brief descriptions of the seeds they observed, labeling them correctly.

2. Supply one flower to each child. Most florists will provide slightly aged flowers for school purposes. To make pressed flowers, sandwich each flower between

layers of absorbent paper and cardboard, and set between two phone books or two boards. (For additional weight, add bricks or more books on the top board to help keep the flowers flat as they dry.) After one week, help the children carefully remove the flowers from their presses. They can glue the pressed flowers onto decorated cardboard strips, and an adult may laminate the strips to create functional bookmarks.

3. Give students access to a colored variety of pipe cleaners, tissue paper and/or crepe paper, cotton balls, yarn, and dots of construction paper. Then using tear-art, they can each create a replica of their pressed flower from Activity Two and glue it onto construction paper. Finally, the children can each write an imaginary story about the travels of their Tiny Seed that bloomed into their flower.

4. Compile a class list of edible seeds including pumpkin, sesame, and sunflower (each of which produces flowers during its life cycle). Bring in samples for the children to examine and then attach to posterboard and label.

5. Give students each a flower seed to paste in the corner of a piece of construction paper and ask them to draw what they think the flower will look like that grows from that seed. Share the drawings and discuss. _____

■ ■ ■ **(5) CONCEPT:** Butterflies and moths go through four life stages: egg, larva or caterpillar, pupa, and adult.

Literature: *Creepy, Crawly, Caterpillars* by M. Facklam (Little, Brown, 1996), 32 pp.

Listed in: *Best Books for Children* (R. R. Bowker, 1998).

Synopsis: A nonfiction book featuring thirteen different types of colored caterpillars as they change into butterflies or moths, it has labeled drawings at the bottom of each page.

Activities After Read-Aloud:
1. Have students each use paper plates on which to glue some dried foods into four clockwise quadrants: white beans for eggs, spiral noodles for larvae or caterpillars, shell macaroni for pupae, and bowtie macaroni for moths or butterflies. When the glue dries, have students label each stage on the plate.

2. Have children each create a caterpillar environment in a glass jar by poking holes in the lid. Students can catch caterpillars, gather leaves from the plants on which they were found, and place them both carefully in the jars. The jars must be kept clean and out of the sun. The class should record predictions, make observations, and compare findings.

3. Create a crayon resist project by having students each divide a large square piece of white construction paper into four equal quadrants. Pressing hard with their crayons, the students should draw and label the four stages in clockwise fashion. Then, using a dark watercolor, they must use even strokes to lightly paint over the papers. Dried papers may be displayed.

4. Allow children to each choose their favorite among the thirteen caterpillars illustrated, and write briefly their reasons for the selection. They may also wish to draw the butterfly or moth that finally emerges in the fourth stage. _____

■ ■ ■ **(6) CONCEPT:** An adult insect has three body parts (head, thorax, and abdomen), one or two pairs of wings, and legs in five sections.

Literature: *Bugs* by N. Parker & J. Wright (Greenwillow, 1987), 40 pp.

Listed in: *Best Books for Children* (R. R. Bowker, 1998).

Synopsis: A nonfiction book gives descriptions and large drawings of thirteen common insects. It also has questions with (rhyming) insect answers on alternate pages.

Activities After Read-Aloud:
1. Assign students to groups and give each a ball of clay to make a model of an insect. Each model will include the body parts, wings, and legs. Let each group name its imaginary insect and then write a collaborative story about it. Encourage groups to share their stories.

2. Prepare with the class a large pictorial chart of the thirteen insects, first placing the names in alphabetical order from Ant to Termite. Then taking turns, pairs of children sketch the insect next to its name, using pencils first and crayons later. Discuss the body parts, wings, and legs.

3. Some children mistakenly consider spiders (or arachnids) as insects, so place transparencies of both a spider and a typical insect (such as a cricket) on the overhead and visually compare the two. Then list the characteristics of each and have students copy the traits. (Spiders are also discussed in the book.)

4. Ask the children each to write briefly about their favorite insect, explaining why a firefly, for example, is the one they like best and describing where they have seen it. Later, have them read their stories aloud. Finally, graph the favorites and discuss. _____

■ ■ ■ **(7) CONCEPT:** Different types of animals leave different types of tracks or footprints.

Literature: *How to Be a Nature Detective* by M. Selsam (Harper, 1966), 32 pp.

Listed in: *Best Books for Children* (R. R. Bowker, 1984).

Synopsis: A nonfiction book, it teaches children to be nature detectives who can tell what animals have been in the area by recognizing the clues, especially different footprints.

Activities After Read-Aloud:

1. Pair students and accompany them on a nature walk looking for clues of animal life on the school grounds, such as nests, holes, footprints, and so forth. Back in the classroom, have them discuss their observations and compare findings.

2. Use a variety of tempera paint colors to paint the bottoms of (individual) students' feet. Have children make tracks across butcher paper and then thoroughly cleanse their feet. Randomly number each set of tracks, keeping a list of which tracks belong to whom. When the prints dry, have students list their guesses as to the owners of the prints, writing reasons for the choices. Later, graph the correct responses, discussing detective skills needed for accuracy.

3. Draw a scenario of "nature clues" on a poster board, including two sets of footprints coming from different directions and then circling each other with only one set leaving the scene. List visual clues about the area, types of animals found there, and so on. Let students write about what might have happened, giving their reasons and listing the clues.

4. Make an interactive bulletin board with numbered pictures of animals on one side and on the other side their labeled footprints. Attach two envelopes to the board: one with blank worksheets and a pencil, the other for completed worksheets. Students take turns completing their Nature Detective worksheets, matching numbers to prints. The class has one week in which to conclude the assignment. _____

■ ■ ■ **(8) CONCEPT:** Backyard insects are numerous and must camouflage themselves for protection from their enemies.

Literature: *Backyard Insects* by M. Selsam & R. Gore (Scholastic, 1988), 40 pp.

Listed in: *Best Books for Children* (R. R. Bowker, 1998).

Synopsis: A nonfiction book, it includes color photos of various insects commonly found in the backyard and divides them into five sections: Hidden Insects, Copycat Insects, Insects with "Warning" Colors, Scary Insects, and Two-Headed Insects.

Activities After Read-Aloud:

1. On a sunny day, take the students outdoors to look for evidence of insects. They must take notes as they try to find tracks, droppings, eaten leaves, and any other evidence of bugs on the school grounds.

2. In groups of four, have children compare and contrast a moth and a butterfly. They should describe the size, color, wing shape, body shape, and food eaten by each.

3. Have the students each draw, color, and cut out from white construction paper one of the insects shown in the book. Then prepare a class bulletin board with a large paper tree in the center, and ask the children to place their "insects", correctly labeled, on or near the tree.

4. Have children each choose their favorite section of insects (as indicated in the book), and write why they prefer it. Encourage some to share or read aloud their choices.

5. Ask the students to investigate one or more insects in their own back yard, and make a sketch of them to share with the class. _____

■ ■ ■ **(9) CONCEPT:**   Everyone must work together to save the environment.

Literature: *The Lorax* by Dr. Seuss (Random House, 1971), 64 pp.

Listed in: *Best Books for Children* (R. R. Bowker, 1998).

Synopsis: A little brown creature called the Lorax tries to ward off pollution and save the Truffula Trees but Once-ler wants them for his business and will not listen to the Lorax.

Activities After Read-Aloud:

1. Set up a rotating schedule for a pollution control patrol to pick up school-site trash after lunchtime for one week. Each child will have a turn and also help keep a class log to find the heavy trash areas. After five days, discuss with the class why some areas are so bad and ask for possible solutions for eliminating/reducing the trash problem.

2. Bring to the classroom several boxes of various items that can or cannot be recycled. (Privately compile a master list of all items properly classified.) Then divide class into groups of four and give each group one of the boxes. Groups must then list which items in their box can be recycled and which cannot. After twenty minutes for group discussion and recording, the class can compare group lists to the teacher's master list and then reevaluate its findings.

3. Discuss with the class the possible project of helping to save the environment by planting one tree: What kind of tree would best fit the school area? Where would it be planted? Who would have to give permission for the planting? Who would plant the tree (or sapling) and what would it cost to buy? Who could take care of it? Divide students into groups to investigate the various aspects of the project and then report back to the entire class.

4. Have children each draw their own version of the Lorax and one Truffula Tree. Encourage them also to write reasons why every tree is important to the environment. _____

■ ■ ■ **(10) CONCEPT:**   Birds of prey have sharp beaks and talons (or claws), and eat other animals in order to live.

Literature: *Birds of Prey* by L. Stone (Children's Press, 1983), 48 pp.

Listed in: *Best Books for Children* (R. R. Bowker, 1994).

Synopsis: A nonfiction book with color photographs, it describes birds of prey generally and then specifically features vultures, condors, hawks, eagles, and owls.

Activities After Read-Aloud:

1. Discuss with the class that birds have different feet to help them in different ways. Birds of prey, for example, are hunting birds and use their feet or claws in order to eat. Distribute pictures of various birds (from swans to hummingbirds) to groups of four or five students. Let each group predict how its bird(s) can use its feet. Encourage the groups to share their predictions with the class.

2. The national bird of the United States is the bald eagle, which was expected to be removed from the endangered list by July 2000. Have the children learn more about that bird of prey and its size, color, diet, and nests. Encourage students to list reasons why they think the bald eagle was chosen to be our national bird and research whether or not it is still endangered.

3. Take the students outdoors and instruct them to stand in a circle on the playground. Choose two children to be "mice" and one child to be "owl." The owl is blindfolded and must catch one of the mice with its "claws" or hands by only using sound. The owl says "Owl" and the mice then say "Mouse." Once the owl catches a mouse, a new owl and mice are chosen. Continue the game for several rounds.

4. Discuss with the class: What makes a bird a bird? Then divide the students into small groups of four or five and give each group whatever materials are available so members can create an imaginary bird to live in a particular environment. (The bird must have feathers, wings, feet, and a beak.) Later, have each group present its bird to the class, and tell where it lives, what it eats, and how or if it flies. Students may choose to give their newly created bird a scientific name. _____

CONTENT STANDARD: PHYSICAL SCIENCES
(with students keeping science journals)

■ ■ ■ **(1) CONCEPT:**   Warm air rises.

Literature: *The Great Valentine's Day Balloon Race* by A. Adams (Macmillan, 1980), 32 pp.

Listed in: *Best Books for Children* (R. R. Bowker, 1998).

Synopsis: Orson Abbot, a rabbit, builds a hot air balloon to enter into the big race. His smart rabbit friend, Bonnie, offers to help fly the balloon, and Orson's parents also become involved. During the race, Orson and Bonnie learn about wind directions and the principles of hot air ballooning.

Activities After Read-Aloud:

1. Make or buy a pinwheel and bring in a hot plate. Warm the plate and then hold the pinwheel over it. The pinwheel will spin as the warm air rises and is replaced by the descending cold air. Discuss with the class what has happened.

2. On a cool day, hang a thermometer from an object placed high in the room. Place another thermometer on the floor. After ten minutes or more, have the class check the temperature on both thermometers to show that warmer air goes toward the ceiling. Discuss.

3. Bring to class a large bowl of very hot water. Partially inflate a balloon and place a tape measure around it to get the exact circumference. Next, place the balloon into the bowl and have class watch it expand. Then measure the balloon again and discuss the size change.

4. Share two other books about animals and ballooning: Mary Calhoun's *Hot Air Henry* (Morrow, 1981) about a cat; and James Marshall's *A Tale of Two Chickens* (Puffin, 1988).

5. Prepare hot chocolate and pour each child a cup. Have the children place their hands a few inches above the paper cups to feel the warmth of the air that is rising. Show that the hot liquid warms the air. _____

■ ■ ■ **(2) CONCEPT:**   Energy takes different forms and is used by all plants and animals.

Literature: *The Science Book of Energy* by N. Ardley (Harcourt, 1992), 29 pp.

Listed in: *Best Books for Children* (R. R. Bowker, 1998).

Synopsis: A nonfiction book with color photographs, it describes simple experiments that explain different forms of energy.

Activities After Read-Aloud:

1. Help the students plant alfalfa seeds in water in glass jars, as shown on pages 8–9. Keep jars in a light, warm place so the seeds can grow into sprouts in a week. Students should make observations and conclude that plants change the

solar energy into *chemical energy* to help their seeds grow. Finally, those who volunteer to eat a small sandwich (made from the alfalfa sprouts and buttered bread), will also be able to conclude that their body can change the energy from the food to a form it can use in order for them to grow. Have them keep a record of their observations.

2. Help the students each make a pinwheel out of a square of stiff paper and a pencil with an eraser, following carefully the instructions on pages 10–11. After they blow on their finished pinwheels and the blades spin rapidly, they should conclude that it is the *kinetic energy* of the moving air that is transferred to the pinwheel. Have them keep notes.

3. Bring in books weighing between one to three pounds and some identical rubber bands. Tie a string around each book and fasten a rubber band to it. Invite a student to lift one book by its rubber band. When the band is stretched to its fullest, measure its length with a ruler and note it on the board. Repeat the steps with each of the other books, with different students. Help them realize that the longer the rubber band becomes in each case, the greater the amount of *kinetic energy* needed to lift the book. Students should be reminded that heavier objects require more energy to lift than lighter objects do. _____

■ ■ ■ **(3) CONCEPT:**   Machines help us do work or move things.

Literature: *Machines at Work* by B. Barton (HarperCollins, 1987), 32 pp.

Listed in: *Best Books for Children* (R. R. Bowker, 1998).

Synopsis: At the construction site on a busy day, all sorts of workers—men and women—use various machines to knock down a building and begin erecting a new one.

Activities After Read-Aloud:

1. Have the children each place a stack of books on a table or desk and try to lift the stack with one hand. Next, have them put one end of a pencil under the stack. Then have the children use a second pencil as a *fulcrum* by placing it under the first pencil. Finally, ask them to push down on the end of the first pencil and try to lift the books. Ask the class: Which method makes it easier to lift the books? Discuss. Define *fulcrum* and have children write the word in their journals.

2. Bring in two bricks, a yardstick, tape, and two thirty-six-inch pieces of string. Tie one end of each string around a brick. First, tape one end of the yardstick to the edge of the table. Set one brick on the floor directly beneath the midpoint of the stick and tie the free end of the string around that midpoint. Have the children lift the free end until the brick is about six inches above the floor, observing the effort required to do the job. Then hold the free end of the string attached to the other brick and lift the brick to the same height, observing the effort required for doing that. Ask the class to decide which method of lifting is easier. Discuss, giving reasons why.

3. Use a paper clip, a tablespoon, and some string to demonstrate a moveable *pulley.* Attach one end of a twelve-inch piece of string to the spoon, and the opposite end of the same piece to the paper clip. Cut a second piece of string (about thirty-six inches long) and tape one end to the edge of a table. Run the string through the paper clip. Have the children raise the spoon by lifting up the free end of the longer string. After discussion, define *pulley,* and have the children write the word in their journals. _____

■ ■ ■ **(4) CONCEPT:**   Magnets have an invisible and natural force that pushes things away or pulls things toward them.

Literature: *What Makes a Magnet?* by F. Branley (HarperCollins, 1996), 32 pp.

Listed in: *Best Books for Children* (R. R. Bowker, 1998).

Synopsis: A nonfiction book offers basic information and a few simple experiments on magnets and how they work.

Activities After Read-Aloud:

1. Bring in an assortment of bar and horseshoe magnets, and have the class observe their sizes and shapes. Students can work cooperatively, experimenting with two different magnets using paper clips, and discover that some magnets are stronger than others. They can make notes, and report back to the class about which was the stronger magnet.

2. Display a lodestone and some small rocks on a table and have the students first guess which one is the *lodestone* (a magnetic mineral containing iron). Then have a child approach the rocks with a strong magnet and let the class observe and discover that the rock that moves back and forth is the lodestone. Ask the students to draw what they have observed and write about it.

3. Show the class a compass with the magnetic needle that tells directions. Review with the students the four directions and discuss some ways in which compasses are used by children and adults, e.g., helping hikers in a large forest.

4. Make three columns on the board: one headed Items, the second headed Predictions, and the third, Magnetic Attractions. In the first column, list crayons, scissors, forks, pencils, books, nails, paper, wooden spools of thread, plastic lids, drinking straws, and so on. In the second column, place a check mark after each item that the class predicts will attract a magnet. Then, distribute writing paper and magnets and have each child copy and complete the third column on his/her paper by experimenting with a magnet and marking items on the list as "yes" or "no." Later, have the class conclude some important facts and write them in their journals about magnets. _____

■ ■ ■ **(5) CONCEPT:**   Some machines depend on the amount of horsepower in their engines in order to do their job.

Literature: *Katy and the Big Snow* by V. Burton (Houghton Mifflin, 1973), unpaged.

Listed in: *Best Books for Children* (R. R. Bowker, 1998).

Synopsis: Katy is a crawler tractor that does many jobs around town. During a bad winter storm, hardworking Katy plows through the heavy snow all over town to help people in need.

Activities After Read-Aloud:

1. Have children each illustrate and/or write a story about the type of equipment they would own in order to help others in an emergency, e.g., "I would own a boat to help during a storm at the lake." Assign them to groups of four to share their stories. Finally, after the stories have been edited, publish them in a class book entitled "Equipment That Helps People in Need" and place it on the library table for all to read.

2. Katy was so strong because her engine had much horsepower. Assign children to groups that will each research how much horsepower exists in *one* of the common machines such as an automobile, school bus, motorboat, motorcycle, lawnmower, and so on. Later, compile a class list about the amount of horsepower in various machines. Discuss.

3. Share with the class related books by the same author, including *Mike Mulligan and His Steam Shovel* (Houghton Mifflin, 1939) and *Choo Choo* (Houghton Mifflin, 1937). Discuss with the children the role of machines in each of the three books (including Katy's). Ask if they are shown in a positive or negative way and how they contribute to the end of the stories.

4. Assemble various materials such as straws, popsicle sticks, macaroni, glue sticks, tape, and fasteners. Let students each design a miniature copy of a new machine that could help others the way that Katy did. This machine can be imaginary or real. Then have them share with the class what their type of machine can do and whom it would help. _____

■ ■ ■ **(6) CONCEPT:**   Changing the state of matter requires adding or taking away energy.

Literature: *How Is a Crayon Made?* by O. Charles (Simon & Schuster, 1988), 32 pp.

Listed in: *Best Books for Children* (R. R. Bowker, 1998).

Synopsis: A nonfiction book with full-color photographs, it describes the manufacture of a crayon from wax to finished product.

Activities After Read-Aloud:

1. Give each student two equal squares of wax paper. Have him/her place some shavings (or small pieces) of crayon on one of the squares and arrange them in some kind of design. Place the other square over the shavings and carefully place the whole thing inside a butcher paper folder. Have each child observe as an adult irons the folders and then pulls the wax paper out. Discuss what happens to the crayons and wax paper after adding heat and then removing it.
2. On a warm sunny day, have each group of children place on a paper plate a piece of crayon, a piece of chocolate candy, and a piece of butter. Have them take the plates outside and leave them in the sun. After an hour or more, have the groups bring in their plates and write their observations. Discuss what causes the change both outdoors in the heat and indoors as materials cool.
3. Make a batch of gelatin with the class, leaving some liquid at room temperature and putting the rest in the refrigerator. Later, as children observe both states, ask what caused any changes and why. Share the refrigerated gelatin.
4. To make hanging designs for a window or mobile, bring in a clear, plastic, nine-ounce, wide-mouth Solo cup for each child. Have students decorate the outsides of the cups with permanent markers. With a paper punch, make a hole near the edge of each cup. Place the cups upside down on foil in oven for ten minutes at 250 degrees. Every three to five minutes, have class check and record what is happening. (The clear plastic turns white, collapses, and cools almost immediately.) With string, hang the designs. _____

■ ■ ■ **(7) CONCEPT:**   A shadow results when an object blocks the light coming from a bright source.

Literature: *Me and My Shadow* by A. Dorros (Scholastic, 1990), 32 pp.

Listed in: *Best Books for Children* (R. R. Bowker, 1994).

Synopsis: A nonfiction book, it explains what shadows are, how and when they exist, and how they reveal the size and shape of things around us.

Activities After Read-Aloud:

1. Darken the classroom and shine a flashlight at a wall or else use an overhead projector. Have the children test a variety of objects to see what sorts of shadows they make. Then have them see how many different animal shapes they can make with their hands. Finally, have them write how they think a shadow is made. Later, after some have shared their ideas, discuss the principle involved.
2. Distribute tagboard and popsicle sticks to the students. Have each choose a different and interesting shape, draw and cut it out from the tagboard, and glue or tape it to the stick. Have the students hold their shapes close to the light and then farther away. Ask them to write in their journals what they observe.
3. The shadow made by a flagpole can be used to check the difference between the positions and lengths of shadows cast at various hours of the day. Place a piece of paper next to the pole and have the children make hourly notes next to each shadowed line they draw. Discuss later what they observed about the length of the shadows as time passed.
4. Take the children out on a sunny morning and group them in pairs. Have each child take turns standing still on the blacktop or cement as the partner uses chalk to draw around the shadow. After they write their names on their shadows, repeat the process four hours later, and ask what has changed and why. _____

■ ■ ■ **(8) CONCEPT:**   Heat causes changes in the shape, color, texture, and state of matter.

Literature: *Fire! Fire!* by G. Gibbons (HarperCollins, 1984), 40 pp.

Listed in: *Best Books for Children* (R. R. Bowker, 1998).

Synopsis: The fire department takes steps to put out fires in four different locations: a city apartment, a country barn, a forest, and a pier on the waterfront.

Activities After Read-Aloud:

1. Discuss fire safety with the children. Then show them several small candles in transparent holders (cup style). Light one candle; next place a nonflammable cover over the holder. Ask the class to observe what happens to the flame and discuss why. Have children brainstorm about other safe ways to put out the flame. Try some of their ideas and later discuss which solutions worked.

2. With tongs, hold a small piece of paper over a flame. Have the class observe what happens to the paper. Repeat the demonstration with a pencil, a paper clip, a crayon, a small plastic object, and so forth, and encourage children to describe the changes in shape, color, texture, and state or condition. Again review fire safety with the students.

3. Discuss the effects of fire on objects and materials. Have the children first predict what could happen to their home if it caught on fire. Compile a brief class list of fire safety rules for the home, and have students copy and read the rules aloud before taking them as homework to read to their parent(s).

4. Contact a local fire station and ask if the firefighter (in charge of community relations) could visit your class. He or she could show some of his/her gear and explain how it is made, tell what happens to things when they burn, describe proper ways of exiting a building on fire, and so forth. _____

■ ■ ■ **(9) CONCEPT:** Everything has color because color is everywhere in an endless variety of shades.

Literature: *A Color Sampler* by K. Westray (Ticknor & Fields, 1993), 32 pp.

Listed in: *Best Books for Children* (R. R. Bowker, 1998).

Synopsis: A nonfiction book introduces the primary, secondary, and intermediate colors, using illustrations adapted from two dozen classic patchwork quilt patterns.

Activities After Read-Aloud:

1. Bring to class several baskets filled with fruits and other items that show the primary colors: red, yellow, and blue. Guide the students to work in groups of three or four so all can learn those colors by sorting the contents of the baskets according to color. Later, have each group describe and identify for the class the names of the items (in each color group) in the basket they chose.

2. Help the children learn about secondary colors by demonstrating palm printing with water paints. Give them each white construction paper (folded into three separate areas). Let them make three sets of overlapping palm prints in red and yellow, red and blue, and yellow and blue to determine secondary colors. Finally, distribute cutout color words and have the children glue them under the correct colors. Display.

3. Guide the students in learning that, when two colors fill areas of very different sizes, the color in the smaller area will jump or "pop out." Give each two large pieces of construction paper of different colors and have them cut a big shape out of the first color and many tiny shapes out of the second so they can glue the tiny shapes onto the big one. Then they can repeat the process with the same colors but reversed so they can see the size effect. Discuss.

4. Separate a color into its component colors through chromatography. Give each group a cup of water, some water-soluble markers, and strips of coffee filter paper one-half-inch wide (four to six inches long). The children choose a marker, make a medium-sized dot about one-half-inch from the end of one of the strips, and then dip that end into the water. They can watch the color break down into its component colors as water runs up the strip. After the strips dry, tape them onto a fact sheet above or below the name of the original color. Discuss and record. _____

■ ■ ■ **(10) CONCEPT:** Sound is caused by vibrations that make invisible movements in the air and are a form of energy.

Literature: *Sound* by A. Webb (Watts, 1988), unpaged.

Listed in: *Best Books for Children* (R. R. Bowker, 1990).

Synopsis: A nonfiction book with color photographs, it explains how sounds vibrate and describes simple experiments.

Activities After Read-Aloud:

1. Guide the students in making a "xylophone" using glass bottles. Have them, in groups, fill four to eight same-sized bottles with different amounts of water, and listen to the notes from the bottles by gently tapping on the necks or tops with a wooden chopstick. Remind them that water levels can be adjusted to produce a musical scale, as pitch is affected when water is added or removed. Have the children record their experiment in their journals.

2. Put into an empty coffee can one or more of the following: dried beans or peas, macaroni, unpopped popcorn, and sand. Next, place the plastic lid on the can and ask different students to tap the top of the can or shake it to produce music. Discuss the difference between sound produced by tapping the can and sound produced by shaking it. Then have the children record the experiment.

3. Introduce the students to some sign language movements as shown in Ruth Gross's *You Don't Need Words!* (Scholastic, 1991). Explain that signing using gestures and hand symbols helps deaf people communicate in a world of hearing and nonhearing people.

4. Divide the children into groups and have them compile lists of School Sounds (heard in and outside the classroom) and Home Sounds. Later, have the groups compare their lists and conclude that sounds of all kinds can be found everywhere. Encourage them to describe some sounds that are pleasing and others that are considered to be noises. _____

CONTENT STANDARD: HEALTH SCIENCES
(with students keeping science journals)

■ ■ ■ **(1) CONCEPT:**   Lungs help us to breathe and use the oxygen in the air.

Literature: *You Breathe In, You Breathe Out: All About Your Lungs* by D. Adler (Watts, 1991), 32 pp.

Listed in: *Best Books for Children* (R. R. Bowker, 1994).

Synopsis: An oversized nonfiction book, it discusses respiration and the lungs, and explains how various parts of the respiratory system relate to each other.

Activities After Read-Aloud:

1. Ask students to each take several 3" × 5" index cards and tape or tie them to various places in and outside of the classroom, e.g., on the side of the teacher's desk. On each card, smear a thin layer of petroleum jelly. After several days, have the class note the amount of pollutants on each card. Which card has the most and why? Ask the children how they feel about breathing in those pollutants daily.

2. Tell the students each to place their hands on their chest and take a deep breath (or inhale). They can feel their chest expand as their lungs fill with air. Then have them exhale or let the air out. Their chest and lungs will get smaller. Remind them that they are always breathing, taking a breath every three or four seconds.

3. Have the students prove that air rushes into their body through their nose or mouth. Ask them each to hold their hand close to their mouth and nose, and then take a deep breath. As they inhale, they will feel the air rushing in. Then, when they exhale, they can feel the air going out.

4. Have children each count how many times a minute they normally breathe, as they watch the second hand on the wall clock. Then make a class graph and dis-

cuss. Later, have the students count the times they take deep breaths for one minute and graph the results.

5. Distribute drawing paper and have the children sketch and label the simplified diagram shown on page 4, explaining how we breathe. (Some may *also* wish to sketch the lung diagram on page 15.) Everyone should write a brief sentence about how air enters the body and where it goes. _____

■ ■ ■ **(2) CONCEPT:**   The five senses are seeing, hearing, smelling, tasting, and touching.

Literature: *My Five Senses* by Aliki (HarperCollins, 1989), 32 pp.

Listed in: *Best Books for Children* (R. R. Bowker, 1998).

Synopsis: A young boy discovers that he is learning about the world through his five senses wherever he goes and whatever he does, any time of the day or night.

Activities After Read-Aloud:

1. Cut some hand-sized holes in a large cardboard box. Then put objects of various sizes and textures into the "feely box." Have several children feel what the objects are, without looking, and tally their guesses. Remind them that the biggest touch organ in their body is their skin.

2. The boy in the book sometimes uses all his senses at once and sometimes only one sense. Ask the children to each write down an activity when they use one sense, and activities when they use two, three, four, or even five senses at the same time. They should list the sense(s) and the activity, e.g., the boy used only one sense (seeing) when he looked at the stars and moon.

3. Obtain enough sterile cotton-tipped swabs so students each will get four for dipping into the following solutions and then touching the swabs to various portions of their tongue: lemon juice (sour taste buds), coffee or tonic water (bitter taste buds), sugar water (sweet buds), and salt water (salty taste buds). Discuss the location of each of the four major types of little bumps called taste buds. Then draw and label the human tongue and taste buds.

4. Develop a class chart of Loud Sounds and Soft Sounds. Remind the students that sounds are measured in decibels and should be below 90 db so as not to damage the ear. _____

■ ■ ■ **(3) CONCEPT:**   Human reflexes such as sneezing and coughing cannot be controlled.

Literature: *Why I Cough, Sneeze, Shiver, Hiccup, & Yawn* by M. Berger (HarperCollins, 1983), 34 pp.

Listed in: *Best Books for Children* (R. R. Bowker, 1998).

Synopsis: A nonfiction book about the human body, it explains reflex actions to help readers better understand why they sneeze, shiver, cough, yawn, and hiccup.

Activities After Read-Aloud:

1. Have students in numbered pairs sit on the floor facing each other and give each pair paper, crayons, and a pencil. (Number Ones will be the first recorders and Number Twos will be the first test subjects.). Twos will close their eyes for one minute until Ones tell them when to open their eyes so that Ones can observe and record any changes in the pupils. Tell partners to exchange materials, switch jobs, and repeat the process. Compare results among the pairs and discuss if it is possible to control this reflex action.

2. (Same paired setup as in Activity One.) Give each pair one popsicle stick and tell them to remove their shoes but keep their socks on. Ones have the popsicle stick first and are told to quickly but gently run the end of it across the bottom of one of Twos's feet, beginning at the heel and proceeding to the big toe. Ones draw the reflex they observed and then exchange materials and jobs with Twos, who repeat the experiment. Next, tell pairs to repeat the steps, but this time try not to react to the pressure of the stick on their foot. Have them record results under the first set of data. Compare results of both foot experiments and discuss if pairs were able to control their reflexes or not.

3. (Same paired setup as in Activity One.) After modeling, have Ones gently blow air into Twos's eyes and record results. Tell pairs to switch jobs and repeat the experiment. Discuss and compare results of Experiments 1, 2, and 3 and conclude whether it is possible to control one's reflexes.

4. After discussion of the experiments, have students write stories that prove why reflexes are necessary. Some may wish to illustrate their stories. _____

■ ■ ■ **(4) CONCEPT:** The food pyramid offers many choices of nutritious foods.

Literature: *What Food Is This?* by R. Hausherr (Scholastic, 1994), 40 pp.

Listed in: *Best Books for Children* (R. R. Bowker, 1998).

Synopsis: A nonfiction book with color photographs on alternate pages, it explains in question-and-answer format eighteen different foods from the four food groups. Answers appear on the back of the questions.

Activities After Read-Aloud:

1. Draw a chart on the board with two columns: Foods and Food Groups. Ask the class to list all the foods shown in the book in the first column and, in the second column, to list which food group each belongs to, e.g., cheese belongs to Milk and Other Dairy Products. Later, at their tables, have children each draw a pyramid with six sections, labeling each section with the name of a different food group. Ask them also to draw and label one food that belongs in each section. Have pairs of children share their papers and discuss them.

2. Bring in some of the foods illustrated in the book and have the students observe the color, smell, size, and other characteristics of each. Encourage them to take notes in their journals. Finally, provide the "food that is needed for all forms of life" and let everyone enjoy a glass or cup of water.

3. Divide the class into groups of three, and assign them to research one of the foods that are called vegetables but are really fruits, i.e., cucumbers, eggplants, peppers, tomatoes, squash, peas, beans, and pumpkins. Later, have each group read or discuss what it learned about its food; some volunteers may wish to draw their foods on the board.

4. Ask the children each to choose three favorite foods and write the true reasons why they like them, e.g., celery because it is crunchy. _____

■ ■ ■ **(5) CONCEPT:** We must eat foods daily from each of the major food groups in order to stay healthy.

Literature: *The Edible Pyramid: Good Eating Every Day* by L. Leedy (Holiday, 1994), 30 pp.

Listed in: Best Books for Children (R. R. Bowker, 1998).

Synopsis: The Edible Pyramid is a restaurant that serves a variety of nutritious and delicious meals. On the day the restaurant opens, the cat waiter introduces his animal customers to the food groups shown in the nutritional pyramid developed by the U.S. Department of Agriculture.

Activities After Read-Aloud:

1. Ask pairs of students to each design a collage of nutritious foods by cutting pictures out of discarded magazines and gluing them onto poster board. Then have them label each item according to the food group to which it belongs. Check to be sure that all groups are represented. Have each pair share its collage with the class before it is displayed on the bulletin board.

2. On Monday, assign students to keep individual lists of all the foods they eat on Tuesday, Wednesday, and Thursday. On Friday, they must categorize into the major food groups what they have eaten during the three-day period. They must also write reports on whether they ate a balanced diet during the three days. Encourage them to list other foods they could have eaten to provide a better diet.

3. Divide the students into groups of four and ask them to create a name for a new restaurant that will serve only nutritious foods. Then each group must plan

three *breakfast, lunch,* and *dinner* menus for its restaurant, making sure that it uses the pyramid as a guide. Menus can be illustrated with markers and shared with the class.

4. Have the children take turns role-playing the waiter and his guests at The Edible Pyramid, using menus from Activity Three and a large table in the classroom. Paper placemats and napkins together with plastic plates, cups, and eating utensils will add to the setting. _____

■ ■ ■ **(6) CONCEPT:**   The human body is a complicated structure controlled by the brain.

Literature: *Human Body* by S. Parker (Dorling Kindersley, 1994), 60 pp.

Listed in: *Best Books for Children* (R. R. Bowker, 1998).

Synopsis: A pocket-sized, nonfiction book, it covers numerous areas of the human body in two-page chapters and uses many illustrations of children.

Activities After Read-Aloud:

1. Have students in pairs made body maps of each other. Give each a large piece of paper and have them take turns lying on the paper. They are to draw around the partner's body, and later add in pencil the heart, lungs, and stomach. Finally, after class discussion of those three important organs, they may each use colored markers over corrected pencil sketches and label the three.

2. Give children each an apple slice and demonstrate how to make a map of their teeth by carefully biting into the slice. Explain that they have incisors (to cut and slice), canines (to tear and spear), and molars and premolars up in their cheeks (to crush and grind). After each child takes a bite of his/her apple and looks at the marks left by some of the different types of teeth, let the children finish eating their apple slices and then discuss reasons for needing different kinds of teeth.

3. Give drawing paper to the children and have them each sketch the two halves (or hemispheres) of the human brain, as shown on page 36. Remind them that their brain is like a huge computer, and scientists used it as a model for developing computers. Then distribute simplified sketches of the inner brain, and have them label the cerebral cortex (which helps them think) and the cerebellum (which controls their muscles and balance).

4. Divide the students into small groups of four and have each group prepare a list of items for a chart headed What We Need Daily for a Healthy Body (e.g., exercise). After the groups compare their lists, assign each to write about one of the important needs of the human body. Share the reports so the students can correct any individual misunderstandings. _____

■ ■ ■ **(7) CONCEPT:**   People and other vertebrates keep their shape because their skeletons are made of bones.

Literature: *Bones* by A. Sandeman (Copper Beach, 1995), 30 pp.

Listed in: *Best Books for Children* (R. R. Bowker, 1998).

Synopsis: This nonfiction book describes what bones are and how they grow and work together in the human body.

Activities After Read-Aloud:

1. Make copies of the bone shown on pages 8–9 and distribute one copy to each student. Have him/her label the three major parts of the bone, and color them in lightly. Remind them that, without bones to hold their organs in place, their body would collapse.

2. Some animals have no bones at all. Have groups of three students each compile a list of as many invertebrates as they can, e.g., ants and crabs. Then compare the group lists as a class and make a final chart of Animals Without Bones.

3. Have the children each feel their backbone or spine so they realize that it is not smooth (like one long bone) but made up of a series of wedge-shaped bones

called *vertebrae*. Finally, have them feel their ribs, which curve forward from the upper spine and come in pairs. Discuss.

4. Ask how many of the students or their friends have broken a bone, especially in the wrist, arm, or leg, and how long it took them to heal. Have them each draw a simple fracture and a compound fracture, explaining in one sentence the difference between the two, as shown on page 26.

5. Have the class examine copies of hardcover books and discuss how the spine of a book compares to a human spine. _____

■ ■ ■ **(8) CONCEPT:**   A balanced diet keeps people and animals healthy.

Literature: *Gregory, the Terrible Eater* by M. Sharmat (Macmillan, 1980).

Listed in: *Best Books for Children* (R. R. Bowker, 1990).

Synopsis: Gregory is a goat who refuses to eat the food that his parents and other goats eat because he prefers good people-food. His parents consult Dr. Ram, who advises them to introduce goat food gradually. Gregory, however, overeats and becomes ill. So his parents decide that it is better to have a healthy son who eats mostly good people-food than a sick son who overeats junk goat-food.

Activities After Read-Aloud:

1. Gregory gets sick eating junk food. Discuss the difference between a goat's idea of junk food and the children's idea of junk food. Have the students compile a list on the board of some foods that their parents would label as junk foods. Ask them, "Why do some foods get that label?" and "Why do we like to eat junk food sometimes?"

2. Gregory likes to eat bread and butter, eggs, fish, cereal, spaghetti, and fruits (like bananas) and vegetables (like beans), and drink orange juice; for dessert, he likes ice cream. Prepare a graph showing Gregory's food choices on the left side and showing the children's names across the bottom. Then complete the graph to see which foods both Gregory and the children like.

3. Make copies of one week's menus from the school cafeteria and give one copy to each group of three students. Ask them to list which of the foods Gregory would eat if he were invited to lunch at the school. Which one of the five days' menus would he like best? Discuss.

4. It is important that all animals and people drink water. Discuss how we could convince Gregory that he should drink water everyday and not just orange juice.

5. Have the class investigate how much water people should drink daily. Ask each student to record how much water he/she drinks during a school day, noting the time (e.g., 7:30 A.M.) and the approximate amount (e.g., one glass). _____

■ ■ ■ **(9) CONCEPT:**   Our body must digest or change the food we eat so it can be used in different ways.

Literature: *What Happens to a Hamburger* by P. Showers (Harper, 1985), 32 pp.

Listed in: *Best Books for Children* (R. R. Bowker, 1990).

Synopsis: A nonfiction book, it explains the digestive process, which begins when food is swallowed and starts a long journey through the body, finally being absorbed in the small intestine.

Activities After Read-Aloud:

1. In each of three small plastic cups, pour three tablespoons of milk. To Cup One, add two tablespoons of water, then cover it with plastic wrap and use a rubber band to hold the wrap in place. To Cup Two, add two tablespoons of a weak acid (like lemon juice), and cover as for Cup One. To Cup Three, add two tablespoons of an enzyme (like meat tenderizer) and cover as for Cup One. After one or two hours, have the class observe the changes that occurred in each cup. Explain that those that occurred in Cups Two and Three are similar to the digestive process in the human stomach.

2. Blow up a balloon and explain that the balloon, like the human stomach, expands when filled. Measure out twenty-three feet of string or yarn for each child, and tell the class that the adult small intestine (where food is absorbed) is this length when stretched out. Discuss.

3. Make copies of a simplified version of the digestive system, much like that shown on page 23. Give students each a copy and have them label and color the eight important organs. Then have a group of volunteers dramatize *What Happens to a Hamburger,* with each one describing his/her part once the burger has been chewed. _____

■ ■ ■ **(10) CONCEPT:**   We depend on muscles to move every part of the human body.

Literature: *You Can't Make a Move without Your Muscles* by P. Showers (Harper, 1982), 33 pp.

Listed in: *Best Books for Children* (R. R. Bowker, 1990).

Synopsis: This nonfiction book explains why muscles are important and describes five of the most important ones.

Activities After Read-Aloud:
1. Have the class practice making faces. Tell them that it takes ten muscles to smile and twelve muscles to frown. Remind them that there are muscles in their eyelids and lips, and ask why these are especially important both at school and at home, e.g., for reading, talking, or eating.

2. Discuss which muscle is the only one in the whole body that never stops working, day or night. Have the children make a simple sketch of the heart, as shown on page 27, that pumps blood around the body and does not look like the heart associated with Valentine's Day.

3. Have three students stand in front of the class to demonstrate an important pair of muscles: First, they must make a fist with their right hand and bring it to their shoulder, causing the upper forearm muscle (the biceps) to get harder. Second, they must unbend that arm by using their lower forearm muscle (the triceps). Explain to the class that muscles often work in pairs because each can only pull. Finally, have the children keep notes in their journals.

4. Muscles need exercise but must be warmed up and stretched to avoid injury. Have the class practice standing and holding stretches for eight to ten seconds, relaxing, and then repeating the stretches. Remind the students to save their muscles by doing this warm-up exercise before most physical activities such as running, jogging, or bicycling, whether at home or at school. _____

CHILDREN'S LITERATURE CITED

Earth and Space Sciences
Aliki.   *Fossils Tell of Long Ago* (HarperCollins, 1990).
Baylor, B.   *Everybody Needs a Rock* (Macmillan, 1985).
Branley, F.   *Earthquakes* (HarperCollins, 1990).
de Paola, T.   *The Cloud Book* (Holiday, 1975).
Fowler, A.   *So That's How the Moon Changes in Shape!* (Children's Press, 1991).
Gibbons, G.   *Stargazers* (Holiday, 1992).
Gibbons, G.   *Sun Up, Sun Down* (Harcourt, 1983).
Krupp, R.   *The Comet and You* (Macmillan, 1985).
Peters, L.   *The Sun, the Wind, and the Rain* (Holt, 1988).
Simon, S.   *Volcanoes* (Morrow, 1988).

Life Sciences
Aliki.   *My Visit to the Zoo* (HarperCollins, 1997).
Aronsky, J.   *I See Animals Hiding* (Scholastic, 1995).
Bjork, C.   *Linnea's Windowsill Garden* (Farrar, 1988).
Carle, E.   *The Tiny Seed* (Picture Book, 1991).

Facklam, M.   *Creepy, Crawly Caterpillars* (Little, Brown, 1996).
Parker, N. & Wright, J.   *Bugs* (Greenwillow, 1987).
Selsam, M.   *How to Be a Nature Detective* (Harper, 1966).
Selsam, M. & Gore, R.   *Backyard Insects* (Scholastic, 1988).
Seuss, Dr.   *The Lorax* (Random House, 1971).
Stone, L.   *Birds of Prey* (Childrens Press, 1983).

Physical Sciences

Adams, A.   *The Great Valentine's Day Balloon Race* (Macmillan, 1980).
Ardley, N.   *The Science Book of Energy* (Harcourt, 1992).
Barton, B.   *Machines at Work* (HarperCollins, 1987).
Branley, F.   *What Makes a Magnet?* (HarperCollins, 1996).
Burton, V.   *Katy and the Big Snow* (Houghton Mifflin, 1973).
Charles, O.   *How Is a Crayon Made?* (Simon & Schuster, 1988).
Dorros, A.   *Me and My Shadow* (Scholastic, 1990).
Gibbons, G.   *Fire! Fire!* (HarperCollins, 1984).
Webb, A.   *Sound* (Watts, 1988).
Westray, K.   *A Color Sampler* (Ticknor & Fields, 1993)

Health Sciences

Adler, D.   *You Breathe In, You Breathe Out: All about Your Lungs* (Watts, 1991).
Aliki   *My Five Senses* (HarperCollins, 1989).
Berger, M.   *Why I Cough, Sneeze, Shiver, Hiccup & Yawn* (HarperCollins, 1983).
Hausherr, R.   *What Food Is This?* (Scholastic, 1994).
Leedy, L.   *The Edible Pyramid: Good Eating Every Day* (Holiday, 1994).
Parker, S.   *Human Body* (Dorling Kindersley, 1994).
Sandeman, A.   *Bones* (Copper Beach, 1995).
Sharmat, M.   *Gregory, the Terrible Eater* (Macmillan, 1980).
Showers, P.   *What Happens to a Hamburger* (Harper, 1985).
Showers, P.   *You Can't Make a Move without Your Muscles* (Harper, 1982).

RECENT AND RECOMMENDED: RELATED BOOKS FOR ADDITIONAL READING

Earth Sciences

Dodson, P.   *An Alphabet of Dinosaurs* (Scholastic, 1995).
> The book presents twenty-six dinosaurs, one for each letter of the alphabet, in full-page spreads. From the familiar to the newly discovered, each is shown in a dramatic painting. The brief text is in large type.

Gans, R.   *Let's Go Rock Collecting* (HarperCollins, 1997).
> An introduction to rocks, the book describes their formation, their composition, and their uses, and also tells how to collect rocks.

Gibbons, G.   *Caves and Caverns* (Harcourt, 1993).
> This introduction to caves tells how they were formed and where they are found, and defines the various types of caves.

Gibbons, G.   *Planet Earth/Inside Out* (Morrow, 1995).
> The book discusses theories of how the earth was formed and provides information about its interior.

Gibbons, G.   *The Planets* (Holiday House, 1993).
> The book devotes two pages to each planet, including information about its size, distance from the sun, and existing conditions. Concepts of rotation, daytime, nighttime, and orbit are also discussed. Illustrations are detailed.

Lauber, P.   *You're Aboard Spaceship Earth* (HarperCollins, 1996).
> The author describes Earth as though it were a huge spaceship.

Locker, T., & Christensen, C.   *Sky Tree: Seeing Science through Art.* (HarperCollins, 1995).
> The shifts in color and form associated with changes in seasons and weather patterns are shown, using the image of a tree on a hill in the foreground of different skyscapes. Each image is accompanied by a question.

McGuire, R. *Night Becomes Day* (Penguin, 1994).

> This book helps children understand the sequence and rhythm of changes over time. It uses universal concepts of evolving themes and events, such as how a stream becomes a river and then an ocean.

Polacco, P. *Thunder Cake* (Philomel, 1990).

> Grandmother cures her granddaughter of her fear of the thunder (from an oncoming storm) by making a thunder cake, complete with a secret ingredient.

Stacey, T. *Earth, Sea, and Sky* (Random House, 1991).

> The book explores mountains, waterfalls, weather, and night and day through a series of questions and answers.

Steele, P. *Rocking and Rolling* (Candlewick, 1997).

> A general introduction to the earth, the book presents basic information about earthquakes, volcanoes, and other geological phenomena.

Zoehfeld, K. *How Mountains Are Made* (HarperCollins, 1995).

> The book uses a simple text to introduce such topics as various kinds of mountains, the earth's interior, and plate tectonics.

Life Sciences

Aliki *My Visit to the Aquarium* (HarperCollins, 1993).

> Narrated from a child's perspective, this book introduces the wide variety of aquatic habitats and creatures that young readers will find in an aquarium.

Arnosky, J. *All about Alligators* (Scholastic, 1994).

> Using watercolor illustrations and a simple text, the book provides young readers with a vast assortment of interesting facts about alligators.

Bischhoff-Miersch, A. & Bischhoff-Miersch, M. *Do You Know the Difference?* (North-South, 1994).

> Double-page comparisons between animal pairs (e.g., a jaguar and leopard) are presented, together with lifelike illustrations and carefully chosen facts.

Bunting, E. *Flower Garden* (Harcourt, 1994).

> A birthday present for her working mother begins as a little girl purchases some flowering plants in the inner city and ends as they are planted in the apartment flower box.

Burnie, D. *Seashore* (Dorling Kindersley, 1994).

> This pocket-sized book offers a beginner's guide to life along the seashore. It gives information about the many plants and animals that live on the beaches, cliffs, or shallow waters of different seashores. It encourages children to observe nature and provides simple projects.

Gibbons, G. *Spiders* (Holiday, 1993).

> Bright illustrations enhance detailed explanations of the physical characteristics, habitats, and behaviors of different kinds of spiders.

Hariton, A. *Butterfly Story.* (Dutton, 1995).

> Clear, full-page illustrations depict birds, animals, and other insects in the butterflies' habitats. Text is straightforward.

Ling, M. *Penguin* (Dorling Kindersley, 1993).

> Full-spread photographs of the stages of penguin growth are in this book intended for early research by young children. Border illustrations are repeated in the endpapers.

Maestro, B. *Bats: Night Flyers* (Scholastic, 1994).

> Information about the types of bats, their habitats, and behaviors is provided with appealing illustrations. Many myths about bats are discussed and dismissed.

Martin, L. *Watch Them Grow* (Dorling Kindersley, 1994).

> Using large print, four general sections ask questions that involve the reader in the development and growth of sixteen familiar animals and plants.

Rauzon, M. *Skin, Scales, Feathers, and Fur* (Lothrop, 1993).

> An introduction to various kinds of animal hides, the book uses simple language and color photographs.

Simon, S.   *Wolves* (HarperCollins, 1993).

> Information is given about the wolf's anatomy, family, and pack life, and hunting behavior in an informal text with color photographs. The relationship of the wolf to the dog is revealed, and myths about wolves are discussed.

Physical Sciences

Ardley, N.   *The Science Book of Magnets* (Harcourt, 1992).

> A series of projects explores the basic properties of magnets and magnetism. Attractive illustrations and clear directions help the young reader.

Branley, F.   *Day Light, Night Light: Where Light Comes From* (HarperCollins, 1998).

> Topics such as darkness, light sources, heat, reflection, vision, and the speed of light are discussed.

Challoner, J.   *Energy* (DK Publishing, 1993).

> The role of energy in our lives is explained in this attractive book, which also describes its uses and sources.

Challoner, J.   *Floating and Sinking* (Raintree Steck-Vaughn, 1996).

> A conversational text with many pictures explores the concepts of floating and sinking.

Fowler, A.   *Energy from the Sun* (Children's Press, 1997).

> This easy-to-read science book introduces solar energy and explains how it is captured and used.

Fowler, A.   *What Magnets Can Do* (Children's Press, 1995).

> This basic introduction to magnets and magnetism uses photos and large type to cover numerous interesting topics.

Gibson, G.   *Hearing Sounds* (Millbrook, 1995).

> Simple activities and projects initiate basic concepts involving sound. There are amusing illustrations and clear instructions.

Gibson, G.   *Light and Color* (Millbrook, 1995).

> Fundamental scientific principles concerned with color and light are revealed in a series of double-page spreads. Each spread has a different project.

Lampton, C.   *Bathtubs, Slides and Roller Coaster Rails.* (Millbrook, 1991).

> This slim volume introduces the wide variety of inclined planes that are all around us from the stairs in our homes to the water slides and soft-drink machines at the park. Inclined planes are one form of simple machines that dominate everyday life.

Vaughn, M., & Mullins, P.   *The Sea Breeze Hotel* (HarperCollins, 1992).

> When it became too windy at the Hotel to swim, fish or beachcomb, Sam decided to fly a kite in the wind. Wonderful things began to happen and there were kites everywhere. Tourists filled the Hotel to fly kites all year, except in April, when Sam and his friends went swimming, fishing, and beachcombing.

Whalley, M.   *Experiment with Magnets and Electricity* (Lerner, 1994).

> Simple experiments using familiar materials cover principles of electricity and magnetism.

White, L.   *Energy* (Millbrook, 1995).

> The book has a series of double-page spreads that describe the uses, properties, and kinds of energy. Brief explanations are followed by simple activities.

Health Sciences

Baer, E.   *This Is the Way We Eat Our Lunch: A Book about Children around the World* (Scholastic, 1995).

> Lunchtime in nine states and twelve other countries are described, together with recipes and food facts.

Berger, M.   *Germs Make Me Sick*! (HarperCollins, 1995).

> An easy-to-read book introduces germs and viruses, and explains their effects on the human body.

Cole, J.   *Your Insides* (Putnam, 1992).

> Clear overlays help the young reader understand the workings of the human body.

Ganeri, A.   *Eating* (Raintree, 1994).
>   With many color photos and diagrams, this book offers a simple introduction to the digestive system.

Ganeri, A.   *Moving* (Raintree, 1994).
>   This book provides a basic introduction to the human skeleton, vertebrae, joints, and muscles. There is a brief text along with many illustrations.

Lambourne, M.   *Down the Hatch: Find Out about Your Food* (Millbrook, 1992).
>   With cartoonlike illustrations and simple text, the story of food and nutrition is presented.

Morrison, L.   *I Scream, You Scream: A Feast of Food Rhymes* (August House, 1997).
>   A humorous collection of rhymes, jokes, and tongue twisters centers around food.

Parsons, A.   *Fit for Life* (Watts, 1996).
>   This beginner's guide to nutrition, exercise, and hygiene also covers the effects of drugs, alcohol, and tobacco.

Perols, S. (illust.) *The Human Body* (Scholastic, 1996).
>   Using transparencies, the skeleton and different systems and organs of the human body are introduced to young children.

Robbins, K.   *Make Me a Peanut Butter Sandwich (and a Glass of Milk)* (Scholastic, 1992).
>   Minimal text accompanied by photos explains how one favorite snack reaches the table.

Royston, A.   *My Body* (DK Publishing, 1991).
>   Using photos and drawings, this book is a basic introduction to the human anatomy.

Sandeman, A.   *Breathing* (Copper Beech, 1995).
>   This exploration of breathing takes readers into the wonder of their own lungs. Photographs and diagrams help explain talking, breathing problems, and so on.

MATHEMATICS AND EMERGENT LITERACY

2+5=

CHAPTER FOUR

MATHEMATICS FOR YOUNG CHILDREN

A superior mathematics program is essential for all students, providing each of them with the opportunity to select among the full range of future career paths. It is also critical for all citizens living in the twenty-first century. The goals in such a program are for students to develop fluency in basic computational skills and an understanding of mathematical concepts; become mathematical problem solvers who not only recognize and solve routine problems quickly but also look for ways to solve as yet unresolved problems; communicate exactly about logical relationships, quantities, and unknown values through the use of symbols, models, graphs, and signs; reason mathematically by gathering and analyzing data; and, finally, make connections among mathematical ideas and also between mathematics and other disciplines (California Department of Education, 1999). Aspects of these goals begin in the early grades.

MATHEMATICS: SOCIETAL NEEDS AND INSTRUCTIONAL PROGRAM PRINCIPLES

In 1998 the National Council of Teachers of Mathematics (NCTM) stated that four *societal needs* for mathematical understanding have never been greater and are continuing to increase. The first is mathematical literacy, because our students live in a world where intelligent decision making often demands quantitative understanding. The second is cultural literacy, because our students should develop an appreciation of the intellectual and cultural achievement of peoples past and present. The third is mathematics for the workplace, because the students will need to use an increased level of mathematical problem solving and thinking in the workplace. The fourth and last need is for more mathematicians, scientists, engineers, and other users of mathematics. These four needs underlie math planning and presentations from the earliest grades.

Principles about instructional programs as developed by the NCTM (2000) apply at many levels of the educational system and so support systemic changes. They include an *equity principle*, because we should promote the learning of mathematics by all students, and a *mathematics curriculum principle*, because we must stress meaningful and important mathematics through comprehensive curricula that are coherent. Further, such programs include a *teaching principle* and a *learning principle*, which both depend on competent and caring professionals who teach all students to understand and use mathematics. An *assessment principle* is needed in order to enhance, monitor, and evaluate mathematics learning of all students and also to inform their teachers. Lastly, a *technology principle* emphasizes the inclusion of technology in mathematics instructional programs so that all students understand math and are prepared to use it in an increasingly technological society.

MATHEMATICAL STANDARDS: CONTENT AND PROCESS

There is a total of five *content standards* according to the National Council of Teachers of Mathematics (2000). Students should learn number and operations; algebra; geometry; measurement; and data analysis and probability. While national standards have been listed and recommended, frameworks for the mathematics curriculum may vary from state to state from those proposed by the NCTM. For example, in the early grades in California (California Department of Education [CDE], 1997) the *content* is summarized as follows:

Kindergarten	By the end of the year, children understand small quantities, numbers, and simple shapes in their daily environment. They count, describe, compare, and sort objects, and develop a sense of patterns and properties.
Grade One	By the end of the year, children understand and use the concept of ones and tens in the place-value number system. They add and subtract small numbers confidently. They measure, using simple units, and locate objects in space. They describe data, and analyze and solve simple problems.
Grade Two	By the end of the year, children understand relationships and place value in addition and in subtraction. They use simple multiplication concepts. They measure quantities with appropriate units. They can classify shapes and see relationships among them by attending to the geometric characteristics. They collect and analyze data and are able to verify answers.
Grade Three	By the end of the year, children have deepened their understanding of place value as well as their understanding of, and skill with, whole number addition, subtraction, multiplication, and division. They estimate and measure. They describe objects in space and use patterns to help solve problems. They represent number relationships and are able to conduct simple probability experiments.

Process Standards

In addition to its five content standards, the NCTM (2000) also lists five standards that define mathematical processes through which students should gain and use their mathematical knowledge. Programs therefore should focus on Standard 6 (or *problem-solving*) and Standard 7 (or *reasoning and proof*); and use Standard 8 (or *communication*). Finally, programs should emphasize Standard 9 (or *connections*) and Standard 10 (or *representation*).

The areas described by the ten Standards are integrated; content can be acquired within the Process Standards and processes can be learned within the Content Standards.

KEY VOCABULARY AND SYMBOLS FOR EARLY CHILDHOOD MATH CONCEPTS

A good math vocabulary often includes many everyday words that are involved in the development of a strong foundation in this content area. Seven groups of such key words (with examples) have been delineated by Smith (1997).

The first category is Comparing Words, which is involved as the child observes differences in characteristics such as size, loudness, or temperature and, therefore, understands words such as *hot/cold* and *large/small*. A second is Directional Words, used during a gym activity or a musical game, which include *forward/backward* and *up/down*.

A third category covers Positional Words, concerned mostly with space concepts such as *in/out* and *apart/together*; the most difficult vocabulary in this grouping refers to the concepts of *right* and *left*. Sequence Words are often experienced by students firsthand as these words provide a sense of order, such as *first/last* and *before/after*.

The Language of Time is the fifth category and, while its acquisition begins before school formally starts, it is not until approximately age nine that girls and boys truly comprehend time concepts (Copeland, 1984). Young children understand the present and can even discuss events in the future, but quickly forget most of the past. Examples of general time words include *morning, night,* and *day*; clock words include *hour, minutes,* and *watch*; and calendar words involve *tomorrow, birthday,* and *holidays.*

Shape Words help young students describe common objects in their environment as *squares* or *triangles*, or as *round* or *flat*. Number Words, the last and especially critical category, concerns our number system. These words help children learn to count, and to compare quantities and recognize relationships such as *greater than/less than*. There are both cardinal numbers (for quantity) and ordinal numbers (for position).

In order to communicate math concepts, symbols (including signs and numbers) are used in place of alphabetic letters. The field of mathematics deals with the quantitative world, and children learn that symbols allow people to transmit quantitative ideas precisely. In the early grades, they are introduced to symbols for *operations* (e.g., + and −), *relations* (e.g., > and <), and *ideas*, including numbers and elements (e.g., 1, 2, x). To a lesser extent, they encounter the symbol for *punctuation* (e.g., the decimal point in problems involving money).

Teachers are advised to help children practice writing complete math sentences by using at least two symbols (for relations and numbers, for example) so the English sentence, "6 is less than 8" becomes the math sentence, "6 < 8." An example of a sentence using three symbols (for relations, numbers, and operations) is 4 × 3 = 12 for the English sentence, "4 times 3 equals 12." Number sentences are written horizontally using the various symbols, and children can write a number sentence for each story problem they can read individually or discuss in cooperative groups.

CONTENT FOR EARLY CHILDHOOD MATH PROGRAMS: STANDARD #1

Boys and girls come to school with an informal knowledge of *Number and Operations.* The school's responsibility, then, is to build on that base with more formal skills because an understanding of number is fundamental to the entire mathematics curriculum internationally as well as in the United States and Canada (Reys & Nohda, 1994). There are three focus areas (NCTM, 2000):

1. An understanding of numbers, ways of representing numbers, relationships among numbers, and number systems;
2. An understanding of the meaning of operations and how they relate to each other; and
3. The efficient and accurate use of computational strategies and tools and an ability to estimate appropriately.

Number Concepts and Their Properties

Young children count everything and learn to associate number words with collections of objects counted by establishing one-to-one correspondence. Primary students enjoy opportunities to develop, use, and practice counting as they measure, solve problems, and quantify. They can learn different counting strategies (e.g., counting by twos or tens or counting backwards), which help them build a foundation for subtraction and multiplication. At this stage, teachers can integrate counting books with storylines, such as *Ten, Nine, Eight* (by Molly Bang), *1, 2, 3 to the Zoo* (by Eric Carle), and *Teddy Bears 1 to 10* (by Susanna Gretz).

Children particularly enjoy counting large numbers, and gradually begin to use grouping techniques to help them count larger numbers. Their sense of numbers develops as they come to understand the size of numbers, develop various ways of regarding and representing them, use numbers as referents, and develop correct perceptions about how operations affect numbers. They slowly develop the ability to mentally visualize numbers and/or think about numbers without using blocks or other physical models.

In the early grades, girls and boys begin to understand place value as they enjoy counting into the hundreds, recognize ten as a special unit, and start to appreciate critical patterns in the numeration system. By developing flexibility in thinking about numbers, they are, at the same time, acquiring an understanding of the base-ten number system. Concrete models, such as connecting cubes or beans, will also allow students to represent numbers in groups of ten and help them make the transition to written symbols. They even learn to group and ungroup by tens. Finally, a useful and inexpensive tool in place-value instruction is the calculator, which lets each child see the patterns involved as the digits change.

Although fractions do not receive major attention in the early grades, the school can build on the ordinary language that young children bring into the classroom, as shown, for example, in *Give Me Half!* (by Stuart Murphy). Instruction should be informal, based on everyday events (e.g., dividing an apple) and integrated into meaningful experiences, which provide the foundation for study in the intermediate grades. Rather than memorizing the fraction notation, it is more important that students understand the language and the concept (e.g., one purple section of a white sheet of paper that has been folded twice evenly is one fourth of the sheet).

Operations and Their Properties

Young students develop an understanding of the meanings of such operations as addition and subtraction through a variety of situations and settings. Some of these are child-initiated and others are through teacher-created stories. When children can model the situations directly with objects or by using counting techniques, they can solve simple joining and take-away problems.

In much the same way, through problem solving and modeling situations, they can acquire a meaning of multiplication (as being the addition of equal groups) and investigate division. They enjoy listening to books such as *The Doorbell Rang* (by Pat Hutchins) and *One Hundred Hungry Ants* (by Elinor Pinczes). While young students may not use the symbols or language that older children do in dealing with addition, subtraction, multiplication, or division, they are still able to find ways to solve a broad range of problems. They are revealing a growing sense of number when they begin naturally to use the *communicative property* ("If I know that $8 \times 3 = 24$, then I know $3 \times 8 = 24$. I can prove the same by drawing an array.") and *distributive property* ("When I multiply 7×42, I can consider it as $7 \times 40 = 280$ and $7 \times 2 = 14$. Then I can add the 14 to the 280 and get 294.").

Children in the early grades must communicate their problem-solving strategies orally first, and then later through drawings or other types of written work. By talking and writing about their thinking, they are better able to solidify their ideas and share different ways of resolving a problem like the one found in *Dollars and Cents for Harriet* (by Betsy and Giulio Maestro). They learn to use both conventional notation as well as their own recording techniques.

Computation and Estimation

Even though young students usually begin to compute by using concrete objects, they slowly shift to doing numerous computations mentally or with the help of paper and pencil. During their explorations with numbers and operations on numbers, they invent strategies for determining and remembering basic arithmetic facts. When combined with those facts, these invented strategies or algorithms provide children with methods for computing with larger numbers, and also help them link intuitive knowledge with more formal arithmetic. One recent longitudinal study concluded that 90 percent of young students surveyed used invented strategies; furthermore, those who did so before they acquired standard algorithms not only showed a better understanding of base-ten concepts but they could also better expand that understanding to new situations (Carpenter, Franke, Jacobs, Fennema, & Empson, 1998). Although individual strategies may, and often do, vary, all children benefit from discussing and examining different approaches to the same problem. In doing so, they also indirectly help the teacher plan additional lessons to raise the levels of mathematical thinking in that class.

Young children must be supported in their efforts to develop their own computational strategies. If they can use those accurately and efficiently, can explain why and how those methods work, and even extend them to new situations, they have gained acceptable competence. Often, those strategies will approximate closely conventional algorithms, whose introduction should be postponed until later in the elementary school program.

A necessary component to the students' acquisition of fluency with both basic skills of addition and subtraction number combinations and computation with larger numbers is practice. It needs to be systematic and motivating and can be conducted in the context of other activities, such as keeping score during a spelling game or listening to (or reading) a book like *Arthur's Funny Money* (by Lillian Hoban).

What matters is that students in the early grades develop a foundation for mathematics that is meaningful to them. Through teacher-directed discussions, they can compare various strategies. Should a problem arise that involves more cumbersome computations, children should be encouraged to use calculators as an aid to solving it (NCTM, 1998).

CONTENT FOR EARLY CHILDHOOD MATH PROGRAMS: STANDARD #2

At an early age, children develop beginning concepts concerned with *Algebra*. They recognize patterns and can make comparisons. Their observations and discussions of how things change gradually promotes the notion of function. In their use of objects and pictures for representing mathematical situations, and in their growing understanding of symbols, they are developing the background for the symbolic representations needed for math study in the intermediate grades. Many of the learning objectives in this content area are attained as students work with Number and Operations (Standard #1). These include the ability to classify and sort, analyze simple patterns, describe change, describe situations mathematically, and develop an understanding and use of the properties possessed by numbers and operations. There are four focus areas for Standard #2 (NCTM, 2000):

1. An understanding of various types of patterns, functions and relations;
2. The use of algebraic symbols to represent and analyze mathematical situations and structures; and
3. The use of mathematical models to represent quantitative relationships; and
4. The ability to analyze quantitative and qualitative change in various contexts.

Patterns, Functions, and Relations

Young children notice the regular arrangements of numbers, objects, and shapes and are able to extend the patterns in order to make predictions. Patterns can even be found outside of the math lessons and represent a way that children can follow to organize their world; they also help children develop the ability to form generalizations. That recognition provides the basis for the notion that two items of a very different nature can still be the same in several important ways. Sorting and classifying are, therefore, important aspects of the mathematical development of students in the early grades; these areas can be reinforced by such read-aloud literature as *Just a Mess* (by Mercer Mayer) and *The Button Box* (by Margarette Reid). Finally, patterns are a precursor to function, so children must learn to record numerical relations in tables. More complex patterns that involve more than one attribute can be created by students using attribute blocks and/or computer technology.

Algebraic Symbols

Young children who have the opportunities to generalize from observations about number and operations are forming the foundation of algebraic thinking (e.g., when two numbers are added, their order does not matter). Although the exact vocabulary involved need not be introduced, the teacher should be aware of the algebraic properties used by students and help the children develop an awareness of what they are doing. They should understand the reversal of operation, working with tools and situations in which processes can be reversed. They should learn to use pictorial, concrete, and verbal representations of numerical situations, including invented notation, and be encouraged to use symbolic notation by activities requiring manipulation of objects and quantities that symbols represent. They should encounter equality, a significant algebraic concept.

Models and Change

Under the guidance of their teacher, young students should learn to make mathematical models of concrete situations, using addition and subtraction of whole numbers. They should make comparisons, describing change both qualitatively (e.g., *higher than*) and quantitatively (e.g., *two feet higher*). Since some changes are predictable, it is important that every child understands that many of them can be described mathematically.

CONTENT FOR EARLY CHILDHOOD MATH PROGRAMS: STANDARD #3

Long before they start school, children develop knowledge about *Geometry* as they explore structures and shapes in their environment. Through block constructions, drawings, dramatic play, and verbal language, they learn to represent two- and three-dimensional shapes. They also use some knowledge about position and direction as soon as they begin to talk, and are able to locate objects by giving and following directions verbally. At this stage, the children's geometric and spatial abilities often surpass their numerical skills. The four focus areas for this standard (NCTM, 2000) are:

1. An analysis of properties and characteristics of two- and three-dimensional geometric shapes and of mathematical arguments about geometric relationship;
2. The description and location of spatial relationships using different representational systems, including coordinate geometry;

A young student colors in a pumpkin drawn on one-inch graph paper.

3. The application of transformations and the use of symmetry in analyzing mathematical situations; and

4. The use of visualization, geometric modeling, and spatial reasoning to solve problems both within and outside of mathematics.

Geometric Shapes and Relationships

The naming and describing of shapes is an important component of the geometry program for young children. While they begin by using their own terms as needed, they can slowly integrate conventional vocabulary as the teacher uses it. Although at first they learn to recognize shapes as wholes, they gradually characterize shapes by their properties or attributes. This recognition is promoted by structured environments and by carefully chosen materials such as pattern blocks and models of geometric solids.

Students can explore geometric properties by combining familiar figures to form new shapes (e.g., folding construction paper squares in various ways). They can work with tangram and attribute puzzles for useful geometric experiences.

In the early grades, children should recognize, name, build, draw, compare, and sort two- and three-dimensional shapes and be able to describe their attributes and parts; locate and recognize geometric structures and shapes in the world; recognize congruent and similar shapes; investigate and predict the results of putting shapes together and then taking them apart; and, lastly, relate geometric ideas to number and measurement ideas.

It is important to note that the major sources for judging the developing geometric knowledge of young children are their conversations, their journal entries, and their pictures. As they draw and discuss their experiences, the teacher can use the information when planning future lessons, some of which can include sharing literature

A first grader proudly shares the artwork he designed using triangles.

that has storylines such as *The Greedy Triangle* (by Marilyn Burns), *The Village of Round and Square Houses* (by Ann Grifalconi), *The Boy with Square Eyes* (by Juliet and Charles Snape), and *Grandfather Tang's Story* (by Ann Tompert). Three nonfiction books (written in rhyming verse) include *The Wing on a Flea* (by Ed Emberley), *The Shapes Game* (by Paul Rogers), and *The Shape of Me and Other Stuff* (by Dr. Seuss).

Spatial Relationships

Teacher-led discussions during the school day extend children's knowledge of relative position in space. Through the following four types of mathematical questions regarding navigation and maps, students develop various spatial understandings: Which way? (direction), How far? (distance), Where? (location), and What objects? (representation). Girls and boys should name, describe, interpret, and apply ideas of (1) relative position in space, and (2) direction and distance in navigating space. They should find and name locations with simple relations (e.g., *next to*) and coordinate systems (i.e., maps).

Children can prepare, with a teacher's help, maps of their own environments by gluing pictures from discarded magazines onto a large sheet of paper. They can learn to read simple maps and develop navigation ideas (e.g., *left, right*) and global directions (e.g., *north, east*). Some computer programs also help children navigate through maps, thereby reinforcing direction, perspective, orientation, and measurement concepts.

Transformations and Symmetry

Young children come to school with intuitive ideas about shapes and how shapes may move. They can use their own physical experiences to learn about transformations such as flips (*reflections*), slides (*transformations*) and turns (*rotations*). In the early grades, students should recognize and apply slides, flips, and turns as they solve puzzles.

Children are able to investigate the effects of various transformations on shapes. As they create similar shapes on the geoboard, for example, they can demonstrate how a change in size does not affect a change in shape. And, with technology, students using certain shapes programs can think about the motions they are using, which in turn can help them abstract ideas about sliding, flipping, and turning. Movement experiences help children increase their understanding of shape and structure, and of spatial skills.

They should also recognize and create rotational and reflectional symmetry of two- and three-dimensional objects. As they work with structured geometric materials like pattern blocks, they can create designs with linear and rotational symmetry, and even prove to their teacher the symmetric characteristics of their work.

Visualization, Geometric Modeling, and Spatial Reasoning

Boys and girls in the early grades should learn to create mental images of geometric shapes (spatial visualization and spatial memory). They should recognize and describe spatial relationships and be able to represent objects from different points of view and different perspectives. Spatial visualization involves building and manipulating mental images of shapes and transformations. A proven foundation for this is work with concrete shapes such as attribute and pattern blocks, tangrams, and other shape sets. To build their spatial reasoning, children can be asked to imagine and predict as they perform assigned shape and transformation activities.

Spatial memory is used by students as they recall, for instance, the configuration of the dots on the dominoes and know instantly the correct number without actually counting the dots. A sample *quick image* activity for developing spatial memory has been described as follows: Children get a brief glimpse of a simple configuration on an overhead projector and then try to reproduce it; the teacher shows the configuration again for a few seconds and encourages the students to modify their drawings; the process is repeated several times so the class can self-correct its work; finally, the teacher asks the children to relate what procedures they followed (Yackel & Wheatley, 1990). Spatial reasoning is also developed through navigation activities, such as (1) visualizing the route the students took to get from their classroom to the library media center, or (2) viewing a block model of the classroom from different perspectives.

CONTENT FOR EARLY CHILDHOOD MATH PROGRAMS: STANDARD #4

The teaching of *Measurement* helps young children advance their initial ideas of spatial understanding as well as build connections between that understanding and number. They need to comprehend what it means to measure as well as what is being measured; such understanding only comes after they have experienced a variety of different activities involving informal measurement, visual comparison, and manipulation of concrete objects. There are two focus areas for this standard (NCTM, 2000):

1. An understanding of measurement attributes, units, and systems; as well as the measurable attributes of objects, and
2. An ability to apply a variety of measurement tools, techniques, and formulae.

For the first focus area, children should recognize the attributes of weight, length, capacity, time, and area; compare and order objects qualitatively by those attributes;

The teacher uses a large manipulative clock to help her young students learn to tell time.

make and use measurements in natural settings; and develop referents for estimation and a sense of the measurement unit through estimation. For the second focus area, boys and girls should use such tools as rulers to measure; learn to measure with the same size unit (standard and nonstandard); and use iteration (repetition of units) to measure area and length.

Measurement Systems and Measurement Attributes of Objects

Measurement starts as primary students classify objects using comparative language. Teachers must plan many experiences for the class to see, compare, and touch objects directly (as during block building) before children can understand the attributes of measurement. When they compare objects in various dimensions, for example, followed by a whole-class discussion of the experience, they are also developing the vocabulary commonly associated with measurement.

Estimation activities should be incorporated throughout measurement because their purposes are threefold: help students understand the attributes and processes of measuring; promote their awareness of the sizes of units; and support their development of number concepts and skills. In many daily situations (e.g., "What time did you eat breakfast?"), exact measurements are sometimes unnecessary for answering the query and, therefore, children should realize that it is often preferable to report a measurement as an estimation (e.g., "between seven and seven-thirty").

The measuring process is the same for any attribute: choose a unit, compare that unit to the object, and report the number of units by counting or by using a measuring tool. Most measurements for early primary children will use nonstandard units; still, students should experiment and become familiar with standard measures such as inches and feet and centimeters and meters by the end of second grade.

Girls and boys in the early grades develop beginning notions of length (as they use yardsticks to record their height); of area (as they make designs with pattern block shapes); of capacity and volume (as they count while filling a box with unifix cubes); and of weight (by using a scale to measure equal amounts of clay for an art project).

Children also need to explore time concepts and ways that time is measured. They need to develop a sense of time intervals and learn about calendars and seasons. Teachers have routine opportunities throughout the day to focus on time as a unit of measure (*It's ten o'clock and time for recess.*) and can also introduce the class to such stories as *Pigs on a Blanket* (by Amy Axelrod), *The Grouchy Ladybug* (by Eric Carle), *Clocks and More Clocks* (by Pat Hutchins), *Cookie's Week* (by Cindy Ward), and *The Very Hungry Caterpillar* (by Eric Carle). Young students should learn to understand patterns of minutes, hours, days, weeks, and months.

Measurement Techniques and Tools

Measurement techniques can be counting, iteration, estimation, or the use of formulas or tools. While measuring tools include such items as rulers, tapes, scales, and clocks, formulas are general relationships that produce measurements, given values for the variables in the formula.

Children need hands-on experiences and the use of concrete materials in order to develop both the skills and the concepts of measurement. If, initially, they use a variety of units, nonstandard and standard, they will begin to understand the nature of units and the need for standard units. Useful experiences include actually measuring with different materials, from toothpicks to tape measures, so students will recognize the discrepancies between certain measurements and the need for standard tools. They will also enjoy listening to (or reading) stories concerned with nonstandard and standard measurements, including *How Big Is a Foot?* (by Rolf Myller) and *Inch by Inch* (by Leo Lionni).

Making a monthly calendar helps the student develop a sense of time intervals.

CONTENT FOR EARLY CHILDHOOD
MATH PROGRAMS: STANDARD #5

The teaching of *Data Analysis and Probability* involves informal activities of sorting, comparing, and counting to promote the start of mathematical understandings of data and data analysis. Young children can ask questions in order to investigate, organize the responses, and create graphs or other representations of their data. Informal experiences may also underlie experimental probability (e.g., tossing number cubes), but the chief purpose for such activities concerns more important strands, such as number. There are four focus areas for this standard (NCTM, 2000):

1. An ability to pose questions and then collect, organize, and represent data to answer those questions;
2. The selection and use of proper statistical methods of data analysis;
3. The development and evaluation of predictions and inferences which are based on data; and
4. An understanding and application of basic notions of probability.

For the first focus area, children can gather data about themselves and their environment in order to answer questions involving multiple responses; they can classify and sort objects and then organize data according to their characteristics; they can represent data to show results quickly by using pictures, numbers, and concrete objects. For the second focus area, children should describe the data as a whole as well the parts; they should identify parts of the data with special traits, such as the category with the most frequent response (e.g., during a Fruits and Vegetables Unit, students can each relate which type of melon is their favorite).

The third and fourth focus areas at this grade level should involve only informal discussions and informal activities. Children should begin to understand certain vocabulary (e.g., *more likely, less likely*) as teachers introduce the beginnings of probability.

ASSESSMENT IN EARLY ELEMENTARY MATHEMATICS

In 1995, the National Council of Teachers of Mathematics defined assessment: first as an evidence-gathering process concerned with students' disposition toward, knowledge of, and ability to use mathematics; secondly, as the process of making inferences from the evidence for various purposes, only one of which is evaluation. According to the Council, evaluation is the process of deciding the worth of something, based on careful judgment following its examination.

Briefly, assessment is a process of describing what children know and can do in mathematics. Its purposes are outlined in four categories (NCTM, 1995): promoting growth by monitoring and documenting student progress in the classroom; helping teachers improve instruction by making decisions linking learning and teaching; recognizing accomplishment by evaluating and reporting student achievement; and evaluating programs by documenting their strengths and weaknesses and then recommending improvements.

Assessment Standards

The 1995 assessment standards of the NCTM include the following:

1. The Mathematics Standard, because assessment reflects the content that all children should be able to do, with the realization that the body of knowledge is changing;

2. The Learning Standard, because assessment enhances mathematics study and should therefore be a critical component of the learning process;

3. The Equity Standard, because assessment must further the mathematics learning of all students, giving everyone sufficient opportunities to demonstrate mathematical power in ways that do not discriminate against boys and girls who are disabled or are non-native English speakers;

4. The Openness Standard, because assessment of what children learn in mathematics should be communicated to all the stakeholders in education (Shaw & Blake, 1998), including students, teachers, parents, and community members;

5. The Inferences Standard, because assessment provides valid inferences from multiple sources to offer evidence of children's learning of mathematics; and

6. The Coherence Standard, because assessment of organized content must be valid, matching the purposes of mathematics instruction with the broad curriculum goals of the district while simultaneously recalling the developmental levels of the children involved.

Assessment Strategies

There are several common techniques for assessing the mathematical efforts of young children, and teachers should choose more than one that they can use comfortably with the particular group of students enrolled at the time. Choices may be affected by the developmental level of the boys and girls, by district mandates, and/or by teacher personal preference. Teachers often combine some of the techniques in order to obtain a more accurate reading of any one child's growth.

The first strategy is *observation*, familiar to both teachers (and parents). It allows teachers to modify a lesson, redirect it during the presentation, or even conclude it earlier or extend it longer than originally planned. In assessing individual children's work, some teachers only watch and listen. Others, however, also take notes, using small self-adhesive pads and then later transferring their observations to a more formal record. These notetakers should focus on only a few aspects at any one time, and may wish occasionally to include social behaviors (e.g., cooperative group efforts) in their observations.

One primary teacher (Fisher, 1995) employs a class evaluation form that she has developed and that she completes as she observes students during a variety of math experiences. She transfers the information periodically to an individual math evaluation profile that covers fifteen items including, for example, place value, estimating, problem solving, and the use of math vocabulary. The profile also has room for dates as well as a key that quickly shows the extent and quality of the item observed.

A second assessment strategy is *interviewing*, which is more time-consuming in its planning and execution because it always demands careful questioning techniques and sometimes incorporates performance tasks. However, it elicits useful information that can supplement informal observations. The teacher must decide whether to interview the entire class in small groups or individually. In either instance, it is important to listen and allow the students to struggle with a problem (Smith, 1997); too much coaching, overcorrecting, or actually completing the assigned task for them should be avoided because it convinces the group that delays are a clever device. Interviews can be conducted informally and routinely during a brief conversation at the child's table, or more formally and less often in a quiet corner as the rest of the class continues to work.

Questioning and discussion comprise a third strategy for assessing the mathematical knowledge and skills of young students. Both occur daily in the classroom, and can be structured to show how well children understand a concept and are able to share their views with each other. Carefully constructed questions, together with manipulatives and pictures, can stimulate discussion, particularly if that discussion is based on an experience during which the children participated together (e.g., using nonstandard means to measure various parts of the classroom).

The questions should be open-ended, requiring higher-level thinking skills, and the teacher at first may need to encourage talk by modeling possible replies. Children must be cautioned to listen to their classmates and to build on each other's responses. Several students should be asked to give answers to the same question, so that the class realizes that there may be more than one acceptable solution to a problem (and the teacher discovers more about how the children think). Sometimes it is valuable to duplicate the questions, distribute copies among student pairs or small groups, and let the pairs or groups decide on the answers before the teacher calls for a whole-class discussion.

Children's drawings and writings are the fourth assessment strategy as even young girls and boys can write (or draw) in their math journals (Black, 2000). They can, for instance, each create a math problem for their partner, exchange and solve it, and then write an explanation of the answer. Some of these problems with correct solutions can later be posted on the Math Board for the rest of the class to see.

Student writing includes lists, charts, concept diagrams, and texts for such wordless books by Tina Hoban as *Shapes, Shapes, Shapes* and *Is It Larger? Is It Smaller?* Both of these consist of color photographs that easily evoke written reactions from a group of children working cooperatively. A project of this nature provides teachers with insight into the math understandings and attitudes of the students although it is not generally graded. However, when the work is dated and kept in a notebook or portfolio, children, teachers, and parents can all review it periodically and note the progress made.

The fifth strategy is *student self-assessment*, which can begin in a whole-class setting as early as first grade when the teacher asks a leading question (e.g., "Who can tell me what we proved in math today?"), and then writes the children's ideas on the board and reviews them with the class. The next step occurs when the assessment is conducted in groups, with the teacher monitoring the activity and prompting the children with additional open-ended questions about their work. Finally, the students are ready to reflect individually on their math assignment and write those thoughts into their journals.

Sample self-assessment questions may include the following: (1) What do you like least and best about our math class? (2) What did you learn this week in math that you did not know last week? and (3) How well did you and your partner (group) work together today? (Smith, 1997). Such questions are among those that can prompt self-evaluation, which can also sometimes include individual and small-group conferences with the teacher perusing the journals.

Performance tasks constitute the sixth assessment strategy, and are equally useful with school beginners and older primary children. The technique calls for children to actually do and use math, whether individually or in groups, in order to solve a problem that interests them. Once it has been selected, the teacher must next decide what kind of a performance is acceptable (e.g., drawings or drama) and how it can be measured (e.g., using a rubric). It is important that, as students work on the assigned task, the teacher observes not only their mathematical skills, but their social skills as well (Stenmark, 1991).

The seventh assessment strategy is *student portfolios*, which often include other evaluative techniques as well. Portfolios are simply collections of dated samples of children's work over time. In this content area, they should contain varied and concrete proof of the students' understanding of mathematics and of their ability to solve problems; items such as graphs, student self-assessments, entries from a math journal, test papers, and photos of projects are all suitable for inclusion (Micklo, 1997). Used in several curriculum areas, student portfolios are well regarded as providing an alternative to traditional methods of assessment. They offer an opportunity for children, teachers, and parents to communicate, based on the evidence collected.

Teacher-made tests comprise the eighth and last assessment strategy concerned with the progress that young children are making in learning mathematics. They should appropriately involve learning activities that directly review previous instruction and indirectly assist in future planning. There should be items that allow students to display and explain their problem-solving skills. Other items could require children to write or draw their answers and justify how they figured out the solutions.

What teachers cannot include, however, are test items that work successfully with older children but only tend to confuse younger learners (e.g., multiple-choice or true–false questions in the area of measurement). Lastly, results of teacher-made tests should be carefully balanced with outcomes from other assessment strategies.

REFERENCES

Black, S. (2000). Math logs. *r.w.t.*, *1*(3), 12–13.

California Department of Education. (1997). *Mathematics Content Standards for California Public Schools: Kindergarten through Grade Twelve.* Sacramento: Author.

Carpenter, T., Franke, M., Jacobs, V., Fennema, E., & Empson, S. (1998). A longitudinal study of invention and understanding in children's multidigit addition and subtraction. *Journal for Research in Mathematics Education, 29,* 3–20.

Copeland, R. (1984). *How Children Learn Mathematics: Implication for Piaget's Research, (4th ed.).* New York: Macmillan.

Fisher, R. (1995). *Thinking and Learning Together: Curriculum and Community in a Primary Classroom.* Portsmouth, NH: Heinemann.

Micklo, S. (1997). Math portfolios in the primary grades. *Childhood Education, 73* (4), 194–199.

National Council of Teachers of Mathematics. (1995). *Assessment Standards for School Mathematics.* Reston, VA: Author.

National Council of Teachers of Mathematics. (1998). *Principles and Standards for School Mathematics: Discussion Draft.* Reston, VA: Author.

National Council of Teachers of Mathematics. (2000). *Principles and Standards for School Mathematics.* Reston, VA: Author.

Reys, R. & Nohda, N. (Eds.) (1994) *Computational Alternatives for the Twenty-first Century: Cross-Cultural Perspectives from Japan and the United States.* Reston, VA: National Council of Teachers of Mathematics.

Shaw, J. & Blake, S. (1998). *Mathematics for Young Children.* Upper Saddle River, NJ: Merrill/Prentice-Hall.

Smith, S. (1997). *Early Childhood Mathematics.* Needham Heights, MA: Allyn & Bacon.

Stenmark, J. (1991). *Mathematics Assessment: Myths, Models, Good Questions, and Practical Suggestions.* Reston, VA: National Council of Teachers of Mathematics.

Yackel, E. & Wheatley, G. (1990). Promoting visual imagery in young people. *Arithmetic Teacher, 37* (6), 52–58.

CHILDREN'S LITERATURE CITED

Axelrod, A.   *Pigs on a Blanket* (Simon & Schuster, 1996).

Bang, M.   *Ten, Nine, Eight* (Greenwillow, 1983).

Burns, M.   *The Greedy Triangle* (Scholastic, 1994).

Carle, E.   *1, 2, 3 to the Zoo* (Putnam, 1968).

Carle, E.   *The Grouchy Ladybug* (Harper, 1977).

Carle, E.   *The Very Hungry Caterpillar* (Putnam, 1981)

Emberley, E.   *The Wing on a Flea* (Little, Brown, 1961).

Gretz, S.   *Teddy Bears 1 to 10* (Macmillan, 1986).

Grifalconi, A.   *The Village of Round and Square Houses* (Little, Brown, 1986).

Hoban, L.   *Arthur's Funny Money* (Harper 1981).

Hoban, T.   *Is It Larger? Is It Smaller?* (Greenwillow, 1985)

Hoban, T.   *Shapes, Shapes, Shapes* (Greenwillow, 1986).

Hutchins, P.   *Clocks and More Clocks* (Macmillan, 1970).

Hutchins, P.   *The Doorbell Rang* (Greenwillow, 1986).

Lionni, L.   *Inch by Inch* (Astor-Honor, 1960).

Maestro, B. & Maestro, G.   *Dollars and Cents for Harriet* (Crown, 1988).

Mayer, M.   *Just a Mess* (Western Publishing, 1987).

Murphy, S.   *Give Me Half!* (HarperCollins, 1996).

Myller, R.   *How Big Is a Foot?* (Dell, 1990).

Pinczes, E.   *One Hundred Hungry Ants* (Houghton Mifflin, 1993).

Reid, M.   *The Button Box* (Dutton, 1990).

Rogers, P.   *The Shapes Game* (Holt, 1989).

Seuss, Dr.   *The Shape of Me and Other Stuff* (Random House, 1988).

Snape, J. & Snape, C.   *The Boy with Square Eyes* (Prentice-Hall, 1987).

Tompert, A.   *Grandfather Tang's Story* (Crown, 1990).

Ward, C.   *Cookie's Week* (Putnam, 1988).

CHAPTER FIVE

FORTY-FIVE LITERATURE ACTIVITIES PROMOTING MATHEMATICAL UNDERSTANDINGS

CONTENT STANDARD #1: NUMBER AND OPERATIONS
(with students keeping math journals)

■ ■ ■ **(1) CONCEPT:** Money consists of coins and bills.

Literature: *Pigs Will Be Pigs* by A. Axelrod (Four Winds, 1994), 40 pp.

Listed in: *Best Books for Children* (R. R. Bowker, 1998).

Synopsis: A family of pigs (father, mother, two piglets) is hungry but there is no food in the house. So, to finance a dinner out, the family engages in a money hunt around the house. Later, after visiting their favorite restaurant, the pigs return home to find the complete mess they created as they hunted for the needed money.

Activities After Read-Aloud:

1. Retell the story and have the students work in pairs, using paper money to re-create the plot. One child can hand the partner the money that is found by the pigs as they "Hunt for money!" The partner must count the money to double-check the amount. Each pair should then write down the moneys exchanged.
2. Reread the story and have the children count and tally the money (from each page) that the pigs found. At the end of the story, have the class add up all the money found by the family to figure out the total amount taken to the restaurant.
3. Make copies of the menu from the story and distribute these to the class. Then ask students to write addition problems from the menu. Later, they can each exchange their paper with a friend and solve each other's problems.
4. Using the same menu, ask the children what change they would get back if they had a five-dollar bill to pay for the stuffed jalapeños, for example, that cost $2.00. Continue to ask similar questions so the children can determine the change they would receive after paying for certain items. _____

■ ■ ■ **(2) CONCEPT:** Numbers can be counted backwards.

Literature: *Ten, Nine, Eight* by M. Bang (Greenwillow, 1983), 24 pp.

Listed in: *Best Books for Children* (R. R. Bowker, 1998).

Synopsis: While observing the bedroom of a little girl getting ready to go to sleep, the reader can count objects backwards from ten to one.

Activities After Read-Aloud:

1. Have the children practice counting down from ten to one with manipulatives such as unifix cubes, crayons, buttons, blocks, or beans. Divide the students into small groups and have them lay out the objects and count backwards as they repeatedly take one away until a single manipulative is left.
2. Have the children each draw their bedroom. Following the book as a model, let each child draw similar objects in his/her bedroom: ten toes, nine stuffed

animals, eight windows, seven shoes, six hanging seashells on a mobile, five buttons on a nightshirt, four arms embracing (as parent and child are hugging), three books on the floor, two eyes reading a book, and one child's bed. Have children write (or dictate) the names of the objects in their picture.

3. Distribute one sheet of construction paper and ten craft sticks or toothpicks to each child. Ask the class to design a picture on each paper. Next, have the children practice removing each stick off the paper while counting backwards from 10 to 1. Finally, have them glue their craft sticks or toothpicks onto their papers and decorate their pictures. Encourage the children to share their work.

4. Prepare a bulletin board of numbers counting forwards from one to ten and backwards from ten to one. Use the display as a learning center and allow children to use pointers to practice their counting with partners. _____

■ ■ ■ **(3) CONCEPT:**   As numbers get bigger, each represents more objects.

Literature: *1, 2, 3 to the Zoo* by E. Carle (Putnam, 1968), 34 pp.

Listed in: *Best Books for Children* (R. R. Bowker, 1998).

Synopsis: This counting book has pictures of a train of animals in boxcars. Each car contains a different species and a different number from one to ten. The final page shows the animals arriving at the zoo.

Activities After Read-Aloud:

1. Have the children take turns dramatizing the pages of the book by creating a train and parading around the room. Have one child pretend to be an elephant at the zoo, two children can be hippopotami swimming, three can be giraffes stretching, four represent lions roaring, and so on.

2. Distribute construction paper so that children can draw and number ten rectangles to represent boxcars. Share the book and assign the children to draw zoo animals on the boxcars, which are marked from one to ten. Let them copy the name of the animal(s) in each car from a list on the board.

3. Prepare a bulletin board with ten boxcars along the bottom of the board. Place numbers one through ten on the boxcars. Then have groups of students create a zoo, cutting out imaginary animals from construction paper and placing them on the board. The number of animals must correspond to the numbers one through ten that were assigned, for a total of fifty-five creative creatures on the board. Have the children discuss their animals.

4. Create a Big Book, numbering each page one through ten. Let the class decide which animals should be represented on each page. Then divide the children into small groups so that each group is responsible for one page by drawing the proper number of animals on construction paper to correspond with the assigned number, and then writing briefly about the animals. The Big Book can be placed on the library table for all to examine. _____

■ ■ ■ **(4) CONCEPT:**   Numbers show how many objects are present.

Literature: *Ten Black Dots* by D. Crews (Greenwillow, 1986), 32 pp.

Listed in: *Best Books for Children* (R. R. Bowker, 1998).

Synopsis: This counting book emphasizes the distinctness of each set of objects (e.g., "5 dots make buttons on a coat"). The text has no storyline and there is no relationship among the various sets of objects, but the end of the book shows bands of black dots in a natural counting sequence. Highlighted is the sub-base of 5, as the larger numbers are represented as $5 + 1, 5 + 2$, and so on.

Activities After Read-Aloud:

1. Hold up 9" × 12" cards, each showing numerals with corresponding dots that represent numbers. Say to the class, "When I hold up a card, you must clap your hands the number of times shown on the card." Repeat several times.

2. Give students each ten pieces of tagboard (9" × 6") with the numbers one to ten printed on them. Then distribute to each student fifty-five gummed dots. Ask the students to put the correct number of dots on each piece of tagboard.

3. To help students understand "greater than" and "less than," give the children each four cards showing sets of dots. Have them put their cards in order from the smallest to the greatest number. Guide the students by saying, for example, "Five is less than eight" and "Seven is greater than six."

4. Distribute to each student one sheet of paper and ten plastic counters. Tell the class to create pictures, using the counters as shown in the book and tracing around them. Reinforce the language from the book by saying, for example, "Three dots can be a triple-decker ice cream cone." Have them share their pictures with others as they write the numerals under each picture and tell (or write) about it. _____

■ ■ ■ **(5) CONCEPT:** Numbers have a specific order.

Literature: *Teddy Bears 1 to 10* by S. Gretz (Macmillan, 1986), 32 pp.

Listed in: *Best Books for Children* (R. R. Bowker, 1994).

Synopsis: Starting with the number one, and adding a new bear on each page, many teddy bears go through a process of getting dirty, being cleaned, and then dyed another color. At the end of this counting book, the newly freshened bears join each other for a tea party.

Activities After Read-Aloud:

1. Have the students each fold a large piece of construction paper into eight squares. Using both sides of the paper, they are to label ten squares from one to ten, leaving eight squares blank. Have them draw bears to represent the numbers in ten squares of the paper. Finally, let the class count in unison from one to ten.

2. Cut out ten bear outlines from construction paper, and paste each on craft sticks to make puppets. Label them from one to ten and distribute the puppets. Choose ten children at random to line up in order from one to ten, holding up their puppets. As they sit down, have them count backwards from ten to one. Repeat the activity until all children have had a turn.

3. Buy a box of Teddy Gram™ (graham) crackers, available at most supermarkets and shaped like small bears. First, have the children use unifix cubes to count forward from one to ten. Then give the children each ten crackers, and have them count backwards in unison as they eat one cracker at a time. _____

■ ■ ■ **(6) CONCEPT:** People in line can be counted with ordinal numbers that show the position of each person.

Literature: *The Bus Stop* by N. Hellen (Orchard, 1988), 18 pp.

Listed in: *Best Books for Children* (R. R. Bowker, 1998).

Synopsis: A diverse group of seven people is waiting in line for the bus for a variety of reasons. (Each page is layered on top of another so that each new person on a page does not cover up the last one. Once the suburban bus arrives, that page is cut so that it goes over all the people, but they are shown through the cut-out windows.)

Activities After Read-Aloud:

1. Line up seven students at the front of the room so that the rest of the class can easily see them. Tell the class where the line begins and then ask: "Who is *first* in line?" Repeat the question with the other ordinal numbers.

2. Pair up different objects (e.g., erasers, paintbrushes, etc.) around the classroom. Allow the students to move around the room and work with partners, asking each other, "Which (object) is *second*?" They must touch the object chosen unless crayons or markers are used; children can say which color is second.

3. Distribute sheets of white paper to the children. Have them draw eight animals of the same species. Then ask them to write the ordinal number under

each animal, i.e., first, second, third, and so on. Encourage children to share their drawings and count their animals, using ordinal numbers.

4. Arrange a "Family Math Project" that students can do for homework with the help of their parent(s). Give children each a large sheet of white paper and have them illustrate several of their favorite toys or books. Ask them to line up the pictures of those toys or books in order of their importance and place ordinal numbers under each of them. _____

■ ■ ■ **(7) CONCEPT:** Less money is needed to buy items when prices are reduced during a sale.

Literature: *Arthur's Funny Money* by L. Hoban (Harper, 1981), 64 pp.

Listed in: *Best Books for Children* (R. R. Bowker, 1998).

Synopsis: Arthur, the chimp, wants to buy a T-shirt and matching cap costing a total of $5.00. Since he does not have enough money, he sets up a bicycle-washing business with his little sister Violet, but runs into problems. Finally, however, there is a sale on the shirt and cap at reduced prices, and Arthur can buy what he wants with his $4.43 of savings and earnings and still have $.18 left for licorice twists!

Activities After Read-Aloud:

1. When Arthur first counts the money in his piggy bank, he finds that he has only $3.78. Ask the class to determine two different equations to help Arthur decide how much more money he needs for his $5.00 purchase.

2. Have the children each list how much money Arthur collected from Norman, Wilma, Peter, and John. Then have them describe what jobs Arthur did to earn that money.

3. Sale items are always reduced in price. Have the class each make a Sale! poster, listing other sports clothes besides T-shirts and matching caps. Discuss which ones Arthur could have bought with his $4.43 if what he first wanted was all sold out.

4. Divide the class into groups of four. Give each group one (different) newspaper page showing a major markdown sale at a local store. Have the children list items at the original advertised prices and then also show the reduced prices. Discuss reasons why a store would have such a sale, just as Arthur's general store did with "Window Samples Reduced." _____

■ ■ ■ **(8) CONCEPT:** A number multiplied by itself produces a square number.

Literature: *Sea Squares* by J. Hulme (Hyperion, 1991), unpaged.

Listed in: *Best Books for Children* (R. R. Bowker, 1998).

Synopsis: Ten sea animals from sharks to squids are introduced in a rhyming text about counting and squaring numbers one through ten. Each double-page spread introduces a new number of a different sea creature, including the written number and also the squared number. (More information about each animal is given at the end of the book.)

Activities After Read-Aloud:

1. Make a (construction paper) octopus with the children, like the one shown toward the back of the book. Use a hole punch to make eight suckers on each of the eight arms. Discuss that if all the holes were counted together, the answer could be the same as multiplying the two original numbers.

2. In the book, pelicans dive for fish and pack them in their pouches. Prepare an interactive bulletin board with the students. Make ten pelicans with paper lunch-bag pouches. Write a multiplication problem on each bag that equals a square number. Inside, put a large number of paper cutout fish. Have the students use the cutouts to figure out the answer. (Later show large fish cutouts that have the answers to the problems.)

3. Divide the class into cooperative groups of four so students can "fish" for square numbers with partners. In the center of each table (where four students

are seated), put some fish-shaped magnets with numbers one through ten on them. Attach a string to one end of a chopstick and fasten a small magnet to the other end of the string, and place one such chopstick at each table. Partners must alternate turns trying to pick up two fish-shaped magnets that have the same number and to give the square number answer. The player who can do this will keep the fish-shaped magnets next to him or her. Have the groups play until the fish pool is gone; then count to see who has the most magnets. _____

■ ■ ■ **(9) CONCEPT:** Division is repeated subtraction, involving smaller but equal groups of items.

Literature: *The Doorbell Rang* by P. Hutchins (Greenwillow, 1986), 32 pp.

Listed in: *Best Books for Children* (R. R. Bowker, 1998).

Synopsis: Ma bakes twelve cookies for Sam and Victoria to share between them. However, each time the doorbell rings, more and more of their friends come to share the plate of cookies, which leaves fewer cookies for Sam and Victoria, until Grandma arrives with an enormous tray of fresh cookies.

Activities After Read-Aloud:
1. Divide the class into pairs. Give each pair twenty unifix cubes and ask them to find various ways to put the cubes into equal groups. Have the pairs record their findings. Then have them repeat the activity two more times, first using eighteen cubes and then using twelve cubes.
2. Call twelve students to the front of the room. Tell them that they may become teams for a playground race later. Ask them to place themselves into two equal groups, then three equal groups, and finally four equal groups. Write the equations on the board to show how division is related to multiplication.
3. Give twelve children each a name tag with one of the characters from the story, including Cousins #1, #2, #3, and #4. Then place twelve paper cookies on a paper plate and obtain a small bell. Now, reread the story slowly as the character Ma, allowing time for the other characters to pantomime the actions. The remaining children in the class are to watch carefully to be sure that the cookies are divided equally. Discuss the operation of division as well as the courtesy of sharing.
4. Have children each choose their favorite kind of cookie and then write about how they would share that kind with a friend, especially if they only had one cookie. _____

■ ■ ■ **(10) CONCEPT:** Coins are one form of money and include pennies, nickels, dimes, quarters, and half-dollars.

Literature: *Dollars and Cents for Harriet* by B. Maestro and G. Maestro (Crown, 1988), 32 pp.

Listed in: *Best Books for Children* (R. R. Bowker, 1994).

Synopsis: Harriet, the elephant, wants to buy a toy that costs $5.00. In her piggybank she only has 100 pennies. She then finds ways to earn the other $4.00 in different denominations of coins.

Activities After Read-Aloud:
1. Divide the class into groups of four and give each group one catalog that includes a children's toy/book section. Let the groups each list toys or books that cost $5.00. Encourage them to read their lists aloud.
2. Since Harriet's piggy bank has one hundred pennies or $1.00, have the children work in pairs to determine other combinations of coins to equal $1.00. One child in each pair draws the pictures of possible coin combinations while the partner writes equations for the same combinations.
3. Develop a chart with the class showing (a) what Harriet did to earn her $4.00, and (b) how much money she made from each job. Then discuss how many pennies she earned from each task to add to her original one hundred pennies, and add this column to the chart.

4. Have the children each write about the ways that they can earn money helping at home or in the neighborhood. They may wish to add the reason for earning the money, just as Harriet worked in order to buy her toy. _____

■ ■ ■ **(11) CONCEPT:**   Animals in line can be counted with ordinal numbers that show the position of each animal.

Literature: *Harriet Goes to the Circus* by B. Maestro and G. Maestro (Crown, 1977).

Listed in: *Best Books for Children* (R. R. Bowker, 1990).

Synopsis: Harriet, the elephant, gets up early to be first in line for the best seat at the circus. She is first, and one by one her animal friends line up behind her. However, the animals then discover that the entrance to the tent is at the other end of the line so they all turn around and Harriet is now last. Happily, inside the tent the chairs are in a large circle and Harriet gets a front seat.

Activities After Read-Aloud:

1. At the beginning of the story Harriet is waking up. Ask the students, "What will she do first? Second? Third? Last?" Then ask them each to write what they do in the morning in the proper order, numbering each action.
2. Bring to class a loaf of sliced bread, a large jar of peanut butter, a jar of jelly, and a butter knife. Ask the students to tell how to make a peanut butter and jelly sandwich, describing what must be done first, second, third, and so on. Follow their directions exactly, even if some are in error, so they understand the importance of sequencing with ordinal numbers.
3. In the story there are twenty-nine sentences. Print them on a piece of large paper and then cut them apart. Have each child choose one or two sentences to copy on tagboard strips. Collect the strips and have the class put them in the correct order, according to the storyline.
4. Develop with the students one story problem concerned with the lineup of the animals at the circus entrance; for example: The last or tenth in line is the owl. In what position will he be when the entrance is moved to the other end of the line? Ask the children each to write one story problem about Harriet and the other nine animals in line to get into the circus tent. They may wish to exchange and solve their problems with friends. _____

■ ■ ■ **(12) CONCEPT:**   A whole item can be divided into parts called fractions.

Literature: *Gator Pie* by L. Mathews (Dodd, Mead, 1979), 32 pp.

Listed in: *Best Books for Children* (R. R. Bowker, 1985).

Synopsis: Two alligators named Alvin and Alice find a pie on a table near their swamp. After they decide to divide it equally, more alligators keep coming until there are one hundred of them to eat one pie. A fight ensues and Alvin and Alice run away with their chocolate marshmallow pie, each eating one half.

Activities After Read-Aloud:

1. Bring in eight aluminum pie tins, each with a cardboard circle that fits the bottom. Leave the first circle whole, cut the second circle into two equal parts, cut the third circle into three equal parts, and so on. Demonstrate to the class that the pieces in a specific circle are all the same size and, when they are put together, they make a whole circle. Explain how to write fractions, and demonstrate on the cardboard circles.
2. Alice Alligator had to try to cut the chocolate marshmallow pie into one hundred pieces. Have the class discuss strategies for doing this and then let the students experiment in groups to see which way would work the best. Encourage them to share findings with the rest of the class.
3. Bring in enough aluminum pie tins so that children can pair up to make pies out of clay to fit into the tins. Before the clay has hardened, have them practice

marking or cutting the pies into the different number of slices described in the story. Ask them to record the fractions.

4. Bring in a real nine-inch single-crust pie to share with the class. Distribute copies of a recipe for a similar pie filling and discuss the fractions used in that recipe (e.g., ¾ cup of sugar). Finally, debate how to divide the pie evenly among everyone in the class. (Some students may suggest earnestly that more pies are needed.) _____

■ ■ ■ **(13) CONCEPT:** Some items can be divided into equal halves.

Literature: *Give Me Half!* by S. Murphy (HarperCollins. 1996), 40 pp.

Listed in: *Best Books for Children* (R. R. Bowker, 1998).

Synopsis: A boy and his sister learn how to share when he has only one pizza and she has only one can of juice. When she tries to hide her package of two cupcakes, her brother gets upset so the package is split in half. When both finish their cupcakes, each child cleans up half of the kitchen!

Activities After Read-Aloud:

1. Have the children draw pizzas on large (nine inches or bigger) paper plates. Instruct them to fold the "pizzas" in half and cut them so they can share even amounts with a friend in another classroom. Then, ask the students, "What would you do if you needed to feed four people?" Encourage them to write the same name of their variety of pizza on both pieces of the paper plate (e.g., pepperoni).

2. Before recess bring to class one half the number of cookies or cupcakes needed to feed the children. Discuss the problem and ask them to write what should be done so that everyone in the class can taste the dessert. After some have read their solutions, share the treats during recess.

3. Before lunch bring to class some large pizzas and guide the students to discover how many cuts will be needed to divide the food evenly so everyone can have a piece the same size. Then serve the hot food on paper napkins or plates. After lunch, have students write briefly the importance and courtesy of sharing equally, whether at home or at school. _____

■ ■ ■ **(14) CONCEPT:** Multiplication and division are opposite operations.

Literature: *One Hundred Hungry Ants* by E. Pinczes (Houghton Mifflin, 1993), 32 pp.

Listed in: *Best Books for Children* (R. R. Bowker, 1998).

Synopsis: One hundred hungry ants are off to a picnic site to get food. They stop to change line formation, showing different divisions of 100, which causes them to lose time. In the end, the slower turtle and snail make it to the site before the ants and have a feast.

Activities After Read-Aloud:

1. Bring in numerous plastic ants (or rice grains dyed black). Have the children in groups of four make the ant formations from the book on construction paper. Show the class how each formation represents a division and multiplication problem: 50 ants in 2 rows equal 100 ants divided by 2 *or* 50 ants multiplied by 2 equal 100 ants.

2. Have the children each use tally marks to represent the ant groups on large sheets of paper. Have them label the groups with numerals (100 ants) and words (one hundred ants).

3. Pretend that the children are ants on their way to the picnic site. Go out on the playground (or push the desks back in the classroom) and try different ways of lining up. The class number must be even, so substitute students in and out or have an aide/teacher participate.

4. Distribute holed-edge strips from continuous-feed computer paper. Have pairs of children make their own lines by showing them how to label strips five holes at a time (with a pencil) to help them keep track as the story is being retold. _____

■ ■ ■ **(15) CONCEPT:**   When a number cannot be evenly divided, the number left over is called a remainder.

Literature: *A Remainder of One* by E. Pinczes (Houghton Mifflin, 1995), 32 pp.

Listed in: *Best Books for Children* (R. R. Bowker, 1998).

Synopsis: Twenty-five beetles parade in rows of two before their Queen. However, she is displeased because one beetle (Joe) has no partner. The group tries marching in rows of three or four but Joe is still the odd man out. Finally, he figures out that if they all march in rows of five, he can join the parade and please the Queen.

Activities After Read-Aloud:

1. Use plastic bugs (or counters) on an overhead projector to reenact the story, using the number 25 to show how the rows look with a remainder and without one. Discuss, and then have the children repeat the process at their tables. If time allows, repeat with the number 35.

2. Have twenty students line up in rows of three at the front of the room. Allow them to discover how many are left over as remainders. Then have them line up in rows of four to see if there are any remainders. Repeat the activity with fifteen students, having them line up first in rows of two, then in rows of four and finally in rows of three. Discuss what it means to be a remainder.

3. Have the students, in small groups, line up twenty-one plastic bugs (or counters) on their table in rows of two, three, four, five, and six to see which numbers will have remainders and which ones will divide evenly. Record findings on the board. Repeat the process, using the number 36.

4. Let the children each illustrate their own Bug Parade. They may choose any number they wish that will have a remainder (like Joe) after the rest of the bugs have been placed in even rows. Some may wish to write a story about their parade, and even involve bugs others than beetles. _____

CONTENT STANDARD #2: ALGEBRA
(with students keeping math journals)

■ ■ ■ **(1) CONCEPT:**   Patterns exist everywhere, in all shapes and sizes.

Literature: *Sam Johnson and the Blue Ribbon Quilt* by L. Ernst (Lothrop, 1983), 32 pp.

Listed in: *Best Books for Children* (R. R. Bowker, 1998).

Synopsis: Sam Johnson is a farmer who learns to quilt when his wife is away visiting. On her return, he wants to join her Rosedale Women's Quilting Club. When the club refuses his membership, he organizes the Rosedale Men's Quilting Club. Both Clubs compete to win the prize at the county fair. A crisis arises before their quilts reach the fair, but the members are able to create a winning design by working together to create the Flying Sailboats pattern.

Activities After Read-Aloud:

1. In addition to the Flying Geese quilt pattern (by the men) and the Sailboats quilt pattern (by the women), fourteen other actual patterns are shown as border designs in the book. Have the children each select one of the sixteen patterns, draw it repeatedly on graph paper, and color it in. The completed patterns, correctly labeled, can be displayed on the bulletin board.

2. Divide the children into pairs. Have one child create and name a pattern on a geoboard and then ask the partner to copy it. Then reverse the roles and have the pair create, name, and copy a new pattern. Write on the board the names of the children and the patterns they created.

3. Ask for several volunteers to come to the board, one at a time, and draw a pattern using only circles and squares. Give each volunteer a number (for identification) and allow no patterns to be duplicated. Remind them that a pattern is an "over-and-over occurrence." Finally, let the class decide which patterns (by number) are the most interesting. Discuss.

4. Distribute beads (of three different colors) and a piece of heavy string to each child. Then announce the pattern(s) the class is to make. _____

■ ■ ■ **(2) CONCEPT:**   Classifying a large group of assorted items into categories is useful and practical.

Literature: *Just a Mess* by M. Mayer (Western Publishing, 1987), 23 pp.

Listed in: *Read Any Good Math Lately?* (Heinemann, 1992).

Synopsis: A "little critter" needs his baseball glove and so must clean his disorganized room in order to find it. He decides to group things that go together (like clothes) and put them away in their proper places. However, he fails to sort them adequately and so does a poor job of organizing.

Activities After Read-Aloud:
1. Discuss with the class how it could devise a better plan to help the little critter organize his room. First, brainstorm a general list of different categories, e.g., outdoor equipment. Then have each child expand the list by writing down specific items that belong in that category, e.g., baseball mitts. Remind them that categories can be useful to help locate items quickly.
2. Have the students each briefly evaluate the little critter's efforts to organize his room, and tell if they would have done the job differently.
3. Have the children each take off one of their shoes and place it in a common pile. List on the board with the help of the class different ways of classifying the set of shoes, e.g., by color.
4. Share with the class Ron Roy's *Whose Shoes Are These?* (Clarion, 1988), which describes in black-and white-photos (on every page) some twenty different kinds of shoes worn by children and adults. This is a question-and-answer book that shows that a given set of objects can be sorted in various ways, and those classifications can sometimes overlap. _____

■ ■ ■ **(3) CONCEPT:**   Addition (and subtraction) sentences can be used to find sums (and differences).

Literature: *Ready, Set, Hop!* by S. Murphy (HarperCollins, 1996), 32 pp.

Listed in: *The Wonderful World of Mathematics* (NCTM, 1998).

Synopsis: A hopping contest in a woodland setting involves two frogs named Matty and Moe that compete to see which takes longer hops. They must determine how many hops it takes each of them to reach specific distances. (Illustrations use loops to indicate the number of hops Matty and Moe take in each situation.)

Activities After Read-Aloud:
1. Review terms used in the book (e.g., *more, less*) and the meanings behind them. Have the students explain how they know when to add and when to subtract to solve a problem. (*More* suggests addition but *less* suggests subtraction.)
2. Place plastic counters in a small pile on the overhead projector. Count them with the class. Add more counters and ask, "How many counters are there *now*?" Repeat with different numbers and ask, "How many counters are there *altogether*?" Remind the students when to use addition when solving word problems by emphasizing the italicized terms. Have them write the equations in their journals.
3. Place plastic counters in a small pile on an overhead projector. Count them with the class. Then take some counters away from the pile and ask, "How many counters are *left*?" Repeat with different numbers and ask the class, "How many counters *are still there*?" Remind the students when to use subtraction when solving word problems, emphasizing the italicized terms. Have them write the equations in their journals.
4. With the class, create on the overhead a new situation for Matty and Moe, using an addition sentence and a subtraction sentence. Have students illustrate the story. _____

■ ■ ■ **(4) CONCEPT:**   Numbers become larger when they are doubled.

Literature: *A Grain of Rice* by H. Pittman (Hastings House, 1986), 65 pp.

Listed in: *Best Books for Children* (R. R. Bowker, 1990).

Synopsis: In fifteenth-century China, a poor farmer wishes to marry the emperor's daughter after he saves her life. The emperor offers him any reward he chooses—except the princess. The farmer then cleverly asks for a single grain of rice doubled every day for one hundred days, and eventually succeeds in becoming very rich and winning the hand of the princess.

Activities After Read-Aloud:

1. Give students each a large piece of unlined paper. First, have them fold it in half and ask them how many sections their paper has. Second, have them fold it in half again and ask them how many sections their paper has now. Continue until there are sixty-four sections in every paper. Finally, remind them that every time the paper was folded, the number of sections was doubled.

2. Give students each a large piece of construction paper and numerous grains of rice (or dried beans or popcorn kernels). Have the students work in pairs to glue the rice (or beans or kernels) to the paper in groups representing the equation $1 \times 2 = 2$, $2 \times 2 = 4$, $4 \times 2 = 8$, and $8 \times 2 = 16$. Remind them that doubling is really multiplying by 2.

3. Help the students relate the story to pennies instead of rice. Divide them into cooperative groups of four and tell them to imagine that each group had a job that paid 1 cent the first day, 2 cents the second day, 4 cents the third day, and so on. Ask how much money the group would make by the end of one week. (Some groups may wish to continue the calculation for two, three, or four weeks.)

4. In the story, the emperor's mathematician used an *abacus* to count the rice. Describe what an abacus is and how it works. Then have the children each use a *calculator* and add each number by itself to get the double number, just as in the story. Let them continue the doubling through Day 20. _____

■ ■ ■ **(5) CONCEPT:** Items can be classified according to shape, color, or size.

Literature: *The Button Box* by M. Reid (Dutton, 1990), 24 pp.

Listed in: *Best Books for Children* (R. R. Bowker, 1998).

Synopsis: A young boy explores his grandmother's box of buttons, grouping or classifying them according to various qualities. He imagines interesting stories behind the different buttons.

Activities After Read-Aloud:

1. Collect numerous buttons from a sewing store or from parents. Give each child ten various buttons and have them sort the objects into piles according to color.

2. Have the children each line up their ten buttons from the smallest to the largest. Then ask them to mix up the buttons and, this time, reverse the order from largest to smallest.

3. Let each group of four students list words describing their forty buttons from Activity One or Two. Then have each group write or dictate a story about the buttons that the four students have.

4. Have the children work in groups of three and give each group thirty buttons. Ask them to sort buttons by color and create pictures according to the color of the buttons they have (e.g., yellow buttons can form the sun; multicolored buttons can make a rainbow). Some groups may wish to share their designs with the class. _____

CONTENT STANDARD #3: GEOMETRY
(with students keeping math journals)

■ ■ ■ **(1) CONCEPT:** Some geometric figures are two-dimensional like a square, but others are three-dimensional like a cube.

Literature: *Flat Stanley* by J. Brown (Harper, 1964), unpaged.

Listed in: *Best Books for Children* (R. R. Bowker, 1990).

Synopsis: When an enormous bulletin board falls on Stanley Lambchop, it squashes him flat and makes him four feet tall, about one foot wide, and one-half inch thick. The story tells how his life changes and what adventures he has until his brother figures out how to return Stanley to his normal size.

Activities After Read-Aloud:

1. Give pairs of children each eight feet of butcher paper and have them cut out two copies of Flat Stanley, four feet tall and one foot wide. Help each pair staple their figure together exactly one-half inch apart. Then the children may color their figure to represent Stanley the way he looks on the title page.
2. Stanley's body is three-dimensional when the story starts, but after the bulletin board accident, he becomes almost two-dimensional. Discuss with the class the difference between two- and three-dimensional objects. Then have groups of students each develop lists of two-dimensional objects (e.g., a sheet of writing paper) and three-dimensional objects (e.g., a book). Compare and correct group lists, and then construct a final chart.
3. Distribute to each student one sheet of construction paper, some toothpicks, and small pieces of clay, miniature marshmallows, or peas so that each one can create two- and three-dimensional geometric shapes.
4. Have each child divide a large sheet of unlined paper into two columns: Two-Dimensional Geometric Shapes and Matching Three-Dimensional Geometric Shapes. The child then draws some items in the first column (e.g., a rectangle). Have a class discussion about corresponding items that belong in the second column (e.g., a brick). List them on the board for the class to copy. _____

■ ■ ■ **(2) CONCEPT:** Polygons are geometric shapes with sides that are straight line segments.

Literature: *The Greedy Triangle* by M. Burns (Scholastic, 1994), 40 pp.

Listed in: *Best Books for Children* (R. R. Bowker, 1998).

Synopsis: A triangle is unhappy with its shape and so keeps asking the local Shapeshifter, again and again, to give it more sides and more angles. When it has many, many sides and many, many angles, it cannot keep its balance and friends begin to avoid it. So it decides to return to the Shapeshifter for the last time and become a triangle again.

Activities After Read-Aloud:

1. Have the children pair up. Have them take turns putting their hands on their hips and having the partner trace the triangle inside their arms. Each child can make a sketch of the partner's "triangle" and explain how to be certain when a shape is a triangle.
2. There are many important jobs for triangles, quadrilaterals, pentagons, and hexagons according to the story. Let students each choose which of the four polygons they would like to be, and then explain orally or in writing the reasons for their choice. Some may also wish to draw and color that shape before sharing with the class.
3. Help the students write riddles about geometric shapes, especially polygons, such as the following: I have five sides and five corners. What am I? Children may like to write their riddles on one side of the paper, and write or draw their answers on the other side.
4. Provide the class with an assortment of construction paper polygons in several different colors. Let each student select one piece and decide what object that polygon could be a part of (e.g. a quadrilateral is a part of a table). Then he or she is to glue the piece onto a sheet of white paper and draw a picture around it. Compile the papers into a book titled "Polygons Are Everywhere" and place it on the library table for all to examine. _____

■ ■ ■ **(3) CONCEPT:** Rectangles have four sides and four corners, triangles have three sides and three corners, and circles have no sides and no corners.

Literature:	*The Wing on a Flea* by E. Emberley (Little, Brown, 1961), 48 pp.
Listed in:	*Read Any Good Math Lately?* (Heinemann, 1992).
Synopsis:	With cartoonlike drawings and rhyming verse, this nonfiction book gives abstract representations of rectangles, triangles, and circles found in everyday objects.

Activities After Read-Aloud:

1. Give children each three sheets of paper and have them label the top of each sheet with one of the following: Circles, Rectangles, Triangles. Ask them to divide each sheet into four sections and draw an item in each section that includes the geometric shape listed at the top, e.g., a full moon (circle), a closed door (rectangle), and a sail (triangle). After the students label the twelve items, have them exchange papers with a partner to see how many shapes each got correctly.

2. As a class, create some couplets or other verses about each of the three shapes mentioned in the book, just as the author did. Write these on the board after ideas have been discussed. Then have each child copy and illustrate his or her favorite verse. Display some on the bulletin board under a heading such as Poetry Takes Shape.

3. Cut sponges into the three shapes studied, and prepare several small pans of different colored paints. Have the students each hold the sponges with a clothespin as they dip them into the paint in order to make several designs on large sheets of white paper. After the sponge paintings dry, let students share and explain their designs. _____

■ ■ ■ **(4) CONCEPT:** Circles and squares are two basic and different geometric shapes.

Literature:	*The Village of Round and Square Houses* by V. Grifalconi (Little, Brown, 1986), 32 pp.
Listed in:	*Best Books for Children* (R. R. Bowker, 1998).
Synopsis:	In a certain Cameroon village on the west coast of Africa, the men live in square houses and the women and children live in round houses. How the custom started is explained in this folktale, which describes a place located at the base of a volcano.

Activities After Read-Aloud:

1. Give each of the students a large square piece of paper and a large round piece of paper. Have them cut out pictures from discarded magazines of square items that belong on the first piece and round items that belong on the second piece. Ask them to paste the pictures on the proper papers and label each one. Discuss and display.

2. On a sunny day, take the children outdoors on a shape walk, looking only for round and square objects. Have them each take a small notepad in which to write down their observations. On returning to the classroom, let the class discuss some of their findings until everyone understands two of the basic geometric shapes.

3. Historical tradition, as described in the folktale, is one reason why houses are built in different shapes. Have a class discussion as to other justifications for houses shaped differently, e.g., climate, availability of certain materials, and so on.

4. Ask the children each to write whether they would like their families to live in a round house or in a square house. They must offer at least one reason for their choice. Have them share stories with partners. _____

■ ■ ■ **(5) CONCEPT:** Besides circles, triangles, rectangles, and squares, other common shapes include hexagons, trapezoids, stars, parallelograms, ovals, hearts, and arcs.

Literature:	*Shapes, Shapes, Shapes* by T. Hoban (Greenwillow, 1986), 32 pp.
Listed in:	*Best Books for Children* (R. R. Bowker, 1998).
Synopsis:	A wordless nonfiction book, it has color photos of the environment showing eleven shapes combined in creative ways.

Activities After Read-Aloud:

1. Prepare numerous, large sheets of white paper with one colored shape on each sheet, such as a red circle or a yellow square. Be sure to have three sets with each combination of shape and color. Place them randomly on the floor, leaving space between the papers. Assign the children by groups of three and have them remove their shoes. Begin the activity by calling out a group number and a colored shape. Have those children find that colored shape and stand on one of the sheets. When all the sheets with that shape are occupied, collect them and call out a new shape and another group. Discuss.

2. As a variation of Activity One, write or draw colored shapes on index cards, e.g. blue oval. Then let the students take turns being the caller, either reading the words or describing the small illustrations.

3. Have children each create a "How Many Shapes Can You Find?" picture, using special paper with a blank space in the top half and lines in the bottom half. Encourage them to combine shapes in the top half, e.g., a *square* sandwich cut into *triangles* and placed on a *round* plate. Finally, have each pair of children trade papers, list on the lines below the shapes they spot, and then outline each shape in a different color. A bulletin board of completed papers could be headed with the title of the assignment. _____

■ ■ ■ **(6) CONCEPT:**   Geometric shapes are everywhere.

Literature: *The Shapes Game* by P. Rogers (Holt, 1989), unpaged.

Listed in: *Best Books for Children* (R. R. Bowker, 1994).

Synopsis: Riddle verses and Matisse-like collages present readers with an introduction to geometric and other shapes. They includes circles, triangles, squares, rectangles, ovals, and diamonds as well as spirals, stars, and crescents.

Activities After Read-Aloud:

1. Give each group of children a paper with a different geometric shape on it. Have them complete a picture around that shape, e.g., a circle could be a clock face. Then have each group write a story about its shape and picture.

2. Distribute construction paper and discarded magazines. Have students find one or more geometric shapes, cut them out, and make a collage on the paper. Ask them to label each shape.

3. Ask pairs of children to select one of the shapes from the book and list objects at school or at home that have that shape.

4. Have children, in groups of three, help each other use their bodies to make geometric shapes. Then have each group present their "shapes" to the rest of the class. List on the board all the body shapes shown. _____

■ ■ ■ **(7) CONCEPT:**   No shapes are ever alike, and some objects even have many shapes.

Literature: *The Shape of Me and Other Stuff* by Dr. Seuss (Random House, 1988), unpaged.

Listed in: *The Wonderful World of Mathematics* (NCTM, 1998).

Synopsis: The silhouetted shapes of a girl and a boy move from page to page as the children explore the shapes of themselves and numerous, different things. The book, written in rhyme, is a general introduction to shapes.

Activities After Read-Aloud:

1. Have the children, using butcher paper and markers, make life-size copies of themselves with partners. Have them do it twice and cut out the body images. When they have finished coloring in a face and clothes, have them each staple the two pieces together, leaving a small opening. Help them stuff their figures with discarded newspapers and finish stapling. Display the completed bodies on a clothesline or elsewhere in the room.

2. Discuss with the class why people, animals, and objects have some of the shapes they do, e.g., giraffes have long necks in order to reach their food.

3. Have children brainstorm things that change shape, e.g., bubblegum, clouds, and balloons. Then give them each some clay to create four different shapes and then change each one. Finally, they must identify and record each of the eight results on paper.

4. Since the book shows shapes in silhouettes, have the children work in pairs to help make silhouettes of their profiles. Set up a bright light to shine on pieces of construction paper. Then have each child stand between the light and the paper while his/her partner traces the shadow. Reverse the roles. Later, the silhouettes are cut out and mounted on black paper. Discuss and display.

5. Discuss the difference between shapes generally and geometric shapes in particular. Ask students to identify one of the latter on the human body (e.g., their face is a circle), and use that geometric shape to draw other objects. _____

■ ■ ■ **(8) CONCEPT:** Symmetry involves balance, and two of the basic kinds are line and plane symmetry.

Literature: *What Is Symmetry?* by M. & H. Sitomer (Crowell, 1970), 33 pp.

Listed in: *Read Any Good Math Lately?* (Heinemann, 1992).

Synopsis: A nonfiction book, it has playful alligators pointing out symmetry in nature and man-made objects.

Activities After Read-Aloud:

1. Have the students complete the folding test for line symmetry: Give them each a piece of fingerpainting paper and have them place some pudding or fingerpaint in the middle of the paper. Ask them to fold the paper together lengthwise so that each side fits exactly over the other, and then open it back up. They now have a design that is a horizontal line for symmetry. Discuss the findings.

2. Give groups of children discarded magazines and have them cut out some pictures of items with horizontal lines of symmetry and some with vertical lines of symmetry. They may glue their pictures on construction paper, placing each kind of line symmetry on a different side of the paper. Finally, have the groups share results.

3. Give children each a piece of paper (8½" × 11") and have them fold the paper in half once and then in half again, both times vertically. Next, help them carefully punch three holes in the folded paper near the second crease. Before they are allowed to open the paper, they must predict how many holes will be in the unfolded paper and where those holes will be. Write their predictions on the board and later have the class compare them with the actual findings, deciding also which is the line of symmetry.

4. Bring in a mirror and have the children each study themselves to prove that their face and the mirror face have the same shape and size, and balance on each side of the mirror. Explain to them that the mirror is not a line but a flat surface, so the balance between them and their mirror image is called *plane symmetry*. Discuss the findings; then draw on a board a house with two identical sides to show that it too has plane symmetry. _____

■ ■ ■ **(9) CONCEPT:** A square is a geometric shape that has four equal sides.

Literature: *The Boy with Square Eyes* by J. Snape & C. Snape (Prentice-Hall, 1987), unpaged.

Listed in: *Best Books for Children* (R. R. Bowker, 1990).

Synopsis: Charlie watches television so much that his eyes turn square and everything else starts looking square also. He cures himself through eye exercises by reading books, drawing pictures, and doing puzzles, just like his doctor ordered.

Activities After Read-Aloud:

1. Have the children each make a drawing of Charlie's lunch plate, as shown early in the unpaged book, with everything square. Then have them make a second drawing of the way the plate looked to his mother, who did not have square eyes. Discuss why the second plate of food would seem more appetizing to the students.

2. Organize groups of three students and have each group begin its own chapter book about Squares. For Chapter One, entitled Things That Are Square, each group first makes a list of different objects that can be square, such as houses, computer screens, and books. Then they draw each object separately on a sheet of paper and write one sentence about it. Remind them that squares have four equal sides. Finally, the group assembles their papers for Chapter One.

3. Following the routine set up in Activity Two, the groups are now ready to prepare Chapter Two, entitled Making Things Out of Squares, not unlike the way that Charlie saw the world for a few hours. Again, the children each draw an object separately on a sheet of paper (e.g., a square flower), and write a sentence describing it. Help the groups assemble both Chapters One and Two, add a title page (Squares) and the students' names, and staple the book for the class to read at the library table. _____

■ ■ ■ **(10) CONCEPT:**   Tangrams are ancient Chinese puzzle pieces of geometric shapes still used today by adults and children.

Literature: *Grandfather Tang's Story* by A. Tompert (Crown, 1990), 32 pp.

Listed in: *Best Books for Children* (R. R. Bowker, 1998).

Synopsis: Grandfather Tang tells his granddaughter, Little Soo, a Chinese folktale about two fox fairies that can change themselves into different animals. As each transformation occurs in the tale, Grandfather rearranges his seven tangram puzzle pieces to depict the new form. Finally, he and Little Soo each arrange their pieces to form a story about themselves.

Activities After Read-Aloud:

1. Give each pair of children one sheet of construction paper and seven tangram pieces: one square, one parallelogram, one middle-sized triangle, and four congruent triangles (two large and two small). Have them assemble the pieces on the construction paper to form a square.

2. Copy the eleven animal shapes arranged with tangram pieces shown in the book. Let each group of three students choose one of the shapes and form it with the pieces that were distributed for Activity One. Read the story aloud again, and this time, at the appropriate places in the story, have the groups discuss and show the shapes each made.

3. Have pairs of children create their own shape with the tans (or seven standard pieces). Remind them that in designing a picture, all seven must be used, touching each other but never overlapping. Next, the pairs must write a story about their new design, and edit it before submitting it for possible publication.

4. Compile a book of the shapes/stories created during Activity Three and entitle it "(Room #......) Tangram Stories." Share it during Open House. _____

CONTENT STANDARD #4: MEASUREMENT
(with students keeping math journals)

■ ■ ■ **(1) CONCEPT:**   Time is made up of minutes, which can be added up to make hours.

Literature: *Pigs on a Blanket* by A. Axelrod (Simon & Schuster, 1996), 32 pp.

Listed in: *Best Books for Children* (R. R. Bowker, 1998).

Synopsis: One hot day, a pig family wants to go to the beach. Delays, however, cause the pigs to reach the water after the beach has closed. (Throughout the book, the amount of time it takes for each delaying action is listed.)

Activities After Read-Aloud:

1. Have the children list all the activities and add how much time passed for each delay. Finally, ask: "Why did the pigs run out of time?"
2. Using a large manipulative clock, adjust the hands to different times shown in the book, and ask the class what time is shown on the clock face. Students taking turns can also come to the front of the room and set the hands for classmates to guess the correct times.
3. Copy clock faces onto construction paper and have children create their own clocks to show different times (for lunch, morning recess, etc.). Make sure the size of the clock will match with the hands, which can be made by using two black paper strips, one large and one small, attached with a brad. Ask the children to each make the hands on their clocks show the different times that their classmates suggest.
4. Have children work in pairs to challenge each other to show different times on their clocks. (Student A asks Student B to show her 11:15 on his clock. After moving the hands to the correct positions, Student B then asks Student A to show 2:30 on her clock.) _____

■ ■ ■ **(2) CONCEPT:**   Time can be shown in hours, half hours, and quarter hours by the movement of hands on a clock.

Literature: *The Grouchy Ladybug* by E. Carle (Harper Collins, 1977), 48 pp.

Listed in: *Best Books for Children* (R. R. Bowker, 1998).

Synopsis: A grouchy ladybug begins at five o'clock in the morning to fight hourly with various insects and animals, regardless of their size and shape. Finally, at six o'clock in the evening, she decides to share her food with a friendly ladybug.

Activities After Read-Aloud:

1. Make a learning center or interactive board featuring a sturdy paper clock. Place cards with various times in an envelope next to the clock. Have the children each take turns drawing a card and moving the hands on the clock to the specified time.
2. The grouchy ladybug had a very busy day. Write short sentences about his activities on oaktag strips. Then have the class put the strips in sequence and read them aloud.
3. Have the children make paper plate clocks and use them to tell the activities of the grouchy ladybug.
4. Have the children practice counting by fives and tens as they move the hands of the clock that they made during Activity Three.
5. Distribute worksheets, each showing a large circle. Ask the students to add numbers and make picture clocks of their weekday schedules. They must write in both words and times (e.g., lunch at 11:30 A.M.). _____

■ ■ ■ **(3) CONCEPT:**   The days of the week go in order from Sunday to Saturday.

Literature: *The Very Hungry Caterpillar* by E. Carle (Putnam, 1981), 32 pp.

Listed in: *Best Books for Children* (R. R. Bowker, 1998).

Synopsis: A hungry caterpillar eats his way through the days of the week. When he is very full, he spins a cocoon so that, in about two weeks, he will become a beautiful butterfly.

Activities After Read-Aloud:

1. Have the children each trace seven circles on green construction paper. Ask them to write in sequence a different day of the week on each circle. Discuss the story sequence; have the children draw or write the events of the story on the circles.
2. Divide the class into small groups. Prepare a set of index cards for each group, making two cards for each day of the week. Give each group a set of cards. Have children match the cards, working together to place them in sequential order.

3. Write the days of the week in random order on several sentence strips. Cut each strip apart before giving it to a group of students. Each group must arrange the words together in correct order and read them. Encourage students to copy the words on a paper that they can take home to share.

4. Make five large lunch graphs, titling each with a day of the school week from Monday through Friday. On each have five columns headed Fruits, Vegetables, Dairy Products, Bread, and Meat. Ask the children each day what they ate for lunch and build a bar graph of the different foods they ate. At the end of the week, tally up each column and determine what type of foods the class ate the most, as compared to the very hungry caterpillar. _____

■ ■ ■ **(4) CONCEPT:**   Size is a relative matter.

Literature: *Is It Larger? Is It Smaller?* by T. Hoban (Greenwillow, 1985), 32 pp.

Listed in: *Best Books for Children* (R. R. Bowker, 1998).

Synopsis: A wordless book filled with color photographs, it introduces relativity and the many ways and reasons that one thing is smaller or bigger than another.

Activities After Read-Aloud:

1. Project on the overhead transparencies of the first two pages and ask the class to tell which leaf is the largest and which pig is the larger. Then project the next page and have the children write which color measuring cup is the largest.

2. Bring in several different sized playground balls including a softball, a soccer ball, a basketball, and so on. Have the class identify each ball as its name is written on the board. Then ask them to write down the names in the order of ball sizes, going from the smallest to the largest. Finally, call on a volunteer to arrange the playground balls in order of size.

3. Have cooperative groups of three each draw or paint a row of five different sized daisy plants in a garden picture. Ask them to sketch the stems in order of their size, going from the smallest to the largest. Then have them choose one color for all of the flowers (so the stem size differences show clearly). Discuss the middle flower to show that it is both larger than some and smaller than others.

4. Have each child choose one photo from the book and write about it briefly, emphasizing different sizes shown.

5. Measure each child (without shoes), using an ordinary growth chart. Remind the class that, while one person is shorter or smaller than another, he or she is also taller or larger than someone else. Discuss. _____

■ ■ ■ **(5) CONCEPT:**   Time moves forward.

Literature: *Clocks and More Clocks* by P. Hutchins (Macmillan, 1970), 32 pp.

Listed in: *Best Books for Children* (R. R. Bowker, 1985).

Synopsis: Mr. Higgins finds a clock in his attic; he does not know if it tells the right time. To find out, he proceeds to buy new clocks for his bedroom, his kitchen, and the hallway, but he still cannot tell which one of his clocks is correct because each shows a different time from the others. He is surprised when the clockmaker proves to him that they are all correct.

Activities After Read-Aloud:

1. Chart the daily schedule on the board. Give copies to each student, and have them draw clocks that tell the time each scheduled activity will begin. Near the board chart, hang a battery-operated clock. At the start of each activity, move the operating clock down so the students can see how the time on their paper clocks matches that of the operating clock. Have children take turns reading the activities and matching times.

2. Use twelve students, standing in a circle, each holding a different card, to represent the numbers on a clock. Choose two more students to represent the minute and second hands. The Second Hand will walk around the circle, starting at 12,

counting to 60. Each time the Second Hand gets to 12, the Minute Hand will take one step forward. After giving all students a chance to be part of the Human Clock, review the concept with the class.

3. Bring in four battery-operated clocks. Show the class how they are all set to the same time. Place them in different areas of the classroom. Have the students move from one area to another, recording the area (e.g., door) and time.

4. Have students write why clocks must always be accurate. Ask volunteers to share their reasons.

5. Discuss briefly the five time zones in the continental United States. Ask the class if anyone has friends or relatives living in a different time zone from that of the school. Some may wish to mark the zones on a simple outline map of this country. _____

■ ■ ■ **(6) CONCEPT:** Linear measuring involves laying out uniform units end to end repeatedly.

Literature: *Inch by Inch* by L. Lionni (Astor-Honor, 1960), unpaged.

Listed in: *Best Books for Children* (R. R. Bowker, 1998).

Synopsis: An inchworm is almost gobbled up by a robin until the bird discovers that the inchworm has a special talent for measuring. So the captive inchworm measures parts of birds (such as beaks, tails) until it is asked to measure the length of a nightingale's song—an impossible task! So, cleverly, it inches its way to freedom.

Activities After Read-Aloud:
1. Have groups of three children each select five items in the classroom that they believe measure one inch. They must write down the items they chose, e.g., a paper clip, and then measure them with a tape measure or ruler and record their findings. Finally, compile a class list of the actual measurements reported by the groups, together with the items.

2. Have pairs of students each write and illustrate another version of the Lionni book. To do so, they must create a large animal that can only measure "Foot by Foot" and list several items that it could easily measure. After the stories have been edited, they can be copied and compiled together with a title page before being placed on the library table.

3. Just as the inchworm measured birds in its outdoor locale, have each child measure three items on the playground, using a tape measure or ruler. Have each one record on a clipboard the items measured and their actual lengths.

4. Have students each draw a one-inch square within a two-inch square of cardboard. Have them take the two-inch square home and fill the one-inch area with one or more kinds of dry items such as cereal, rice, beans, or seeds. Ask them to glue the items to the one-inch cardboard square and return the squares to school. After discussion, trim and assemble the squares into a classroom inchworm. ___

■ ■ ■ **(7) CONCEPT:** An estimate is a thoughtful guess or mental calculation.

Literature: *Betcha!* by S. Murphy (HarperCollins, 1997), 33 pp.

Listed in: *Best Books for Children* (R. R. Bowker, 1998).

Synopsis: Two boys estimate and then count many different things in the city, from the number of people on their bus, the number of cars stuck in a traffic jam, the amount of money they need to buy all the toys in the store window, and so forth.

Activities After Read-Aloud:
1. Use a small jar, such as a pint jar, and place some pinto beans in it. Have each child write down the number of beans he or she thinks is in the jar. Then use the overhead to count out the pinto beans to see whose estimate was closest to the actual number. Ask the best estimators, "How did you get your answer?"

2. Use a larger jar, such as a quart jar, and place enough pinto beans in it to fill it. Have each child write down the number of beans she or he thinks is in the jar. Now use the overhead to count out the pinto beans to see who estimated the

number closest to the actual number. (It would be best to place the beans into groups of ten on the overhead so that everyone can count them more easily.) Ask the best estimators, "How did you get your answer?" (This time the answers should be larger because the jar is larger.)

3. Use the larger jar from Activity Two, but this time place in it enough lima beans to fill the jar. Have each child write down the number of beans he or she thinks is in the jar. Then use the overhead to count out the number of lima beans to see who estimated the number closest to the actual number. When the best estimators are asked, "How did you get your answer?" they should say that the lima beans take up more space than the pinto beans.

4. One of the boys in the story estimates the number of passengers on a city bus. Have the bus riders in the class make some estimates about the number of children riding the school bus every morning. Then appoint two of them to check with the bus driver the following day and report back to the class as to whose estimate was closest. _____

■ ■ ■ **(8) CONCEPT:**   There are both standard and nonstandard ways of measuring.

Literature: *How Big Is a Foot?* by R. Myller (Dell, 1990), unpaged.

Listed in: *Best Books for Children* (R. R. Bowker, 1998).

Synopsis: The king decides to surprise his wife on her birthday with a bed made especially for her (in the days when there were no beds). However, the apprentice carpenter makes a bed that is too small for the queen and is jailed until he solves the problem.

Activities After Read-Aloud:

1. The king used his feet to measure the queen for the bed. Have the children each trace around their shoes or feet on a sheet of paper. Have each cut out the paper foot and use it to measure various items in the classroom. They should estimate measurements first, using a worksheet with three columns headed, Object, Estimate, and Actual Measurement.

2. Give children each a ruler and have them measure their thumbs and feet to see how nearly their body parts come to an inch, a foot, and so on. Ask the class why many of our measurements today were based on body parts originally.

3. Let the children choose partners and measure each other's wrists, ankles, arm lengths, and leg lengths with pieces of string. Then distribute foot rulers and yardsticks. Ask the students to write down their findings after they have placed their string pieces on a ruler or yardstick to determine the standard measurement. Ask the students to write down their findings.

4. Discuss with the class different measures and group them on the board as standard (being always the same size) and nonstandard (not always the same size). Tell the students to write down which kind of measurement they prefer and give the reason for their choice. _____

■ ■ ■ **(9) CONCEPT:**   It is important to know how heavy or light something is, but weight does not always correlate with size.

Literature: *Heavy Is a Hippopotamus* by M. Schlein (Children's Press, 1984), 32 pp.

Listed in: *Best Books for Children* (R. R. Bowker, 1990).

Synopsis: A nonfiction introduction to weight, it is addressed to the reader and begins with the concepts of *light* and *heavy* before moving on to standardized measures.

Activities After Read-Aloud:

1. Brainstorm with the children some examples of things that are heavy and some that are light, besides those that are mentioned in the book. Chart the replies on the board.

2. Divide the class into cooperative groups and give each several objects of varying weights. Ask them to list the objects in order from heaviest to lightest. Then have

the groups use a balance scale to determine their orders more accurately. Ask, "Why do some objects that look different actually weigh the same?" Discuss.

3. The book states that sixteen doughnuts weigh about one pound. Have students use a marked scale to weigh other things in the classroom that weigh about one pound (e.g., a small vase). Bring in various grocery items that weigh one pound so the students get accustomed to how heavy a pound feels to them. Remind everyone how different one item weighing one pound can look compared to another item of the same weight, e.g., one pound of unpopped popcorn next to one pound of popped popcorn.

4. Different standards of weight are used to measure different items. Have groups of four children each compile a list of everyday items together with the standard measures used to weigh them, e.g., apples are weighed in pounds. Compare and correct group lists before making a final class list. _____

■ ■ ■ **(10) CONCEPT:** There are seven days in a week.

Literature: *Cookie's Week* by C. Ward (Putnam, 1988), unpaged.

Listed in: *Best Books for Children* (R. R. Bowker, 1990).

Synopsis: An incorrigible kitten named Cookie has several adventures in the course of one week. The days of the week are sequenced through Cookie's antics.

Activities After Read-Aloud:

1. Cut out seven cats (complete with tails) for each student, using an Ellison die cut machine. Write (or have the students write) the days of the week on each cat. Then write the corresponding number for each day of the week on the cat's tail. Have children sequence their cats in order to show the days of the week.

2. Give students each a worksheet divided into seven sections, with the names of the days of the week written at the top of each section. Have students draw (or write) what Cookie did on each day. Then students can share their work.

3. Write each of the days of the week on separate sentence strips. Then write each of Cookie's antics on a separate strip. Have the students take turns using a pocket chart to match the day of the week with one of Cookie's adventures, reading both strips aloud to the class.

4. Divide the class into seven groups, naming each of them after a day of the week. Each group will write (or dictate) sentences about an animal other than a kitten that can cause mischief around the home or yard. The seven group stories can be illustrated and placed in a class book entitled "Seven Days With Our Pets."

CONTENT STANDARD #5: DATA ANALYSIS AND PROBABILITY
(with students keeping math journals)

■ ■ ■ **(1) CONCEPT:** Graphs and charts are different ways of organizing and presenting data.

Literature: *Charts and Graphs: Fun, Facts and Activities* by C. Arnold (Watts, 1984), 32 pp.

Listed in: *The Wonderful World of Mathematics* (NCTM, 1992).

Synopsis: A nonfiction book, it uses drawings and photographs to illustrate real-world examples using various kinds of graphs as well as common charts concerned with schedules, mileage, the telephone book, and the calendar.

Activities After Read-Aloud:

1. Tell the students that a *time line* is a kind of graph that shows when things happen. Then help them each make a time line of their typical school day, using a sheet of paper, a pencil, and a clock, while following the directions on page 21. Post completed time lines on the bulletin board.

2. A popular type of graph is a *bar graph*, which helps a reader compare things. Help the class make a bar graph titled "Favorite Kinds of Ice Cream" adapting it from

the graph shown on page 8; the three columns will be Chocolate, Vanilla, and Strawberry. When the class graph has been completed, each column can be colored differently before the bar graph is displayed.

3. On a sunny day, help the children make a giant circular or *pie* graph on the (paved) playground so that everyone knows where each student was born (either in the United States or elsewhere). Follow the directions on pages 10–11 to make a living pie graph.

4. Let the students each make their own phone book (or *chart*) of the numbers of their friends, using seven sheets of paper (9 × 12 inches), a pencil, and a stapler. After folding and stapling the papers properly, each child writes one letter of the alphabet at the top of each page and then asks friends to place their names and phone numbers in "This Phone Book Belongs to...." Further details are on pages 26–27. _____

■ ■ ■ **(2) CONCEPT:**   Collecting and organizing data help people make good decisions.

Literature: *Moira's Birthday* by R. Munsch (Annick Press, 1987), unpaged.

Listed in: *Literature for Science and Mathematics* (California Department of Education, 1993).

Synopsis: Moira invites all the 200 children in her school to her birthday party although her parents were expecting only six children. Only ten (not 200) pizzas and only ten (not 200) birthday cakes arrive in time. The rest of the food arrives after the guests leave so Moira decides to have another party the next day for the 200 guests with plenty of pizzas and cakes.

Activities After Read-Aloud:

1. Help the children in groups of four prepare a Birthday (Bar) Graph by the month for the classroom, using graph paper, pencils, and markers. The left or vertical side of the graph should be titled Number of Students, the bottom (or horizontal) side, Months of the Year. Each month's tally should be a different color. Discuss.

2. When the guests come to Moira's party, they spread out all over the house, including the basement and the roof. Have cooperative groups each draw a picture of all these places on a large sheet of paper, and then give every group 200 counters to divide evenly in each area. Ask, if there were an equal number of guests in each area, how many would there be? Is it possible that there would be an even number in each area? Discuss.

3. Moira generously ordered 200 birthday cakes and 200 pizzas for her 200 guests. She expected each child to eat one whole cake and one whole pizza. Discuss with the class if Moira needed to order that much food. If not, help the class determine how many cakes and pizzas would be needed to feed 200 guests.

4. Have the students, working in groups of four, make a pie graph of their favorite kinds of pizza. Then help the class make a large pie graph incorporating all the information from the small group graphs. Which kind of pizza is the most popular? Which one is the least popular? Discuss. _____

■ ■ ■ **(3) CONCEPT:**   Statistics are important in the field of sports.

Literature: *Fleet-Footed Florence* by M. Sachs (Doubleday, 1981) 48 pp.

Listed in: *Best Books for Children* (R. R. Bowker, 1985).

Synopsis: A famous baseball hero named Matt has a daughter named Florence, who becomes the fastest runner in the East, West, North, and South. She joins her father's old team, the North Dakota Beavers, and sets many, many records.

Activities After Read-Aloud:

1. Since Florence was such a fast runner, have the children research the speed records for both female and male runners in the Olympics and/or in city-wide marathons like those in Boston or Los Angeles. How do the female and male runners' records compare? Plan a class race for a sunny day during one physical education period, and let the girls and boys each record their own speeds.

2. Professional baseball has many statistics. Have the class find out if statistics are kept for Little League teams and how they compare to those of the pro teams. The author refers to RBIs, ERAs, and BAs. Have the class determine what these three sets of initials mean. Have groups of three students each choose a different professional baseball player and research his three important statistics. Then have the groups report their findings to the class.

3. There are other sports besides baseball in which statistics are kept. What statistics are used in basketball, soccer, and football? Distribute one copy of the sports section of the local paper to each group of four students and help them locate some sports statistics. Ask if anyone knows why statistics are important in sports.

4. Some students may wish to research statistics on Olympic events, either in the winter or summer games. Help them locate sources for these statistics. _____

■ ■ ■ **(4) CONCEPT:**   The most common kinds of averages are the mode, the median, and the arithmetic mean.

Literature: *Averages* by J. Srivastava (Harper, 1975), 33 pp.

Listed in: *Best Books for Children* (R. R. Bowker, 1985).

Synopsis: A nonfiction book with drawings on almost every page, it explains with examples and easy-to-understand language that the type of average used (mode, median, or arithmetic mean) depends on the type of problem that needs to be solved.

Activities After Read-Aloud:

1. The common or usual kind of average is called the *mode* because it tells about the largest part of a group. Have the students each remove one shoe and put it in one of three or four rows (by color or type). The mode is the row that has the most shoes in it.

2. The second kind of average is the *median*. Since it is the middle of a group (when its items are arranged in an order), have the children line up alphabetically to see if there is one boy or girl who is the median. (This activity only works in classes with odd-numbered enrollment.)

3. Choose five children to line up in order of height, reminding the class that it does not matter if two children are the same height or who stands ahead of whom. Let the rest of the students sketch pictures of the standing group in order to understand the concept. Then explain to the class that the height of the child standing in the middle of the line is the median height for the group. Discuss.

4. The third kind of average is the *arithmetic mean* (found by doing arithmetic—adding and dividing), and it represents the kind of average usually computed in school. Collect many pencils of different lengths and give each child three of them, as well as a long piece of string and a pair of scissors. Then read the directions on page 23 to the class so that the children can each figure out the mean length of their pencils. _____

■ ■ ■ **(5) CONCEPT:**   Statistics are numbers collected and organized to give information.

Literature: *Statistics* by J. Srivastava (Crowell, 1973), 33 pp.

Listed in: *Best Books for Children* (R. R. Bowker, 1990).

Synopsis: A nonfiction book with drawings on every page (except one), it explains how statistics are gathered and used, and how they can be communicated through graphs and tables.

Activities After Read-Aloud:

1. Have the students each begin a booklet about themselves entitled "My Vital Statistics"; it should have a construction paper cover and three sheets of paper stapled together. It should include one or more of the following statistics: the number of people in the family (together with ages, heights, and shoe sizes), the

number of pets the family has, the number of books the student reads monthly, the number of sports that he/she plays, and so on.

2. After completing Activity One, the children should compare their own statistics with those of other students by drawing a *bar graph* (as shown on page 14) about one of the common items (e.g., shoe sizes). If a class graph is drawn on the board, everyone can participate and also discuss which size is the most common.

3. Many countries (like the United States) take a census every ten years to count the number of people who live in that country and gather other statistics about the country. Have each child choose one statistic from the U.S. census that he or she thinks is interesting (e.g., the three largest cities). Then compile all the statistics for a bulletin board entitled "Statistics from the U.S. Census."

4. Ask the students if they know which fruit the children like best in the first, second, and third grades in the school. Explain about their taking a sample poll, as described on pages 10–11. When the statistics are completed, help the class prepare a list (or table) with two columns: Number of Children and Fruit Liked Best. _____

CHILDREN'S LITERATURE CITED

Number and Operation
Axelrod, A.   *Pigs Will Be Pigs* (Four Winds, 1994).
Bang, M.   *Ten, Nine, Eight* (Greenwillow, 1983).
Carle, E.   *1, 2, 3 to the Zoo* (Putnam, 1968).
Crews, D.   *Ten Black Dots* (Greenwillow, 1986).
Gretz, S.   *Teddy Bears 1 to 10* (Macmillan, 1986).
Hellen, N.   *The Bus Stop* (Orchard, 1988).
Hoban, L.   *Arthur's Funny Money* (Harper, 1981).
Hulme, J.   *Sea Squares* (Hyperion, 1991).
Hutchins, P.   *The Doorbell Rang* (Greenwillow, 1986).
Maestro, B. & Maestro, G.   *Dollars and Cents for Harriet* (Crown, 1988).
Maestro, B. & Maestro, G.   *Harriet Goes to the Circus* (Crown, 1977).
Mathews, L.   *Gator Pie* (Dodd, 1979).
Murphy, S.   *Give Me Half!* (HarperCollins, 1996).
Pinczes, E.   *One Hundred Hungry Ants* (Houghton Mifflin, 1993).
Pinczes, E.   *A Remainder of One* (Houghton Mifflin, 1995).

Algebra
Ernst, L.   *Sam Johnson and the Blue Ribbon Quilt* (Lothrop, 1983).
Mayer, M.   *Just a Mess* (Western Publishing, 1987).
Murphy, S.   *Ready, Set, Hop!* (HarperCollins, 1996).
Pittman, H.   *A Grain of Rice* (Hastings House, 1986).
Reid, M.   *The Button Box* (Dutton, 1990).

Geometry
Brown, J.   *Flat Stanley* (Harper, 1964).
Burns, M.   *The Greedy Triangle* (Scholastic, 1994).
Emberley, E.   *The Wing on a Flea* (Little, Brown, 1961).
Grifalconi, V.   *The Village of Round and Square Houses* (Little, Brown, 1986).
Hoban, T.   *Shapes, Shapes, Shapes* (Greenwillow, 1986).
Rogers, P.   *The Shapes Game* (Holt, 1989).
Seuss, Dr.   *The Shape of Me and Other Stuff* (Random House, 1988).
Sitomer, M. & Sitomer, H.   *What Is Symmetry?* (Crowell, 1970).
Snape, J. & Snape, C.   *The Boy with Square Eyes* (Prentice-Hall, 1987).
Tompert, A.   *Grandfather Tang's Story* (Crown, 1990).

Measurement

Axelrod, A.   *Pigs on a Blanket* (Simon & Schuster, 1996).
Carle, E.   *The Grouchy Ladybug* (HarperCollins, 1977).
Carle, E.   *The Very Hungry Caterpillar* (Putnam, 1981).
Hoban, T.   *Is It Larger? Is It Smaller?* (Greenwillow, 1985).
Hutchins, P.   *Clocks and More Clocks* (Macmillan, 1970).
Lionni, L.   *Inch by Inch* (Astor-Honor, 1960).
Murphy, S.   *Betcha!* (HarperCollins, 1997).
Myller, R.   *How Big Is a Foot?* (Dell, 1990).
Schlein, M.   *Heavy Is a Hippopotamus* (Children's Press, 1984).
Ward, C.   *Cookie's Week* (Putnam, 1988).

Data Analysis and Probability

Arnold, C.   *Charts and Graphs: Fun, Facts and Activities* (Watts, 1984).
Munsch, R.   *Moira's Birthday* (Annick Press, 1987).
Sachs, M.   *Fleet-Footed Florence* (Doubleday, 1981).
Srivastava, J.   *Averages* (Crowell, 1975).
Srivastava, J.   *Statistics* (Crowell, 1973).

RECENT AND RECOMMENDED: RELATED BOOKS FOR ADDITIONAL READING

Number and Operations

Adler, D.   *Fraction Fun* (Holiday House, 1996).
   A concise introduction to fractions; uses numerous real-life situations as examples.

Becker, J.   *Seven Little Rabbits* (Walker, 1994).
   Seven rabbits leave home to visit Toad. However, on the way, one rabbit after another gets tired and stops at Mole's house to sleep. Finally, all seven are tucked into Mole's bed and he must sleep in a chair. (Subtraction concepts are introduced.)

Calmenson, S.   *Dinner at the Panda Palace* (Scholastic, 1991).
   There are ten occupied tables of various animal guests at the Panda Palace, including lions and pigs. (Children learn to add numbers from 1 to 10.)

Chandra, D.   *Miss Mabel's Table* (Harcourt, 1994).
   One frying pan, two teaspoons of salt and three glasses of milk through ten dashes of yeast are sequentially set on the table by Miss Mabel as she prepares to fix pancakes for ten friends. (Counting is the theme.)

Dunbar, J.   *Ten Little Mice* (Harcourt, 1990).
   A narrative rhyme concerns ten mice who are returning to their nest, one by one, before a thunderstorm strikes. (This is a simple lesson in subtraction.)

Fleming, D.   *Count!* (Holt, 1992).
   A minimal-text number book with pictures of toucans, giraffes, and other lively creatures that present the numbers one to ten and then twenty, thirty, forty, fifty. Each representation shows the proper number of creatures and rectangular counters as well as the numeral and word name. (Multiples of ten are introduced along with counting from one to fifty.)

Giganti, P.   *Each Orange Has Eight Slices* (Greenwillow, 1992).
   Based on the familiar verse, "As I Was Going to St. Ives," the book emphasizes that math problems can be found everywhere. They are presented in parallel formats, varying in concepts involved from multiplication and addition to counting.

Hubbard, W.   *2 Is for Dancing: A 1, 2, 3 of Actions* (Chronicle Books, 1995).
   A counting book with zany characters uses minimal text to convey numerals one to ten; also included as a bonus is *C is for Curious: An ABC of Feelings,* which is found when the counting book is turned over.

Leedy, L.   *Fraction Action* (Holiday House, 1994).
   Cartoon animal characters, including Miss Prime and her students, discuss fraction concepts, focusing on solving such problems as selling lemonade or dividing food.

Lottridge, C.   *One Watermelon Seed* (Oxford, 1990).

> Max and Josephine plant their garden from one watermelon seed to two pumpkin seeds to ten corn seeds. Each seed results in a tenfold harvest (and children realize the power of grouping by ten).

Merriam, E.   *Twelve Ways to Get Eleven* (Simon & Schuster, 1993).

> This book presents twelve combinations of numbers that add up to eleven, such as nine pinecones and two acorns. (Children learn early counting and addition in a colorful format.)

Micklethwait, L.   *I Spy Two Eyes: Numbers in Art* (Greenwillow, 1993).

> A variation of the "I Spy" game asks the reader to examine twenty famous paintings to find the number of objects named, such as four fish in Matisse's "Goldfish." (Children are challenged with simple counting during an art appreciation lesson.)

Morozumi, A.   *One Gorilla* (Farrar, Strauss, 1990).

> Each scene in the book shows a gorilla with a different number of animals (such as pandas), from one to ten. Some are partially camouflaged in their environment. (Children learn simple counting in a book that earned a *New York Times* award.)

Nikola-Lisa, W.   *One, Two, Three, Thanksgiving!* (Whitman,1991).

> A Thanksgiving dinner, from preparations to cleanup, provides the context for a story about ten family members on a holiday. (Children learn counting as well as the concepts of "one more than" and "one less than.")

Reiser, L.   *Christmas Counting* (Greenwillow, 1992).

> The story centers on a growing family whose members establish their own Christmas traditions. (Through both text and illustrations, children can count and recount the accumulating holiday decorations.)

Ryan, P. & Pallotta, J.   *The Crayon Counting Book* (Charlesbridge, 1996).

> Even numbers from zero to twenty-four and odd numbers from one to twenty-three are shown as two more crayons are added to represent each new set. (Children learn about odd and even numbers through rhyming verses.)

Sendak, M.   *One Was Johnny* (HarperCollins, 1991).

> A boy named Johnny lived alone. When nine visitors came, he sent them away by counting backwards.

van Noorden, D. (Ed.)   *The Life-size Animal Counting Book* (Dorling Kindersley, 1994).

> Close-up photographs of animals appear almost life-size, extending over the borders of double-page spreads. (Children learn numbers from one to ten, twenty, and one hundred as well as numerals and number names.)

Voss, G.   *Museum Numbers* (Boston Museum of Fine Arts, 1993).

> Opposite each art reproduction is a page designed in two colors that tells the number to be counted. (Children learn numerals from one to ten in this attractive, cardboard counting book.)

Wise, W.   *Ten Sly Piranhas: A Counting Story in Reverse* (Dial, 1993).

> Ten piranhas gradually diminish in number. (Children learn to count backwards from ten to one in a book set in the Amazon jungle.)

Algebra

Anno, M.   *Anno's Magic Seeds* (Philomel, 1994).

> A wizard gives Jack a magic seed that he plants, so his family prospers from crops (from many seeds) until a hurricane wipes out all but ten seeds. (Children learn number patterns from the pictures.)

Bulloch, I.   *Patterns* (Thomson Learning, 1994).

> Close-up, color photos of various projects (centered on geometric patterns) help readers understand the explicit directions for construction. (Young children will need adult assistance making mosaics, etc.)

Demi   *One Grain of Rice* (Scholastic, 1997).

> Another version of the folktale from India relates how a village girl named Rani outwits the rajah to gain food for her people. (Children learn the value of doubling numbers.)

Martin, B. & Carle, E.   *Polar Bear, Polar Bear, What Do You Hear?* (Holt, 1991).
>   Animal sounds from ten different animals are featured in this predictable book. (Children learn the patterns in the repetitive text.)

Murphy, S.   *A Pair of Socks* (HarperCollins, 1996).
>   Patterns of stripes and dots and colors of red, blue, yellow, and green are all shown in different combinations of socks. (Children learn to match socks and also look for other patterns and matches in the world around them.)

Murphy, S.   *Too Many Kangaroo Things to Do* (HarperCollins, 1996).
>   Set in Australia, the story told in verse concerns Kangaroo and his surprise birthday party given by four friends who bring food and gifts. (Children learn four equations with an appropriate number of objects to represent each situation.)

Pluckrose, H.   *Pattern* (Children's Press, 1995).
>   Tennis shoe soles, carpets, dishes, flowers, and so on are all shown in color photos as examples of patterns. (Children learn, through this simple text, to become aware of the patterns around them and to create original designs.)

Pluckrose, H.   *Sorting* (Children's Press, 1995).
>   Objects are first shown in a pile and later in sets and subsets, always in color photos. (Children learn to sort objects after they decide, individually, what the objects have in common.)

Geometry

Anno, M.   *Anno's Math Games III* (Philomel Books, 1991).
>   As pictures drawn on grids are stretched and shrunk from side to side or from top to bottom, Kross and Kriss explore what changes and what remains the same. Triangles alone are explored in one chapter. (Children learn geometry and spatial sense through puzzles and a simple text.)

Dodds, D.   *The Shape of Things* (Candlewick Press, 1994).
>   A variety of shapes are introduced in a rhythm-and-rhyme text. (Children learn how shapes can be simplistic representational pictures of objects in daily life.)

Ehlert, L.   *Color Farm* (HarperCollins, 1990).
>   Shapes are used to create farm animals (e.g., a hexagon becomes a duck when an octagon is added). (Children learn to compare the shapes and patterns of animals.)

Feldman, J.   *Shapes in Nature* (Children's Press, 1991).
>   The book explores the world of shapes through the use of color photos of the natural world. Every page has a shape drawn at the top, followed by a photo that highlights the shape. (Children learn to look for shapes in the great outdoors.)

Friedman, A.   *A Cloak for the Dreamer* (Scholastic, 1994).
>   This book tells the story about four cloaks designed for the Archduke, one with rectangles, another with squares, a third with triangles, and the fourth with circles. The last is not acceptable to the Archduke so it is redesigned for the tailor's dreamer son. (Children learn how basic shapes are often used in designing clothes.)

Grover, M.   *Circles and Squares Everywhere!* (Harcourt, 1996).
>   Colorful illustrations show circles and squares in an urban environment, with increasingly complex scenes. (Children learn to focus on two-dimensional shapes in a three-dimensional world.)

Hoban, T.   *Shadows and Reflections* (Greenwillow, 1990).
>   Distortions may appear when shapes are reflected in mirrors, ponds, etc. but certain attributes remain unchanged. (Children learn to analyze shapes in these color photos, by comparing objects with their shadows and reflections.)

Rogers, P.   *Surprise! Surprise!*. (Scholastic, 1990).
>   Ten gifts of various sizes and shapes are shown on the opening page, and readers must guess what is inside. Hints are given before each movable flap. (Children learn to make intelligent guesses and to observe carefully the box shapes and sizes.)

Sharman, L.   *The Amazing Book of Shapes* (Dorling Kindersley, 1994).
>   Two-page color spreads connect geometric shapes and patterns to the real world. Each spread focuses on one concept and is accompanied by a project. (Children learn about three-dimensional shapes through step-by-step directions for each project.)

Turner, G. *Shapes* (Viking, 1991).

>A cutout book introduces squares, circles, triangles, rectangles, hearts, and stars, using common pictures. (Children learn that shapes can be found in the environment.)

Measurement

Allen, P. *Who Sank the Boat?* (Sandcastle, 1990).

>Five animal friends get into the boat, one by one. The waterline approaches the rim of the boat, but only the final scene reveals the answer to the title. (Children learn concepts of volume and capacity.)

Axelrod, A. *Pigs in the Pantry* (Simon & Schuster, 1997).

>When Mrs. Pig is ill, her family insists on cooking her favorite dish: firehouse chili. Unfortunately, the family does not understand the measures of different ingredients and the story ends with the arrival of the fire department. (Children learn measurement equivalents for cooking as well as some vocabulary that cooks use in their work.)

Edens, C. *The Wonderful Counting Clock* (Simon & Schuster, 1995).

>The text shares what happens at specific times between one o'clock and midnight on a unique clock tower. A missing numeral on each clock face corresponds to the number to be counted. (Children learn to tell exact times, such as 3:39, and also review counting from one to twelve.)

Hopkins, L. (Ed.) *It's About Time!* (Simon & Schuster, 1993).

>Poems chosen for this anthology represent appropriate activities and thoughts for specific times of the day, from 7:00 A.M. to midnight. A clock face appears in the corner of each double page. (Children learn to tell time through poetry.)

MacKinnon, D. *What Size?* (Dial, 1995).

>Close-up photos of children in familiar settings illustrate comparative size. Each double-page spread has a photo on the left side and a question about size on the right. (Children learn pairs of opposites, such as *long/short*, as well as same and different sizes.)

McMillan, B. *Jelly Beans for Sale* (Scholastic, 1996).

>Various combinations of coins and groupings of jelly beans are used throughout the book. (Children learn the values of coins and their interrelationships as well as different ways to partition numbers.)

Murphy, S. *The Best Bug Parade* (HarperCollins, 1996).

>A flower garden is the setting for trios of friendly bugs, each trio introducing a different size concept, such as *small/smaller/smallest*. The trios then join together to enjoy a bug parade. (Children learn size comparisons.)

Viorst, J. *Sunday Morning* (Atheneum, 1992).

>Two little boys have been told not to disturb their parents until 9:45 A.M. on Sunday morning, but they are noisy and the parents cannot sleep. The placement of a clock face with the illustrations shows the passage of time. (Children learn to estimate the minutes to and after the hour.)

Wells, R. *Bunny Money* (Dial, 1997).

>Max and Ruby set out to buy Grandma's birthday present. They spend their money in many ways but have no bus fare home. (Children learn the importance of spending money wisely, and can also dramatize the story with the "bunny money" on the inside book covers, which can be photocopied.)

Zimelman, N. *How the Second Grade Got $8205.50 to Visit the Statue of Liberty* (Albert Whitman, 1992).

>A class trip demands fund-raising projects. (Children can keep records of how much money the second graders are accumulating toward their goal.)

Data Analysis and Probability

Kirby, D. *Sorting* (Rigby, 1996).

>A nonfiction book with color photographs and drawings, it discusses surveys, tallies, and various kinds of graphs and even poses some problems about them that need solving.

Murphy, S. *The Best Vacation Ever* (HarperCollins, 1997).

>A good context for beginning data exploration, the story concerns a little girl who believes her busy family needs a vacation. She polls all the members, records their responses, and finally determines that only one place will fit all their expectations.

Pittman, H. *Counting Jennie* (CarolRhoda Books, 1994).

Jennie Jinks counts compulsively (from meatballs to monkeys, from pies to pigeons) on the bus trip to school through a bustling city. The rich watercolors reflect the incredible intensity of the morning rush hour and Jennie's equally intense need to classify and enumerate. The book is a springboard for discussing and collecting all the data around us.

Time-Life for Children (Eds.) *Play Ball: Sports Math* (Time-Life for Children, 1993).

Statistics, probability, and measurement are some of the topics in this multiconcept book that has colorful drawings on every page. Of its eighteen sections, five involve statistics and two concern probability.

Time-Life for Children (Eds.) *The Search for the Mystery Planet: Space Math* (Time-Life for Children 1993).

This multiconcept book of fourteen sections (with colorful drawings on every page) begins with data analysis in its first series of problems. It also includes statistics in two of its other sections. The format and problems throughout are motivating and concern the development of math skills rather than space concepts.

SOCIAL STUDIES AND EMERGENT LITERACY

CHAPTER SIX

SOCIAL STUDIES FOR YOUNG CHILDREN

The overall goal of education in the United States is to prepare students for their role as citizens in a democracy. It is the field of social studies that appears especially suited for providing our students with the skills, knowledge, and attitudes needed to begin to participate in miniature democracies in their classrooms, their homes, and their neighborhoods. It is also believed that it is in the early childhood years that the necessary foundation is best laid for later attainment of this overall goal.

NATIONAL DEFINITION AND CURRICULUM THEMES/STANDARDS

The National Council for the Social Studies (NCSS; the primary membership organization for social studies educators) has adopted the following definition:

> Social studies is the integrated study of the social sciences and humanities to promote civic competence. Within the school program, social studies provides coordinated, systematic study drawing upon such disciplines as anthropology, archaeology, economics, geography, history, law, philosophy, political science, psychology, religion, and sociology, as well as appropriate content from the humanities, mathematics, and natural sciences. The primary purpose of social studies is to help young people develop the ability to make informed and reasoned decisions for the public good as citizens of a culturally diverse, democratic society in an interdependent world. (NCSS, 1994, p. 3).

Furthermore, social studies is distinct from other fields of study because it integrates many areas across the disciplines and because it emphasizes and promotes civic competence.

The ten themes forming the framework of the (1994) social studies standards are:

1. Culture or *anthropology*
2. Time, continuity, and change or *history*
3. People, places, and environments or *geography*
4. Individual development and identity or *psychology*
5. Individuals, groups, and institutions or *sociology*
6. Power, authority, and governance or *political science*
7. Production, distribution, and consumption or *economics*
8. Science, technology, and society
9. Global connections
10. Civic ideals and practice

The first seven standards are based on the major concepts in history and the social sciences; the last three are more broadly based themes encompassing several subject areas.

Significance of National Standards

For many decades, the federal government played only a small role in the U.S. school system, which is primarily decentralized and local. However, the people's recent lack of confidence in the public schools has increased the desire for greater accountability from the schools, according to Chapin and Messick (1999), and that concern in turn has led to the creation of national educational standards. Although those standards are called voluntary, they do influence textbook publishers and have an impact on the many states, such as California, that have history and social science standards.

CALIFORNIA HISTORY–SOCIAL SCIENCE STANDARDS (K–3)

Before entering kindergarten, most children have acquired important spatial, temporal, and causal understandings, and teachers must recognize the crucial role that the "home base" plays in every child's life. They must therefore begin each year by concentrating first on the student's immediate world and understandings already introduced. Then studies begin that move both outward, to develop links with the larger geographic and economic world, and backward, to develop historical links with the people and times past (California Department of Education [CDE], 1997).

Kindergarten: Learning and Working Now and Long Ago

There are three major goals for this grade level:

1. Learning to work together
2. Working together: Exploring, creating, and communicating
3. Reaching out to times past

For the first major goal in the kindergarten, children daily *learn to work together* at centers during both whole-class and small-group activities. While they are always encouraged to participate, they still require gentle but firm guidance in acquiring the intricate skills needed in relating to peers and adults. They must learn to share the teacher's time and attention. Many must also learn to share classroom books and equipment and take turns at the learning centers.

It is important that teachers take advantage of classroom mini-crises (e.g., sharing two pairs of scissors at a table with six children), and use them as opportunities for critical thinking and problem resolution. Teachers can guide the class into analyzing the problem, considering alternative solutions and how these might be effective, and, finally, learning to work with a conclusion acceptable to all, or nearly all, of the students. The class must have time to discuss more desirable behaviors than grabbing or shoving, for example, and try them out until everyone can learn and work together in harmony.

In support of these learnings, teachers can introduce nursery rhymes, folktales, and current picture books that involve conflict and raise issues with which young children can identify. Examples include *Goldilocks and the Three Bears* (retold by Jan Brett) and *Arthur's New Puppy* (by Marc Brown). Following the read-alouds, children can discuss the behaviors of the character and how those affected others, decide why the character acted as he or she did, and, finally, consider whether other behaviors would have changed the results. Slowly, the class members will begin to ponder the consequences of their actions and develop individual responsibility.

A second major goal of the kindergarten is helping children *work together by exploring, creating, and communicating*. Under the teacher's guidance, girls and boys should have many opportunities to explore the school and its environment. A walk-

Kindergarten children learn to share and work together at the listening center.

ing trip around the neighborhood will offer the children information about its workers, its streets, its transportation system and its varied public structures and private businesses.

From such school and community walks, the children will bring back to the classroom ideas that they can transform into imaginary neighborhoods by using large blocks and small vehicles, together with materials from a classroom box filled with a variety of objects (e.g., workers' hats). Initial experiences with map work for young children can occur naturally through group activities centered about the newly created neighborhoods. Finally, as children want to learn more about the places they are developing, they will need to become acquainted directly with picture files and books. Indirectly, they will slowly begin to realize the value of literacy in their search for additional data.

A third major goal of the kindergarten curriculum is to help the children make their initial efforts to *reach out to times past*. Carefully chosen stories can promote simple understandings of how people lived in other times and places and how the children's own lives would have been affected had they lived in another century or in another country.

Grade One: A Child's Place in Time and Space

There are three major goals for this grade level:

1. Developing social skills and responsibilities
2. Expanding children's geographic and economic worlds
3. Developing awareness of cultural diversity, now and long ago

Six-year-olds begin to understand how important it is for individuals and groups to work together and, therefore, with the teacher's guidance they can *develop social skills and responsibilities* for classroom chores, cooperative group work, and school participation. These include the values of fair play, respect for the viewpoints and rights of peers, and acceptance of rules by which their classroom society abides.

When social dilemmas arise, children can practice problem-solving skills even as they start to realize that problems occur repeatedly and often in daily life. In this instance, besides those that happen in school settings, problems can also be found in stories carefully chosen by the teacher for read-alouds followed by discussions. Children better understand the significance of responsible behavior when they have heard stories such as *Did You Carry the Flag Today, Charley?* (by Rebecca Caudill) and *Peppe the Lamplighter* (by Elisa Bartone).

Most first graders, excepting those who are recent arrivals to the area, are already familiar with their neighborhoods. Now, however, the teacher can *expand the children's geographic and economic worlds* and help them develop an understanding of how their own communities relate to other places, both near and far, especially those that supply basic needs. Should the school be located in a changing region (with new construction of highways and shopping malls, for example), there is even a practical and greater chance for students to increase their geographic and economic beginnings.

One activity that first graders can complete is a three-dimensional floor or table map of their immediate geographic area (CDE, 1997), which will help clarify concepts of geographic distance and scale, promote observational skills, and clarify spatial relationships among the features of the region. Small milk cartons and building blocks can simulate structures (such as the post office and the library), especially when the front of each carton or block is identified by a taped photo taken on an initial walking trip. To represent the various human activities occurring in that community, street signs, mailboxes, buses, delivery trucks, signals, and so forth can be constructed and added. This also gives the teacher an opportunity to supply study prints, textbooks, and picture files that will lead the class to better comprehend the workplaces and workers.

When the floor or table map is finished, the children can then compare it to a picture-symbol map of the same area. At that point, they can more readily see that

A young student prepares to show the class his solution to a problem.

the picture-symbol map can reveal the same facts as their floor or table model, but on a smaller scale. It can also be hung upright without changing the spatial arrangements of the features (such as the post office and the library) or their relationship to each other (e.g., the library is still north of the post office). Such basic understandings underlie all subsequent map skills.

Once the children have become fully acquainted with their neighborhood, they are prepared to begin a study of its numerous economic and geographic links to the larger world. A short unit on The Airport or The Harbor will help girls and boys connect their community with peoples around the world, including those that supply goods and services. It will also introduce economic understandings.

Finally, first graders, under the direction of their teacher, can begin to *develop an awareness of cultural diversity, now and long ago*. They discover through selected literature the many similarities and differences among the cultural groups represented by families in the school. Later, they can be introduced to other cultures as well, both from the past as well as the present, again through such literature as *When I Was Young in the Mountains* (by Cynthia Rylant), *Umbrella* (by Taro Yashima), *The Snowy Day* (by Ezra Keats), and *Nine for California* (by Sonia Levitin). Children will further their appreciation for many cultures but, even more importantly at this grade level, they will become convinced of the genuine pleasure of reading.

Grade Two: People Who Make a Difference

There are three major divisions for this grade level:

1. People who supply our needs
2. Our parents, grandparents, and ancestors from long ago
3. People from many cultures, now and long ago

Seven-year-olds can develop an appreciation of the many *people who supply our daily needs,* including those who grow and/or harvest crops on farms, those who supply dairy products, as well as processors and distributors who move those crops and products to market. Large three-dimensional floor or table maps can again be created, much as they were in the first grade, except that the emphasis now is on linkages among children's homes, the places where food is produced, and the transportation system needed to move products to processors and then to markets. Picture maps, flowcharts, and even air photos and regional maps can be introduced to help children locate places where the economic activities occur. During the geographic lessons, boys and girls can begin to differentiate between the map and the globe and to learn cardinal directions; some may be ready as well to read and interpret map symbols with the use of a legend.

Ongoing throughout the unit is the development of basic economic concepts about human needs and wants, choice and scarcity, and specialization in the workplace. International trade can be introduced, using examples of foods with which the children can identify, e.g., bananas from Central America or cocoa from South America or Africa.

Literature is useful to help children better relate to the workers and producers of goods and services needed and to the concept of economic interdependence. Two examples include, *Where Does the Mail Go?: A Book about the Postal System* (by Melvin and Gilda Berger) and *The Milk Makers* (by Gail Gibbons).

Most second graders are capable of developing a beginning sense of history by constructing a family history of their *parents, grandparents, and ancestors of long ago.* This must be done cautiously in a classroom setting, with sensitivity to family privacy, because some children and parents may prefer not to include their backgrounds in this activity. For that group of students and parents, the teacher may suggest the alternative of each child preparing a biography of a famous American of special interest to the individual student.

Children can illustrate their family history by painting or coloring pictures or by using photos (with parental permission). They can write the story of family adventures, and invite parents or other members of the family to visit the classroom to relate their experiences. Class discussions can center on the various places and nations represented by the students and their families. Maps and a globe can help locate places of origin.

Selected literature pieces can also help boys and girls better understand the many cultural traditions and values that exist among the peoples in this country, how they began, and are being preserved. Examples from three different cultures include, *The Patchwork Quilt* (by Valerie Fluornoy), *How My Parents Learned to Eat* (by Ina Friedman), and *Laura Charlotte* (by Kathryn Galbraith).

In the final unit of the second grade, children should learn about *people from many cultures, now and long ago,* whose contributions they can understand and appreciate. Such men and women will include scientists, artists, musicians, athletes, authors, and others who have become role models for their achievements, courage, and sense of responsibility. By listening and reading biographies especially prepared for primary students, girls and boys can better comprehend how much people truly matter, whether we know their names or not and whether they are living now (as described in *A Picture Book of Rosa Parks* by David Adler) or lived in days past (as detailed in *A Weed Is A Flower: The Life of George Washington Carver* by Aliki).

Grade Three: Continuity and Change

There are two major divisions for this grade level:

1. Our local history: Discovering our past and our traditions
2. Our nation's history: Meeting people, ordinary and extraordinary, through biography, story, folktale, and legend

A second grader is preparing to mount photos of his family history to share with classmates.

Children who had spent time in the second grade constructing their family history are now ready to proceed with a construction of the *local history* of the city/town and state where they live so they may discover its past and its traditions. Since geographic settings affect where and how localities develop, third graders should begin with a study of their natural landscape. Uniquely valuable are field trips, which provide firsthand information; these can be augmented by the use of slides, videotapes, and photos.

A teacher must not assume that students are knowledgeable about the region where they live. On the contrary, experience has shown that often children are unfamiliar with places close to their homes. For this reason, the class should build a terrain model of the topography of the local area (CDE, 1997). The research required for the model will reveal the physical setting of the region's history, including major landforms. That information, in turn, will lead children to discover who the first settlers were, and how they used the natural resources, and modified the environment. Native Americans who once inhabited the region should be presented authentically through the aid of museum publications, artifacts, and pictures.

At this point, a classroom time line is needed to help children understand the sequence of events as each successive group of explorers and settlers arrived in the region and impacted the economy, the landscape, and the tribes of Native Americans. Boys and girls need to observe how their community has changed over the years (e.g., in its means of transportation), yet how in many respects it has remained the same (e.g., in its wheat farms). Through historical photos, local newspaper files, and publications of certain community organizations, children can see how a given place (such as City Hall) looked long ago and how it appears today. They may enjoy role-playing immigrant arrivals in years past as compared to modern newcomers, and be helped to contrast past history to ongoing changes and issues.

Together with an introduction to their local history, children should begin their study of the *nation's history* by becoming acquainted with its many groups of people over its four centuries of existence, who were both ordinary persons and extraordinary heroes. Literature appropriate for third graders includes stories of immigrants both past and present (as described, respectively, in *Squanto and the First Thanksgiving* by Joyce Kessel and in *Molly's Pilgrim* by Barbara Cohen). It further includes, from the past, biographies of adult achievers (such as *Dear Benjamin Banneker* by Andrea Pinkney) and stories of child heroes (as described in *The Drinking Gourd* by F. Monjo). The class can listen to books about the risk-takers, past and present, child and adult, and begin to appreciate those who opened new opportunities for others.

HISTORY, GEOGRAPHY, AND ECONOMICS: CRITICAL CONCEPTS

Social studies for young children today is an integrated course. However, teachers must be aware that each of the three major areas comprising the field of social studies demands an understanding of certain critical concepts peculiar to that area. Furthermore, they must also realize that, if genuine learning is to take place, those concepts must be presented in ways appropriate to the development of children in the early grades.

History

Once defined as a time-oriented study that refers to what we do know about the past, history can be introduced as involving the concepts of *time* (its measurement and passage), the inevitability of *change* (in schools, neighborhoods, nature, and the children themselves), the *continuity of human life* (through the family, intergenerational contacts, and holiday celebrations), *the past*—both immediate and distant (through people and objects), and the *methods of the historian* (Seefeldt, 1997).

Young children can learn to differentiate time present, time past, and time long, long ago (National Center for History in the Schools, 1995). They will find history both interesting and meaningful when it is centered around themselves, their families, and their community. They can appreciate it when it involves myths, legends, stories, and biographies. In order for them to get a firsthand look at the lives of people who lived long ago, children need records of the past including photograph albums, diaries, letters, artifacts, and family documents. Finally, they will begin to use the methods of the historian as they learn to question and identify a problem, gather information, observe and analyze the data, and, eventually, reach conclusions.

Geography

Defined as the field of study that enables people to find answers to queries about the world around them, geography is much more than memorizing the names of countries/states and their capitals or locating them on a map. Instead, the Geography Education National Implementation Project (1987) integrated place geography with the study of human–environment relationships and structured geographical studies around five critical concepts, all of which can be studied in some form in the early grades:

1. The earth as the place in which we live: This includes both physical characteristics (from landforms and bodies of water to natural vegetation and animal life) and the human actions and ideas that have shaped their character;

2. Direction and location: This is developed in young children through active experiences (e.g., moving through space). Helpful tools for locating such self in space are maps, and these the students can begin to make and use long before they can read them;

3. Relationships within places: As environments and humans are related, girls and boys can be introduced to the concept that, while humans have acquired control over their environment, nevertheless humans are also controlled by that environment. People live in different communities and are spread unevenly around the world; they interact with other persons by communication and travel, and by using products and ideas that arrive from environments beyond their own communities;

4. Spatial interactions: No matter where people live, they can interact with others far away in order to secure food, clothing, and additional products, as well as to share information by television, newspapers, telephones, radio, and other communicative means;

5. Regions: These are defined as places on Earth that have certain physical characteristics that dictate the ways in which its inhabitants live in societies and use the land. All children live in communities of some kind, and regions (or very large communities) represent convenient units on which to build a working knowledge of the world.

As they gain a basic understanding of geographic concepts, young children are also able to learn to ask geographic questions, acquire geographic information, organize and analyze that information, and, finally, answer their geographic questions (Geography Education Standards Project, 1994).

Economics

According to the National Council for the Social Studies (1989), all children need powerful and useful economic knowledge as well as the formal development of critical thinking skills. Economics represents the study of how services and goods are produced and distributed and how industry and trade generate wealth. Concepts appropriate for students in grades K–3 are those concerned with scarcity and production. These involve the use of barter and money to purchase goods, the necessity of decisions regarding the use of resources, the function of production (which is to meet consumer wants), and, most importantly, scarcity. The latter concept is basic to all economic understandings, and children experience it daily as they conserve their limited resources of time, materials, and energy.

While young students can be introduced to a few economic concepts, that introduction must occur through experiences, whether structured or incidental. Dramatic activities involving "producers" and "consumers" have proved to be especially effective (e.g., making, selling—and eating—cookies).

ANALYSIS SKILLS FOR HISTORY AND SOCIAL SCIENCES

Students in the elementary school (grades K–5) can demonstrate reasoning, reflective, intellectual, and research skills, according to the California Board of Education (1998). Therefore, teachers of kindergarten and primary children should modify the following twelve analysis skills and adapt all those that meet the needs of their particular classroom population.

CHRONOLOGICAL AND SPATIAL THINKING
1. Children can interpret time lines, and place key events and people in chronological sequence and within a spatial context.
2. Children can apply time-related terms correctly, including *past, present,* and *future,* and including *century, decade,* and *generation.*
3. Children can explain how the present connects to the past and identify similarities and differences between the two; they can also relate how some things change over time and others do not.
4. Children can use map and globe skills to determine absolute locations of places and also interpret information available through the map's legend, scale, and symbols.
5. Children can judge the importance of the relative location of a place (e.g., close to a harbor) and analyze how those relative advantages or disadvantages can change over time.

RESEARCH, EVIDENCE, AND POINT OF VIEW
1. Children can distinguish between primary and secondary sources.
2. Children can develop relevant questions about events mentioned in historical documents, eyewitness accounts, oral histories, diaries, letters, artifacts, maps, photos, art, and architecture.
3. Children can differentiate between fact and fiction by comparing documents involving historical events and people with fictionalized events and characters.

HISTORICAL INTERPRETATION
1. Children can summarize important events of the era they are studying and explain their historical contexts.
2. Children can identify human and physical characteristics of the places they are studying and explain how those features establish the unique character of those places.
3. Children can identify and interpret the numerous causes and effects of historical events.
4. Children can conduct cost/benefit analyses of current and/or historical events.

ATTITUDES AND VALUES: AN IMPORTANT PROCESS

Social studies educators emphasize the importance of addressing democratic values in the classroom, both as objects of study and as concerns to be taken into account when making decisions (Brophy, 1990). Nevertheless, due to their very nature, controversy continues over which attitudes and values should be taught and how they should be presented. Both deal with personal beliefs and feelings and, therefore, many persons advocate that values and attitudes should be taught at home or in the church or temple, not in the public classroom.

Realistically, however, there can be no argument about the role of the schools and teachers in the transmission of values, because nothing actually occurs in the primary grades, according to Seefeldt (1997), that is not influenced by, or bound up in, values and attitudes.

From the earliest grades, states the CDE (1997), students should learn the kind of behavior needed for the functioning of a democratic society. They should learn to share and take turns, and have opportunities both to lead and to follow. They should learn how to choose leaders and resolve routine disputes fairly and rationally. They should learn to respect the rights of the minority, even if it is a minority of one. Briefly, then, these democratic values should be taught through the curriculum, and in the daily life of the classroom and school.

Acquiring Attitudes and Values

Values and attitudes may be acquired through one of several approaches, the first of which is through *modeling*. Boys and girls in the early grades accept the attitudes and values of those around them, especially authority figures they love, such as their parents and other significant family members with whom they are in close contact. They also model their teacher's attitudes and values because he or she also represents an authority figure who protects them and cares for them. Too, they will model the attitudes and values of persons in the entertainment world as well as individuals who are prestigious figures in our culture; children can readily identify with both groups through the media.

Finally, because the expectations of any social group influence an individual's values, young students are affected by peers in their school. Teachers can, therefore, model the attitudes and values in a democratic classroom as they encourage whole-class participation in rule setting; permit each child to express ideas and feelings; value individual dignity and the rights of all children to feel safe; and insure that everyone understands that he or she bears some responsibility to others in the school and community and must endeavor to be a cooperative member of the school society.

A second approach by which children can acquire attitudes and values is through *reinforcement*. We know that, when students behave in a particular way and that behavior is recognized, it will be repeated. The same kind of conditioning applies also to the acquisition of attitudes and values. Consequently, girls and boys who respond in ways consistent with their beliefs and then are rewarded appropriately will have those beliefs reinforced. Under this approach, it becomes the teachers' responsibility to reward only those student attitudes that are consistent with democratic values in the classroom.

Still another approach to value and attitude formation incorporates the *cognitive theory*, which suggests principles of growth and development. It was Piaget who believed that children's attitudes and values coincide with their thought processes, and that their learning of moral values involves both interactions with others as well as maturation. Only through interactions are children allowed to make choices and experience their consequences, and, thereby, construct a sense of right and wrong. In the primary grades, according to Riley (1984), choices for the children become gradually more numerous and complex, while the teacher's choices to make for the class members diminish.

A final means to the acquisition of values and attitudes by young children is the *eclectic approach*, which combines all three of those already described. This gives teachers greater freedom, but increased responsibility, in deciding under what circumstances and with which groups of children they should employ a particular approach.

Understanding Democratic and Civic Values

An important curricular goal, which starts, with age-modification, in the early grades, is an understanding of: (1) national identity and constitutional heritage, together with the civic values involved, and (2) the responsibilities and rights of all citizens (CDE, 1997). To attain an understanding of the nation's identity, children must recognize that U.S. society is now, and always has been, multicultural and pluralistic. They must understand that the U.S. creed extols freedom and equality, and, therefore, the status of women and minorities has evolved over time in U.S. history. Furthermore, they must understand the unique experiences of immigrants from Latin America, Asia, Africa, and Europe, and the special role of the United States in world history as a nation of immigrants. Lastly, children should be led to realize that true patriotism incorporates the moral strength of the United States as a nation because it unites as one people the descendants of the many ethnic, religious, racial, and cultural groups.

To acquire an understanding of the constitutional heritage of the United States, children must apprehend the basic principles of democracy and learn the historical beginnings of such basic concepts as representative government, separation of powers, and trial by jury. In order to appreciate civic values, responsibilities, and rights, children must gradually come to understand what is required of all citizens in a democracy and, particularly, what one's individual responsibility is in the democratic system. Critical thinking and active participation are both skills attained through practice and deemed essential to good citizenship in a democratic setting.

ASSESSMENT IN EARLY ELEMENTARY SOCIAL STUDIES

For social studies in the early grades, most assessment is informal and maintained primarily to gain information about student learning that may lead to the overall improvement of instruction in this content area. Once teachers have developed appropriate goals in alignment with social studies standards set by national professional organizations and/or state departments of education, they are ready to integrate assessment as an ongoing and comprehensive activity. The tasks they use to evaluate children's learning are real instances of learning and connect to students' daily experiences. In this way, authentic evaluation

1. Clarifies goals that help describe the extent of student learning and growth;
2. Helps teachers determine the effectiveness of their whole-class instruction as well as their instruction of individual students;
3. Provides information to parents regarding their children's learning and development in this curricular area; and
4. Stimulates creative ideas for alternative techniques that may promote a revised and improved set of educational goals and classroom practices.

Five Alternative Assessment Techniques

Since children's literacy skills may vary widely in the early grades, there are other strategies besides paper and pencil testing that are useful for evaluating social studies instruction. These include:

1. *Journal summary entries created by the whole class:*   Once the class has orally compiled the important understandings from a particular lesson, the teacher can copy them on a flip chart for later review. In this way, a whole-class journal can be kept with one or more chart pages for each unit, and children will enjoy reading it during their free time. The chart is especially effective when contributors' names are posted after each entry in the journal.

2. *Use of word cards containing key concepts:*   Keyboards can be written on the overhead to help beginning writers with assignments concerned with an understanding of, and reaction to, some aspect of the unit. Word cards can then be used in packs by small groups or pairs for sorting or sequencing the steps involved, for example, in a particular production, such as the making of a quilt. Lastly, the cards can serve during an introductory reading/writing assessment in which the teacher reads statements about the words on the cards and the students respond by circling the correct yes or no answers on their work papers.

3. *Carousel assessment involving scribes from upper grades:*   This technique, especially geared for end-of-unit assessment, involves older and more capable readers and writers who work individually with each group of three or four younger children assigned to a different color marker (Alleman & Brophy, 1999). In preparation for the lesson, teachers write open-ended questions relevant to the major objectives of the unit; then they print each question, using a different color ink, at the top of a large sheet of newsprint.

As the groups assemble at their "stations" and are assigned questions, each begins at the site where the question matches the color of its marker, reads the question, and writes its response. Then the carousel starts, and each group reads the previous group's response and then places a question mark next to any part of that response with which it disagrees. Each group then privately discusses and records its own response to the question at the top of the sheet. The carousel continues until all groups have answered all the questions and returned to their original sites. There, they review all of the responses to the question at their "station" and plan how to expand their answers during the large-group or whole-class discussion that follows.

4. *Verbal response sharing in pairs, small groups, or whole-class:*   When it comes time for the class to reflect on, or react to, an important concept in the unit, the teacher opens the lesson by posing an open-ended question or reading a statement. After a sufficient period of time for individual reflection, children are each asked to discuss their responses with a partner or with their table group. Thus, they have the opportunity to learn from each other before reaching a satisfactory conclusion. Time permitting, the pairs or small groups can share one or more of their conclusions with the entire class.

5. *Student portfolios accompanied by informal interviews:*   Collections of dated samples of children's work are especially helpful when they are used during interviews with the teacher. Students can then explain their thinking on some of the social studies assignments that they completed. In turn, the teacher can help girls and boys select workpapers, maps, or drawings that were particularly challenging or reveal a special talent or interest. Furthermore, according to Meisels and Stelle (1991), parents may share an opportunity to select appropriate work samples to contribute to the portfolio.

Among the variety of items that can be included in the social studies portfolio are: copies of journal pages (with temporary spelling preserved); logs of books (rele-

Informal interviews by the teacher can be used to assess young students' understanding of social studies concepts.

vant to the units) that have been read to or by the children; dictated or written stories about social studies; photos of students engrossed in a unit project; and tape recordings made during a performance.

A Sixth and Popular Alternative Assessment Technique

Student performance during role-playing sessions, or informal interviews or during teacher observation is another assessment technique. To assure the success of a *role-playing* performance, the teacher must be involved in each enactment and allow sufficient time for preparation by the performers. He or she must carefully explain to the members of the young audience what, specifically, they must listen or look for (e.g., the sequence of workers involved in the production of *A New Coat for Anna* [by Harriett Ziefert]).

Interviews can be held during free play (supervised outdoors) or free classroom time, which allows the teacher and child to meet informally. Sometimes manipulatives (such as objects or study prints) can be used to help demonstrate understanding of a particular concept that young children have difficulty explaining in words alone. For this kind of evaluation to be authentic, there should be no time limits, so that girls and boys have all the time they need to consider their responses and elaborate on them if they wish.

Observations by teachers are being made continually and are generally unrecorded. Nonetheless, for assessing the significant goal of positive social behavior among young children, which involves learning to work with others and developing personal responsibility, it is critical to record behaviors observed. It can be done on a daily basis with a few children (in order that every student is observed weekly), and completed on self-adhesive notes, which are later transferred to a more permanent file. Teachers must focus on a few specific objectives and not attempt to record all behaviors every single time. Some districts require checklists whenever the goal can be divided into a list of traits or procedures (absent or present) that can be readily marked with *yes/no* answers.

REFERENCES

Alleman, J. & Brophy, J. (1999). Current trends and practices in social studies assessment for the early grades. *Social Studies and the Young Learner, 11*(4), 15–17.

Brophy, J. (1990). Teaching social studies for understanding and higher-order applications. *Elementary School Journal, 90,* 351–419.

California Board of Education. (1998). *California History-Social Science Standards: Grades Kindergarten—Six.* Sacramento: Author.

California Department of Education. (1997). *History-Social Science Framework.* Sacramento: Author.

Chapin, J. & Messick, R. (1999). *Elementary Social Studies: A Practical Guide,* (4th ed.). New York: Longman.

Geography Education National Implementation Project. (1987). *K–6 Geography: Themes, Key Ideas, and Learning Opportunities.* Macomb: Western Illinois University, National Council for Geographic Education. Washington, DC: U.S. Department of Education.

Geography Education Standards Project. (1994). *Geography for Life: National Geography Standards 1994.* Washington, DC: National Geographic Society.

Meisels, S. & Stelle, D. (1991). *The Early Childhood Portfolio Collection Process.* Ann Arbor, MI: Center for Human Growth and Development.

National Center for History in the Schools. (1995). *National Standards: History for Grades K–4.* Los Angeles: Author.

National Council for the Social Studies (1989). *Charting a Course: Social Studies for the 21st Century.* New York: Author.

National Council for the Social Studies. (1994). *Expectations of Excellence: Curriculum Standards for Social Studies.* Washington, DC: Author.

Riley, S. (1984). *How to Generate Values in Young Children.* Washington, DC: National Association for the Education of Young Children.

Seefeldt, C. (1997). *Social Studies for the Preschool-Primary Child,* (5th ed.). Upper Saddle River, NJ: Merrill/Prentice-Hall.

CHILDREN'S LITERATURE CITED

Adler, D. *A Picture Book of Rosa Parks* (Holiday, 1993).

Aliki *A Weed Is a Flower: Life of George Washington Carver* (Simon & Schuster, 1988).

Bartone, E. *Peppe the Lamplighter* (Lothrop, 1993).

Berger, M. &. Berger, G. *Where Does the Mail Go?: A Book about the Postal System* (Chelsea House, 1994).

Brett, J. *Goldilocks and the Three Bears* (Dodd, 1987).

Brown, M. *Arthur's New Puppy* (Little, Brown, 1993).

Caudill, R. *Did You Carry the Flag Today, Charley?* (Holt, 1966).

Cohen, B. *Molly's Pilgrim* (Lothrop, 1983).

Flournoy, V. *The Patchwork Quilt* (Dial, 1985).

Friedman, I. *How My Parents Learned to Eat* (Houghton Mifflin, 1987).

Galbraith, K. *Laura Charlotte* (Philomel, 1990).

Gibbons, G. *The Milk Makers* (Macmillan, 1985).

Keats, E. *The Snowy Day* (Puffin, 1962).

Kessel, J. *Squanto and the First Thanksgiving* (Carolrhoda, 1983).

Levitin, S. *Nine for California* (Orchard, 1996).

Monjo, F. *The Drinking Gourd* (Harper, 1970).

Pinkney, A. *Dear Benjamin Banneker* (Harcourt, 1994).

Rylant, C. *When I Was Young in the Mountains* (Dutton, 1982).

Yashima, T. *Umbrella* (Viking, 1958).

Ziefert, H. *A New Coat for Anna* (Knopf, 1986).

CHAPTER SEVEN

FORTY LITERATURE ACTIVITIES PROMOTING SOCIAL STUDIES UNDERSTANDINGS

CURRICULUM STANDARD FOR KINDERGARTEN: LEARNING AND WORKING, NOW AND LONG AGO

■ ■ ■ **(1) CONCEPT:** It is not polite to use something that belongs to others without first asking for their permission.

Literature: *Goldilocks and the Three Bears,* retold by J. Brett (Dodd, 1987), unpaged.

Listed in: *Best Books for Children* (R. R. Bowker, 1990).

Synopsis: This traditional folktale is lavishly retold and highlighted by unusual designs.

Activities After Read-Aloud:

1. Obtain other versions of this tale as retold and illustrated by L. Cauley (1981), J. Dyer (1984), J. Marshall (1988), J. Stevens (1986), or T. Rose (1992). Read all of them to the children on different days. Then, ask each child to choose a favorite and explain his or her choice. Finally, make a class graph depicting student preferences.

2. Dramatize the story during a circle time by having the children portray the bears and Goldilocks. Ask the "bears" how each felt when "Goldilocks" entered their home and used their things. Ask "Goldilocks" how she felt, using what did not belong to her. Finally, discuss manners and ask children what they would do if they found another child playing with their toys who had not asked permission.

3. Have each student draw a picture of Goldilocks and Baby Bear's broken chair. Then, have them each copy "I'm Sorry" from the chalkboard, writing it in a speech bubble linked to Goldilocks. Discuss how important it is for positive personal relationships and strong self-esteem to apologize sincerely when one has offended or harmed someone.

4. Remind the class that the Three Bears never had a chance to talk to Goldilocks about her not asking permission to use their things. Ask the children to decide a new way to end the story, possibly with the Bears being able to talk to Goldilocks. Have them dictate (or write) their own endings. Then, share these different endings with the class. _____

■ ■ ■ **(2) CONCEPT:** Children must teach their pets good manners so that everyone in the family is happy.

Literature: *Arthur's New Puppy* by M. Brown (Little, Brown, 1993), 32 pp.

Listed in: *Best Books for Children* (R. R. Bowker, 1998).

Synopsis: Arthur the aardvark gets a new puppy that tears the living room apart, refuses to wear a leash, and causes other problems until Arthur teaches him some basic manners.

Activities After Read-Aloud:

1. Give children each four to six paper squares and ask them to draw themselves helping with home chores, showing a different chore in each square. Next, give each child a piece of butcher paper and have him or her glue a photo or self-portrait in the center, with spokes extending from the photo. At the end of each spoke, the child glues one paper square. Finally, the children each dictate (or write) a sentence about every chore shown on their squares.

2. Invite the children to suggest ways that they can or do help at home and create a class Home Helpers Chart. Each child then prepares his or her own chart by selecting different chores that can be completed on different days of one week. The charts may go home and, when completed, be returned for class display on a board titled "How I Can Help at Home."

3. Procure a class pet and discuss the responsibilities of caring for it. As a class, develop a list of the jobs involved in taking care of that pet and assign jobs on a weekly basis. Have the students each keep a record about the pet, and draw or write about the responsible care that it demands.

4. Share with the children another book by Marc Brown about Arthur the aardvark. An especially appropriate one is *Arthur Writes a Story* (Little, Brown, 1996) in which he tells how he got his new puppy. _____

■ ■ ■ **(3) CONCEPT:**   Dinosaurs are large extinct animals that lived a long time ago.

Literature: *Patrick's Dinosaurs* by C. Carrick (Houghton Mifflin, 1983), 32 pp.

Listed in: *Best Books for Children* (R. R. Bowker, 1998).

Synopsis: When his brother discusses dinosaurs, Patrick imagines he sees them in the street and outside his window. Finally, he learns that they all died millions of years ago.

Activities After Read-Aloud:

1. Make a collection of cards with facts about dinosaurs on one side and "What If?" questions on the other. Read and discuss the facts with the class. Then, divide the children into groups (named after dinosaurs) with leaders who each select one card for their group to discuss such questions as:

   a. "What if you could have a dinosaur for a pet?"

   b. "What if people had been living back in dinosaur times?"

2. Introduce children to various theories of dinosaur extinction. Show pictures and explain in simple terms how these are only guesses. Make a chart with student names on one side and symbols or simple pictures representing theories on the other side. Let children vote for the theory they like best (e.g., Earth hit by a large asteroid), and graph the results.

3. Read Carrick's *What Happened to Patrick's Dinosaurs?* (Houghton Mifflin, 1988) and explain this is Patrick's funny guess about what happened to make dinosaurs extinct. Tell children to create their own guesses and dictate or write their ideas. They may illustrate them, too.

4. Play "I Spy" by first placing large posters or pictures of dinosaurs near the children. Then, demonstrate the game, saying "I spy with my little (colored) eye a dinosaur that…," inserting a fact about one of the pictured dinosaurs. Whoever guesses correctly is the next player. _____

■ ■ ■ **(4) CONCEPT:**   Children ride the school bus together to get to school and later to get back home.

Literature: *School Bus* by D. Crews (Greenwillow, 1984), 32 pp.

Listed in: *Best Books for Children* (R. R. Bowker, 1998).

Synopsis: Many kinds of school buses pick up children for school and bring them home again.

Activities After Read-Aloud:

1. Take a class poll on how children get to school (car, bus, bicycle, walking). Help the class graph the results by taking poster board and labeling numbers (for

students) up the side, and forms of transportation across the bottom. Fill in with grid lines and compile the results of the poll. Discuss.

2. Begin a project on school buses by asking children what they know about them ("They are yellow.") and what they would like to find out. Provide books about buses generally, such as Judy Hindley's *The Big Red Bus* (Candlewick, 1995), and school buses in particular, such as Sharon Denslow's *Bus Riders* (Macmillan, 1993). Arrange for a class visit by one of the district bus drivers who can discuss his or her job and the importance of being a good rider.

3. Adapt the familiar song, "Wheels on the Bus," to reflect the school bus: "The wheels on the bus go round and round, round and round, round and round; the wheels on the bus go round and round, *on the way to school.*" Let children create their own lines in the song, such as "The backpacks on the bus go bump, bump, bump," and so on.

4. On a large map of the school community, help the children highlight the route each takes to get to and from school. (For those who take the bus, first check with the drivers for the correct routes.) Work with the children to place colored plastic thumbtacks to identify the locations of their homes and the school. Connect thumbtacks with yarn and display on a bulletin board. _____

■ ■ ■ **(5) CONCEPT:**   Everyone in a family must follow certain rules so that everyone is safe.

Literature: *The Story About Ping* by M. Flack (Viking, 1933), 32 pp.

Listed in: *Best Books for Children* (R. R. Bowker, 1998)

Synopsis: Over in China, a little duck lives on a boat in the river with his parents and sixty-five relatives. They all lead an orderly life with morning and evening rules. One day, Ping accidentally becomes separated from his family when he is late returning home. He spends a perilous night on the river, escapes with his life, and is finally reunited with his family. He has learned to appreciate the importance of following rules.

Activities After Read-Aloud:

1. Have children tell about an adventure that they would like to have (go on a space shuttle). Tape their responses, and allow them to listen to their stories at the listening center.

2. Discuss the importance of having rules. Have children think of rules at school that help keep everyone safe and the classroom orderly. Then distribute duck-shaped books with blank pages on which students can dictate (or write) three school rules. Finally, ask them to go home and think of three rules they have there to keep the family safe and the home orderly. Let the children dictate (or write) the home rules in their duck-shaped books to share in class.

3. Divide the class into small groups. Give each group a problem to solve, such as "Find a way to make a ramp from the table to the floor, using unifix cubes, just like the bridge (or ramp) Ping and his family used to reach the shore from their boat each day." Encourage the children to work together to solve the problem. When each group is finished, have the members share their solutions with the class. _____

■ ■ ■ **(6) CONCEPT:**   Being honest is an important part of daily life.

Literature: *Jamaica's Find* by J. Havill (Houghton Mifflin, 1986), 30 pp.

Listed in: *Best Books for Children* (R. R. Bowker, 1998).

Synopsis: Jamaica finds a little stuffed dog in the park and decides to take it home and keep it for her own rather than turning it in at the Lost and Found Office. Finally, with help of her family, she solves her dilemma and so meets the little girl who had lost her stuffed dog. They become friends.

Activities After Read-Aloud:

1. Help the children make two-sided paper plate masks showing a person feeling happy on one side and a person feeling sad on the other. Encourage the class to

use their masks to show how the little girl who lost her stuffed animal felt, first when she lost it, and then when she got it back. Then, have the children use their masks to show Jamaica's feelings at the beginning and end of the story.

2. Brainstorm with the children other feelings that they have experienced, e.g., disappointment. Chart a list of Words About Feelings and discuss what situations may cause some of those feelings. Have students dictate (or write) one sentence that begins: I feel (.......) when (.........). Share the writings.

3. Discuss what should be done when we find items that belong to someone else, e.g., put an ad in the paper or go to the Lost and Found Desk at the school. Let the children pretend that they have each lost a favorite toy or pet and then create a poster so others can help find the missing item. Each poster should have pictures and words. _____

■ ■ ■ **(7) CONCEPT:** Children and adults must be respectful to each other.

Literature: *Lilly's Purple Plastic Purse* by K. Henkes (Greenwillow, 1996), 32 pp.

Listed in: *Best Books for Children* (R. R. Bowker, 1998).

Synopsis: Lilly the mouse loves everything about school, and especially her teacher, Mr. Slinger. One day, however, when he asks her to wait a while before she shows the class her new purse, she does something for which she is very sorry later.

Activities After Read-Aloud:

1. Prepare flash cards that give students 2-, 3-, and 4-step directions. Have children take turns choosing one card, handing it to the teacher, and following the directions read to them. Let the class orally repeat the sequence of directions.

2. Have children create their own alliterations, like "purple plastic purse," about an item that is a container. Then, have them think of three items that begin with the same sound and would fit into their alliterative container, e.g. Susie's pretty, pink pocket holds pennies, pencils, and pins. Finally, have them illustrate their alliterations, dictating (or writing) their alliterations below the pictures.

3. Develop with the class a definition of the word *respect*. Then, discuss with the class the ways in which Lilly was disrespectful and impolite to her teacher, and ask the students "How do people show respect at school?" On 4" × 6" white construction paper, have students each draw one way that they are respectful at school. Invite them each to dictate (or write) a sentence about their picture. Cut large letters spelling RESPECT from bright-colored construction paper and glue the letters in the center of a long piece of dark-colored butcher paper. Finally, glue the student pictures around the word. _____

■ ■ ■ **(8) CONCEPT:** Friends are special and they make adjustments for each other because they care.

Literature: *Frog and Toad Are Friends* by A. Lobel (Harper, 1970), 64 pp.

Listed in: *Best Books for Children* (R. R. Bowker, 1998).

Synopsis: The first of four books about two animals who become friends emphasizes cooperation and the adjustments that the two make to help each other in many ways.

Activities After Read-Aloud:

1. Have children brainstorm ideas about what is special about Frog, what is special about Toad and what special qualities they share. Record their ideas on a Venn diagram. Next, instruct them to draw a picture of a special friend and then dictate (or write) what they like about her/him.

2. Have students think about what friendship means by asking them to brainstorm a list of descriptive words to complete the sentence, "A friend is...." Write the words on cards that contain the sentence starter. Display them on the bulletin board for review and for the class to read aloud.

3. Introduce a classroom pet for which the children can care. They will learn that they must sometimes sacrifice their own wants for the needs of another and also learn the value of caring.

4. Have the children make a Big Book featuring some of the friendly behaviors they have seen in the classroom. Ask each child to draw a picture that shows a classmate doing something "friendly." Then, have each one dictate (or write) a description of the illustration at the bottom of his or her page. Staple the pages together with a cover and title the booklet "Friends Do Special Things for Each Other."

5. Read Frog's letter (p. 62) aloud to the class. Just as Frog sent a letter to Toad, have students dictate (or write) a short letter to children in another class. (If the Internet is available, children may E-mail a new friend from the E-mail Classroom Exchange: *http:www.iglou.com/xchange/ece/index.html* _____

■ ■ ■ **(9) CONCEPT:**	Many things contribute to a final product, which often must be shared.
Literature:	*The Cake That Mack Ate* by R. Robart (Little, Brown, 1991), unpaged.
Listed in:	*Best Books for Children* (R. R. Bowker, 1998).
Synopsis:	The value of sharing is related to this cumulative tale of farm life. The story lists items that went into the cake that Mack ate, but the reader does not learn who Mack is until the end.

Activities After Read-Aloud:

1. Create a class book by assigning one item from the story to every two children. Instruct each pair of students to illustrate that item to accompany the text. Compile the illustrations sequentially into a book (with the title of the story) and place it on the library table for all to enjoy.

2. Since this book builds on prior text, much like "The House That Jack Built," have children create their own (small group) cumulative stories based on a topic of their choice. First, the group introduces its topic ("This is the shirt that Joshua wore."). Then they build on their text by telling either how the item came to be or something that happened to it ("This is the stain on the shirt that Joshua wore. This is the pizza that made the stain on the shirt that Joshua wore."). Depending on the size of the group, either the children may each memorize their lines or an adult aide may write down the short cumulative tale.

3. Have the students brainstorm about how a chocolate cake could be made. Write their recipes on chart paper and number the steps in possible sequential order. Have the class read the steps in unison and discuss.

4. When a special treat is set on the teacher's desk in the morning for all to see, say to the class, "It's mine! And I'm not sharing!" Before recess, ask children how they feel when someone (like the teacher) refuses to share her or his treat. Discuss, stressing why it is polite to share things. Then divide up the treat equally before class is dismissed. _____

■ ■ ■ **(10) CONCEPT:**	It is important to care about yourself and other people, animals, and things.
Literature:	*Pierre* by M. Sendak (Harper, 1962), 48 pp.
Listed in:	*Best Books for Children* (R. R. Bowker, 1998).
Synopsis:	A young boy's motto is "I don't care." Then a lion eats him after hearing him say that motto, and teaches Pierre the importance of caring for himself. (Story told in verse.)

Activities After Read-Aloud

1. Have children create stick puppets of each character in the story, then let them dramatize and retell the story in small groups.

2. Create a student form stating, e.g., "(*Susie*) cares about her (*cat*)." Have students each think of one thing or person that matters to them. Give each child a copy of the form to complete. Later read and discuss the sentences, and make a chart of all the suggestions, e.g., pets, books, friends, and so on.

3. Develop "Caring Discussion Cards" with simple scenarios and a question to prompt children's thinking skills, for example:

When Jenny's cousin Steve came to school one day, he looked very sad. When Jenny asked him why he looked sad, Steve told her that his dog had been hit by a car. What are some things Jenny could do or say to show her cousin she cared?

4. Each day, draw a child's name at random from a jar of student names. Tell the class that, throughout the day, everyone should think of what is nice about that student. At the end of the day, compile a chart of the children's ideas. When there are at least five complete sentences about the Student of the Day, have the class read them in unison. Then, roll up the chart, tie it with a yarn bow, and give it to the student to share at home. _____

CURRICULUM STANDARD FOR GRADE ONE: A CHILD'S PLACE IN TIME AND SPACE
(with students keeping social studies journals)

■ ■ ■ **(1) CONCEPT:** One hundred years ago, many jobs in the United States were very different from jobs today.

Literature: *Peppe the Lamplighter* by E. Bartone (Lothrop, 1993), 32 pp.

Listed in: *Best Books for Children* (R. R. Bowker, 1998).

Synopsis: A poor immigrant Italian family in New York City "a long time ago" must allow their young son Peppe to take a job lighting the gas street lamps in his neighborhood, after his father becomes ill and cannot work.

Activities After Read-Aloud:

1. Create a class chart of the things we have today that the people in the story did not have, and tell how those items were or are used. Three columns will be needed: Now, Then, and Uses. Discuss.
2. Have children each choose one item from the chart (in the "Now" column in Activity One), and write what would be different in their lives without that item and what they would have to do to make up for not having it, e.g., electricity.
3. Brainstorm with the students the different jobs in today's society and what the people do who have those jobs. List them on the board and let the children each choose one job they would like to have when they get older. Using markers or chalk, have them illustrate themselves doing the job after writing a brief description of it. Share the pictures and sentences.
4. Ask each student to interview an elderly adult to discover a career or job that people had years ago that no longer exists. Later, have the students discuss their findings with the class.
5. Encourage the class to discuss why Peppe's sister Assunta thought his was the best job because it scared the dark away. _____

■ ■ ■ **(2) CONCEPT:** Responsibility can be a reward.

Literature: *Did You Carry the Flag Today, Charley?* by R. Caudill (Holt, 1966), 96 pp.

Listed in: *Best Books for Children* (R. R. Bowker, 1998)

Synopsis: Each day one child is chosen to lead the boys and girls to the bus and carry the flag. This is the highest honor at The Little School, and only given to the student who is most helpful. One day Charley finally achieves the award.

Activities After Read-Aloud:

1. Pair up the students and have each pair decide how everyone in the class will get a turn to lead the Pledge of Allegiance while holding the flag. When all the students are finished, have them share their answers with the class. Discuss and decide on the best way to handle the honor.

2. Have each child brainstorm the various jobs in the school. Then, have them each respond to the following question in writing and/or drawing: What job do you consider to be the most important one at our school? How would you choose people to do that job?

3. Divide the class on Monday morning into committees by table groups (or rows). Develop committee clipboards listing daily jobs and students for each table. Have each child check the clipboard daily and perform any committee work necessary (sharpening pencils, collecting homework, distributing writing paper, etc.). On Friday afternoon, have each committee share the importance and success of their efforts with the class.

4. Make a poster graph to place on the board, listing possible home responsibilities (take out the trash, feed the dog, etc.). With the class, discuss the jobs that they have at home, and make an "x" on each home responsibility that the children have. Then, discuss the graph, counting which category has the most "x's" on it. Ask the children if they think one job is more important than another, and what type of reward they receive at home for doing chores. Stress that people do not always receive money or gifts for doing jobs responsibly. _____

■ ■ ■ **(3) CONCEPT:**   Through their own efforts, people should make the world more beautiful in some way.

Literature: *Miss Rumphius* by B. Cooney (Puffin, 1982), 32 pp.

Listed in: *Best Books for Children* (R. R. Bowker, 1998).

Synopsis: Miss Rumphius is told by her grandfather that she is to leave something beautiful to the world through her life. She travels the world, comes home to live by the sea, and leaves her mark of beauty for future generations by planting lupine seeds.

Activities After Read-Aloud:

1. Brainstorm with the students some ideas of how to make the neighborhood (their part of the world) a more beautiful place. Include some negative aspects that they could help remove, e.g., litter on the ground. Then, have the children write a short story explaining what they would do to beautify the world, how they would do it, and how others would benefit. Share the stories.

2. Help the class trace the travel route that Miss Rumphius took on her travels, using a globe or world map.

3. Give students each some wildflower seeds, a clean, empty container (from eggs or milk), some soil, and information about planting and watering the seeds. Have them observe the growth twice a week and record changes in their journal. (They should save some of their seeds and plant them in their neighborhood, with parental permission.)

4. Tell the class to pretend that they are the architects of a large city skyscraper project that needs a rooftop garden for relaxation and beauty. In small groups, children can plan such a garden, including small trees, plenty of flowers, birds, and so on. Ask them to use markers to color their garden that will help make the large city more beautiful. _____

■ ■ ■ **(4) CONCEPT:**   Friends are important and should be kind to each other.

Literature: *Bargain for Frances* by R. Hoban (Harper, 1970).

Listed in: *Best Books for Children* (R. R. Bowker, 1998).

Synopsis: Frances, a badger, is warned by her mother to "be careful" as she goes to play with her friend Thelma, because Thelma often tricks her in some way. After various complications involving a tea set, Frances and Thelma choose to be friends and enjoy each other's company.

Activities After Read-Aloud:

1. Encourage the children to share some of the things that they have learned from their friends. Then, have them draw pictures of themselves learning something

from a friend ("I learned to play hopscotch"). Finally, ask them each to write a sentence explaining their picture.

2. Send a note home with each child, stating that the class will participate in preparing and eating a Friendship Fruit Salad. Ask the parent which fruit he or she would like to contribute to the giant class salad from the following list: bananas, cherries, apples, pears, melons, oranges, pineapples, or other (preferably fresh) fruits that can be cut up into bite-sized pieces. Confirm the responses and set aside a day to prepare a Friendship Lunch that everyone can enjoy.

3. On the chalkboard, brainstorm with the class a list of characteristics that describe a good friend. Then explain that these traits will be used to create a free-form class poem. To encourage responses, write the following brief sample on the board:

A Good Friend

Plays with you,
Laughs with you,
Talks with you,
And listens to you.

4. Prepare several scenarios (on separate pieces of paper) that depict problems that may arise between friends. Put the pieces in a jar, divide the class into groups of four, and let each group pick a scenario piece from the jar. Each group will read the scenario (with help, if needed), decide how to solve the problem, and dramatize the solution for the class. _____

■ ■ ■ (5) CONCEPT: Children enjoy being outdoors in the snow, but should always play safely.

Literature: *The Snowy Day* by E. Keats (Puffin, 1962), 40 pp.

Listed in: *Best Books for Children* (R. R. Bowker, 1998).

Synopsis: A boy named Peter, who lives in a city apartment, enjoys his first snowfall and even takes a snowball home in his pocket.

Activities After Read-Aloud:

1. Have children fold white tissue or copy paper and cut out snowflakes from a variety of sizes, keeping the designs simple and being sure not to cut into the middle of the snowflake. They must tape a piece of heavy string or yarn to the top of every snowflake. Class mobiles can be made by stringing the smaller snowflakes to the larger ones. Hang mobiles from hangers or windows or even from the ceiling.

2. Cluster on the board some new vocabulary from the story such as *crunch, morning, stick, night, tracks, Peter,* and so on. Have the children each write a story entitled "Peter's Fun," and use three or more of the new words. Ask them to take turns reading their stories to a partner.

3. Share with the class other Keats' books about Peter, including *Goggles!* (Macmillan, 1987), *Whistle for Willie* (Puffin, 1964), and *Peter's Chair* (Harper, 1967). Have the children each vote (secretly) for the one they liked best. Discuss the idea of opinions and how any of the four books would be an appropriate choice for some student. Remind the class that everyone does not have to like the same book, but should have a logical reason for his or her opinion.

4. Using black construction paper, construct a class-sized mural of a winter snow scene. Sponge the paper with white tempera paint, allow it to dry, and then attach cutouts of green fir trees and other winter objects. Assign children to groups so everyone can participate in rotation. _____

■ ■ ■ (6) CONCEPT: Many families traveled to California during the Gold Rush of 1849.

Literature: *Nine for California* by S. Levitin (Orchard, 1996), unpaged.

Listed in: *Best Books for Children* (R. R. Bowker, 1998).

Synopsis: Ma and her five children journey West by stagecoach to join Pa in the California goldfields, and they overcome many obstacles along the route.

Activities After Read-Aloud:

1. Display a large map of the United States and highlight the trail taken in the story (and shown at the beginning of the book). Point out to the students various geographical features such as lakes, rivers, mountains, plains, and so forth, and discuss what the terrain was like in each area. Then, divide the class into groups, assigning each a specific type of terrain, e.g., mountains. Using tear art, have each group create a scene for its type of terrain. Finally, display the art on a bulletin board in the order of the terrain encountered by the characters in the story as they traveled to California.

2. Have students practice letter writing as they pretend to be on the stagecoach going West. They each choose a friend or family member and tell him or her about their experiences and feelings during the journey. Children may elect to write one letter that takes a whole week to write, or they can write a short letter for each day of the week. They should relate where they slept, what they ate, and so on. Distribute envelopes so children can "send" their completed letters, properly addressed, but not stamped. Display the envelopes filled with letters.

3. Give the students each a piece of large white construction paper and ask them to sketch the stagecoach that Ma and the children took. (Remind them to include the horses that pulled the stagecoach.)

4. Discuss with the class some reasons why the trip took nine days then. Ask, "Why is travel faster today?" _____

■ ■ ■ **(7) CONCEPT:**   Family life can be happy no matter where one lives.

Literature: *When I Was Young in the Mountains* by C. Rylant (Dutton, 1982), 32 pp.

Listed in: *Best Books for Children* (R. R. Bowker, 1998).

Synopsis: Two children live with their grandparents in this story of poverty in the Appalachian Mountains. They enjoy a warm family life and pleasant community activities.

Activities After Read-Aloud:

1. Make a Venn diagram. Have the class brainstorm what activities people do (a) in the mountains, (b) in the local community, and (c) in the mountains and the local community.

2. Have students brainstorm what kinds of things they would do if their family moved to the mountains to live. Using crayons or sticks of colored chalk, have each child draw a picture of him- or herself living in the mountains and doing one or more of the activities mentioned. Captions can be added.

3. Have children pretend that they are living in the mountains and wish to write a short letter to a friend. They must explain what is different about their new home and school.

4. Pass around examples of picture-postcards in case some children are not familiar with the format. Then give the students each an 8" × 5" unlined index card to turn into a "picture-postcard" of their own design, drawing on one side a place where he or she would like to live. A short sentence or caption must be added to the back of the "postcard." _____

■ ■ ■ **(8) CONCEPT:**   Sharing is important but must be done fairly.

Literature: *Tops and Bottoms* by J. Stevens (Scholastic, 1995), 32 pp.

Listed in: *Best Books for Children* (R. R. Bowker, 1998).

Synopsis: Hoping to rise above the poverty level, clever Hare takes unfair advantage of lazy Bear during a garden project in which Bear contributes the land and Hare provides the labor for a profitable harvest.

Activities After Read-Aloud:

1. Have the children explain clearly how Hare shared with Bear. Then discuss specific items shared around the home such as dishes, books, and furniture. Then, consider items such as toothbrushes that are not shared due to hygienic reasons. List those items on chart paper and chant them in the following verse

> It's good to share,
> Unless germs are there,
> So please don't share your....

Make copies of the rhyme and invite children to add their own illustrations and finish the verse.

2. Give children each a piece of drawing paper and show them how to fold it in half lengthwise once and then again. There should be four equal rectangles when it is unfolded. Have the children number the rectangles from 1 to 4, and then draw pictures in each to tell the story in sequential order from left to right. Ask volunteers to share their drawings and retell the story.

3. List the vegetables that Hare and his family grew. Ask the children to write which of those vegetables each prefers to eat and why. They may illustrate their stories with markers before reading them to partners.

4. Discuss why it is important that friends share equally when dividing items, and why it becomes more difficult when more than two people are involved. _____

■ ■ ■ **(9) CONCEPT:** Not every day in life is perfect.

Literature: *Alexander and the Terrible, Horrible, No Good, Very Bad Day* by J. Viorst (Macmillan, 1972), unpaged.

Listed in: *Best Books for Children* (R. R. Bowker, 1998).

Synopsis: Alexander wakes up to a bad day and things get progressively worse all day long, until he decides that he may run away and go to Australia.

Activities After Read-Aloud:

1. Design a large, blank bulletin board scroll and entitle it "The Best Day Ever." Use it to record all the good things that happen in the classroom each day for one week. Then let the class decide which day was the best one this week and why.

2. Make a list with the children of all the things that happened to Alexander that awful day. Read the list in unison. Then encourage them each to share one thing that happened on their own terrible, horrible, very bad day.

3. Discuss in small groups how Alexander felt when he went to bed that night, and why he probably will have a better day tomorrow. Have the students help plan a good day for Alexander to make up for one "no good" day.

4. On a world map, locate Australia. Then share a picture book such as David Truby's *Take a Trip to Australia* (Watts, 1981) or Rod and Emilie Cooper's *Journey through Australia* (Troll, 1994). Ask the children if running away to another country would be the best answer to Alexander's day. Discuss. _____

■ ■ ■ **(10) CONCEPT:** Learning to be patient is important and has its rewards.

Literature: *Umbrella* by T. Yashima (Viking, 1958), 32 pp.

Listed in: *Best Books for Children* (R. R. Bowker, 1998).

Synopsis: A little girl, born in New York City, eagerly waits for a rainy day so she can use the new boots and umbrella she received for her birthday.

Activities After Read-Aloud:

1. Give each child a piece of construction paper with a large shape of an umbrella. Then have each student cut out the shape and design an umbrella (for themselves or as a gift for a friend or parent). They may use scrap paper and cloth, glitter, markers, glue sticks, and so on. Remind them to be patient as they share the decorative materials.

2. Discuss with the class how hard it is to wait for some things. Using chart paper, brainstorm a list of those activities that require patience (e.g., waiting for a tooth to come out). Then have students each make individual lists of events that demand patience.

3. Divide the students into groups of four. Have each group prepare to dramatize a time when they had to wait for something. Encourage them to discuss strategies for waiting patiently, and include those in the dramatization to be presented to the whole class later.

4. Tell the children that they are going to make something special to eat. Then have the class, with volunteer help if possible, prepare vegetable soup in a crockpot. When it is finally ready, serve and ask the children the following: Was it hard to wait for the soup to be done, when it smelled so deliciously? Was it worth the wait? _____

CURRICULUM STANDARD FOR GRADE TWO: PEOPLE WHO MAKE A DIFFERENCE
(with students keeping social studies journals)

■ ■ ■ **(1) CONCEPT:** Rosa Parks is a brave African American who has played a critical role in promoting civil rights for everyone.

Literature: *A Picture Book of Rosa Parks* by D. Adler (Holiday, 1993), 30 pp.

Listed in: *Best Books for Children* (R. R. Bowker, 1998).

Synopsis: This is the life story of the modest seamstress whose brave stand in 1955 began the Montgomery, Alabama bus strike that helped the civil rights movement in the United States.

Activities After Read-Aloud:

1. Discuss what contributions Parks made to the African Americans in the story and then chart them on the board. Then ask the children to each write a poem in five or six lines about Rosa Parks, using some of the information from the board.

2. Review briefly some of the facts about Parks's life. Then, have the children dramatize a version of the bus episode. First, arrange two rows of chairs (to represent the sides of the bus) and then divide them in the middle (to indicate discrimination). Then choose the "passengers" by gender and tell them they may only sit in their designated section. Finally, select the "bus driver" and one new "passenger" whose bus section is full. After the presentation, discuss with the students their reactions to the episode.

3. Share some of the U.S. stamps that honor deceased Americans like Presidents, inventors, and authors. Then ask the class to design a postage stamp to honor Rosa Parks someday. Finally, have the children each write how and why they would wish to be remembered on a postage stamp.

4. Examine Rosa Parks and Gregory Reed's *Dear Mrs. Parks: A Dialogue with Today's Youth* (Lee & Low, 1996), and read a few of the letters sent to Parks from younger children and the replies Parks sent back. _____

■ ■ ■ **(2) CONCEPT:** George Washington Carver was a great African American scientist whose work helped all of us.

Literature: *A Weed Is a Flower: The Life of George Washington Carver* by Aliki (Simon & Schuster, 1988), unpaged.

Listed in: *Literature for History-Social Science: Kindergarten through Grade Eight* (California Department of Education, 1991).

Synopsis: Carver was a great African American agricultural chemist who discovered many new uses for peanuts, soybeans, and sweet potatoes. He succeeded despite many obstacles.

Activities After Read-Aloud:

1. Brainstorm about the four elements plants need to grow, light, water, air, and nutrients. Discuss how Carver helped people to grow plants by focusing on the four important elements. Then have the children talk and write about how these elements affect plant growth.

2. Use KWL to ask children what they *know* about Carver's life and contributions. Then ask what they *want to know* and record both the "K" and the "W" comments on charts. (When the mini-unit is done, record responses on a third chart headed What We *Learned*.)

3. Divide children into groups of three and have them choose a topic related to Carver's life or his scientific achievements. After the groups have completed their study, have each make a banner with Carver's name and important facts about his life or work. Display the finished banners and hang them around the room.

4. Have the students each write "A Tribute to George Washington Carver." After the first drafts have been edited and revised, give each child special paper on which to make a final copy of the "Tribute" to be posted (or published). _____

■ ■ ■ **(3) CONCEPT:** Delivery of U.S. mail is an important and detailed process.

Literature: *Where Does the Mail Go? A Book about the Postal System* by M. Berger and G. Berger (Discovery Readers, Chelsea House, 1994), 48 pp.

Listed in: *Best Books for Children* (R. R. Bowker, 1998).

Synopsis: Marty writes a letter and drops it into the mailbox; later he writes another letter and puts it into a fax machine. Both ways of sending mail are described in this book about the U.S. Postal Service and its many workers.

Activities After Read-Aloud:

1. Have each child create his or her own book. Each page will have pre-written words on it, describing the process of mail delivery. The student will illustrate each of the pages. When the class is finished, children can each read their stories with a partner.

2. Ask children to each write a letter to their parent(s). Supply each one with writing paper, an envelope, a stamp, and a return mailing label with the school address on it. After children have each finished writing their own letter, they insert it carefully into the envelope, address that envelope, and put the return label and stamp on it. (The letter should announce a forthcoming school event.)

3. Arrange for a visit to the local post office. Have the students bring with them the letters to parents (from Activity Two) so they can drop the letters into the mailbox themselves. The class may possibly get to see the actual processing of the mail before it is delivered to homes and businesses. (If a visit is not possible, have the class take a walking trip to the nearest mailbox.)

4. Share with the class two recent fiction books about the post office: Cynthia Rylant's *Mr. Griggs' Work* (Orchard, 1989), which tells about a postal worker who loves his job, and Catherine Siracusa's *No Mail for Mitchell* (Random, 1990), which describes the adventures of a dog postman who never gets any letters for himself. Both are picture books. _____

■ ■ ■ **(4) CONCEPT:** Personal family history is important.

Literature: *The Patchwork Quilt* by V. Flournoy (Dial, 1985), 32 pp.

Listed in: *Best Books for Children* (R. R. Bowker, 1998).

Synopsis: A young girl named Tanya helps her grandmother make a beautiful quilt using scraps cut from each family member's old clothing. The patchwork quilt tells the family story.

Activities After Read-Aloud:	1. Give children each a square of colored construction paper (5" × 5") and ask them to write their name and draw the cover of their favorite book, both on the square. Use several different colors of paper so that, when the class is finished, the children can paste their individual squares on one large sheet and make a colorful Book Quilt to hang on the board.
	2. Give each student two pieces of white paper (8½" × 11"), and show them how to make a flip book by folding the sheets in half. On the top or title page the children write "The Patchwork Quilt." On the bottom edge of the next half page (offset by one-half to three-fourths inch), the class writes "The grandmother showed she cared by...." On the remaining two flaps (again offset by one-half to three-fourths inch), the class writes "Another way the grandmother cared was by..." and "I care for my family by...." When the sentences have been completed and the flip books are finished, the children may choose to share some of their thoughts.
	3. Discuss that family history has sometimes been shown on an oval-shaped shield, divided into three or four equal sections. Give children each one sheet of construction paper (11" × 14") and have them create their own family shield. In each section can be drawn one clue to a trait about their personal family, e.g., a shamrock to show Irish heritage. On the back of the shield the students must explain why they chose certain traits.
	4. Quilt patterns are often based on geometric designs or patterns. Distribute one plain sheet of paper and one piece of graph paper to each child. Have the children develop individual quilt patterns on the practice paper and then transfer them to the graph paper with markers. _____

■ ■ ■ **(5) CONCEPT:** People in different cultures have different eating habits.

Literature: *How My Parents Learned to Eat* by I. Friedman (Houghton Mifflin, 1987), 32 pp.

Listed in: *Best Books for Children* (R. R. Bowker, 1998).

Synopsis: John, a U.S. sailor, and Aiko, a Japanese girl, meet when John's ship is stationed in Japan. They try in secret to learn each other's eating habits, and finally succeed.

Activities After Read-Aloud:	1. Give children each a simple outline map of the United States and Japan. Have them label the two countries and the Pacific Ocean. Let the class discuss why the food and the ways of eating it might be different in the two countries.
	2. Divide the class into special interest groups to begin researching Japan. One group might develop a list of words and phrases spoken by the Japanese, including simple greetings. A second group might create an illustrated chart of interesting facts about Japan. A third might draw travel posters that invite visitors to Japan. When all the groups have finished, they can share what they have learned.
	3. Discuss chopsticks and forks, as well as Asian food and U.S. food. Display some different chopsticks and forks, and ask the children to write the differences between the two and which one they would prefer to use.
	4. Cook boil-in-a-bag rice for a snack, and have the children learn to eat with chopsticks just as John did in the story. (It is difficult to eat rice with chopsticks unless the rice is sticky or the plate is held close to the mouth.) _____

■ ■ ■ **(6) CONCEPT:** Hand-me-down toys and other mementos can help boys and girls maintain a contact with their family's past.

Literature: *Laura Charlotte* by K. Galbraith (Philomel, 1990).

Listed in: *Best Books for Children* (R. R. Bowker, 1998).

Synopsis: Mama tells Laura the story of Charlotte, the toy elephant made by her grandmother and given to her as a child. It connects Mama to her childhood and it now becomes a gift to Laura to be a part of both their lives.

Activities After Read-Aloud:

1. Discuss what Laura learned about her family from her mother the day she received Charlotte. Then have the children each write what they consider to be the two most important ideas about Laura's family.
2. Ask the children to bring a favorite toy (or other family memento) that their parent(s) have given them. Invite the students to tell stories about their toys and why the toys are important to them. Prepare a one-day-only Toy Fair so all the toys can be properly appreciated.
3. Have each student prepare a story that his or her parent(s) (or even grandparents) often tell about their childhood. Before sharing their stories, the children will draw pictures on white construction paper to illustrate and accompany the personal stories from their families' past.
4. Cut a tree trunk out of brown tagboard and then cut a treetop out of green tagboard. Attach the two to a bulletin board and place on a wall. Ask the children to bring family photographs that can be displayed on the tree. (Be sure that the students write their names on the backs of their photos before pinning them to The Family Tree.) _____

■ ■ ■ **(7) CONCEPT:** Milk is produced by cows and distributed by the dairy industry to markets and to people.

Literature: *The Milk Makers* by G. Gibbons (Macmillan, 1985), 32 pp.

Listed in: *Best Books for Children* (R. R. Bowker, 1998).

Synopsis: The book describes in detail how cows produce milk and how it is processed and delivered daily to stores to supply our dairy needs.

Activities After Read-Aloud:

1. Bring in different forms of cow's milk for taste testing, including powdered milk, homogenized milk, nonfat milk, lactose-free milk, and so on. Set out small numbered paper cups and have each student taste each type of milk. The children then each prepare a secret ballot by writing: "I vote for number _____ because _____." The ballots are collected and counted.
2. Ask each child to select one milk product indicated in the story and write the name of the product (or draw its container) on a piece of paper. Using a web, students will each list five ways of using their chosen milk product.
3. Display several different dairy products other than milk such as yogurt and cheese. Ask students to identify each product and match it with the correct name from a stack of flash cards. After discussion, everyone shares in tasting the milk products.
4. Distribute construction paper, colored chalk, brushes, and small containers of buttermilk to each group of four children. They may either dip the chalk into the buttermilk or brush the paper with buttermilk. Then they use the chalk to create designs. Tell the children as they work what buttermilk is and how it is made and used today. _____

■ ■ ■ **(8) CONCEPT:** After the parents divorce, a child may become part of two families, instead of just one family.

Literature: *Boundless Grace* by M. Hoffman (Dial, 1995), 32 pp.

Listed in: *Best Books for Children* (R. R. Bowker, 1998).

Synopsis: A sequel to *Amazing Grace* (1991), the story describes a trip to The Gambia in Africa taken by Grace and her grandmother to visit Grace's father and his new family.

Activities After Read-Aloud:

1. Since both the illustrator (C. Binch) and the author traveled to The Gambia to insure the accuracy of background details (from trees to foods to lifestyle), have the class chart a description of that country and its people after discussing the book.
2. The stamp on the envelope of the letter sent to Grace from her Papa had a picture of a crocodile on it. Explain to the children that countries often print

stamps showing some of the animals that live there. Then have them each design a United States stamp that has one of our native animals on it. The children must each write briefly the reason for their choice. Stamps may be displayed and should show a variety of animals.

3. Grace decided after visiting her Papa that she would write a story about belonging to two families living in different places. Divide the class into small groups and ask each group to help Grace write her story about families living happily after a divorce but not in the same place. Encourage the groups to read their stories during sharing time.

4. Plan a Family Tea to which each student will bring a relative (a grandparent, if possible). Students can write invitations to the chosen relatives. (This can be a genuine Friday afternoon visiting time, with cookies and punch, or simply a simulation during which children discuss three interesting facts about their extended families.) _____

■ ■ ■ **(9) CONCEPT:** A single-parent household can offer love and compassion despite many struggles, including money problems.

Literature: *A Chair for My Mother* by V. Williams (Greenwillow, 1982), 32 pp.

Listed in: *Best Books for Children* (R. R. Bowker, 1998).

Synopsis: After fire damages their apartment, Rosa, her mother, and her grandmother all work and save their money in a big glass jar until it is full. Then they shop for a comfortable armchair to replace the one lost in the fire. Everyone enjoys the new chair.

Activities After Read-Aloud:
1. Discuss with the children how hard it is to save money for a special reason. Have them write what they are saving their money for at this time. Let them share their goals if they wish, but only after each has written a personal purpose.

2. Ask how each of the characters contributed coins to the glass jar. What did their actions show about the kind of a family they were? Discuss.

3. Tell the children to each choose a new chair for their home and draw a picture of the kind of chair they would select. On the back, they should write the reasons for their choice.

4. Instead of saving their coins in a glass jar, the family could have opened a savings account at a local bank. Discuss why Rosa's family preferred to save their money at home. Was this a wise thing to do? Debate.

5. Encourage the children to hear or read other books about Rosa's family. Vera Williams' *Something Special For Me* (1983) and *Music, Music for Everyone* (1984) also concern saving money in the big glass jar. _____

■ ■ ■ **(10) CONCEPT:** Several different kinds of workers must sometimes cooperate to complete one job.

Literature: *A New Coat for Anna* by H. Ziefert (Knopf, 1986), 40 pp.

Listed in: *Best Books for Children* (R. R. Bowker, 1998).

Synopsis: Anna needs a new winter coat, but her mother has no money. However, Anna's mother finds responsible ways to ask different workers to help make her daughter a new coat.

Activities After Read-Aloud:
1. Give children each a sheet of paper with a circle that has printed in the center: MAKING A COAT. Then have them make a web of all the different workers that helped make Anna's new coat.

2. With the class, develop a definition of the term *teamwork* that includes the kinds of behavior and attitudes that are needed. Encourage children to write on their papers some of the jobs that require teamwork, and later discuss their choices with the class.

3. Divide children into small groups and have each group list community activities that involve teamwork (e.g., managing a holiday parade). Suggest that they

think of different places where they have been in the last week and saw people working together. Ask what activities there suggested that good teamwork was happening. Discuss.

4. Develop as a class some short guidelines for effective teamwork and post these on a chart. Have children read and review them weekly. _____

CURRICULUM STANDARD FOR GRADE THREE: CONTINUITY AND CHANGE
(with students keeping social studies journals)

■ ■ ■ **(1) CONCEPT:** Water is necessary for the survival of all living things.

Literature: *Bringing the Rain to Kapiti Plain* retold by V. Aardema (Dial, 1981), 32 pp.

Listed in: *Best Books for Children* (R. R. Bowker, 1998).

Synopsis: This rhyming book is a folktale from Kenya that uses a cumulative style to tell of animals caught in a drought, and how a young boy brings the rain and so restores life to the Kapiti Plain.

Activities After Read-Aloud:

1. In small groups have the students list all the ways we use water. As a class, develop a large chart of the group responses. Then, one by one, eliminate those uses that we do not need for survival. Discuss the reasons for the exclusion and inclusion of certain uses.

2. Give the children lima bean seeds on wet paper towels to put into plastic baggies. Close the bags and watch for a few days. When the seeds sprout, have the students move them to paper cups filled with dirt and keep them watered. Children must monitor the plants' growth and document how much water was used to water their plants. Discuss how much the amount might be if it were needed for the plains of Kapiti or a farm field in the United States.

3. For homework, on Monday ask the students to keep a week's list of all the ways that water is used (or wasted) in their homes. One week later, have them bring in their lists and let the class discuss ways to conserve water because it is an important resource.

4. Plan a field trip to a local water treatment plant or else assign groups to research the topic in the library media center. Have students draw and write summaries of what they learned about how and why to purify water. _____

■ ■ ■ **(2) CONCEPT:** Pilgrims still come to the United States today for religious freedom, just as they did nearly 400 years ago.

Literature: *Molly's Pilgrim* by B. Cohen (Lothrop, Lee, 1983), 32 pp.

Listed in: *Best Books for Children* (R. R. Bowker, 1998).

Synopsis: Molly, whose Jewish family has emigrated to the United States from Russia, must make a pilgrim doll for a school Thanksgiving assignment. When her mother creates a likeness of Molly in her traditional Russian clothes, Molly is criticized by her classmates until the teacher explains what a pilgrim really is.

Activities After Read-Aloud:

1. Have the children each write how they would feel if they came from a different country and were laughed at and picked on by some of their classmates. Then they may illustrate their stories and paste them together on large pieces of construction paper.

2. Distribute clothespins or popsicle sticks and have children each make their own modern pilgrim doll (boy or girl). They can attach a paper face with eyes, nose, ears, and yarn hair. Clothes can be made from cloth and string, and boots or shoes and hats from construction paper.

3. Discuss with the class the first Thanksgiving and then ask the students to each imagine the foods the Pilgrims and Native Americans shared. Have them draw a scene of that feast.

4. Molly's Mom explains that "it takes all kinds of Pilgrims to make a Thanksgiving." Have the students write what they think is the true meaning of Thanksgiving. Those who wish may share their feelings with the class. _____

■ ■ ■ **(3) CONCEPT:**   Native Americans had great respect for, and a strong bond with, the buffalo.

Literature: *Buffalo Woman* by P. Goble (Macmillan, 1984), 32 pp.

Listed in: *Best Books for Children* (R. R. Bowker, 1998).

Synopsis: This legend from the Plains Indians is about a buffalo that turns into a beautiful girl. When a young warrior marries her, his people reject her. He must then survive several tests before he can be turned into a buffalo and allowed to join the Buffalo Nation of his wife.

Activities After Read-Aloud:

1. Ask the students to list all the possible reasons why the Native Americans regarded the buffalo so highly.

2. Have each child choose a favorite line from the book, and write it on a sentence strip. Collect the strips and let the students arrange the lines to create a class poem. Then have each child illustrate his or her line on a half sheet of paper. The poem and illustrations can be displayed on the board.

3. In cooperative groups, have the students recreate the story settings. They may use plastic models, clay, or other available materials. When the settings are completed, the groups can retell the legend in sequence.

4. Discuss the ending of the story, and then ask the children each to write another story about what happened to the young warrior after he became a buffalo. __

■ ■ ■ **(4) CONCEPT:**   According to legend, wolves are the friends of Native Americans.

Literature: *The Friendly Wolf* by P. Goble and D. Goble (Bradbury, 1974), unpaged.

Listed in: *Best Books for Children* (R. R. Bowker, 1985).

Synopsis: Little Cloud and Bright Eyes are Plains Indian children who get lost in the hills. A wolf befriends them and helps them find their way home. This all happened years ago, but since then wolves and Native Americans have been friends.

Activities After Read-Aloud:

1. Have the children each design a book entitled "The Friendly Wolf," which illustrates, with captions, the main events of the story in sequence. When all books are done, the students may each read theirs with a partner.

2. Review with the students what they already have heard about the wolf from folktales such as "Little Red Riding Hood" and "The Three Little Pigs." Then ask them if they think this story about the wolf is believable or not. Finally, have them complete in writing the sentence: "I liked the story about Little Cloud and Bright Eyes because...."

3. Share with the class some well-illustrated informational books about wolves, such as Emilie Lepthien's *Wolves* (Children's, 1991) and Carol Greene's *Reading about the Grey Wolf* (Enslow, 1993). Then have the class prepare a short list of True Facts about Wolves that can be put on a chart and read.

4. In groups of four, have the students create a legend involving an animal they have seen at the zoo. Later they may share the legends with the class. _____

■ ■ ■ **(5) CONCEPT:**   Designing and building a national memorial takes years of planning and cooperation by many different people.

Literature: *The Lincoln Memorial* by D. Kent (Children's Press, 1996), 30 pp.

Listed in: *Best Books for Children* (R. R. Bowker, 1998).

Synopsis: This account of the design and construction of the Lincoln Memorial in Washington, D.C. documents the numerous difficulties as well as the triumphs of its creation. It is a massive marble building with a large statue of President Abraham Lincoln. It finally opened in 1922.

Activities After Read-Aloud:

1. Have the students create a journal with construction paper covers, and lined notebook sheets stapled together. As they learn about each event in the Memorial's construction, have them document what they believe the architect thought. Encourage them to read and discuss their responses.

2. As a class, have the children list all the events in the book that required cooperation and also list the different people working on the Memorial to get it completed. Then, have students each choose the one person whom they think was the most important in building the Lincoln Memorial and list reasons for their selection.

3. Bring in numerous photographs of the Lincoln Memorial and share them with the students. Let them write a belated class letter to Henry Bacon, the architect who designed the Memorial, telling him what they like best about it and how it attracts nearly three million visitors a year.

4. Divide the children into groups, each of which must choose a famous person in U.S. history. They must then find a location in the country in which to build a memorial to him or her and present reasons for choosing that site. Finally, they must draw or write how the memorial will look. _____

■ ■ ■ **(6) CONCEPT:** The Pilgrims who arrived in 1620 survived with the help of Native Americans like Squanto.

Literature: *Squanto and the First Thanksgiving* by J. Kessel (Carolrhoda, 1983), 48 pp.

Listed in: *Best Books for Children* (R. R. Bowker, 1998).

Synopsis: Born near Plymouth, Massachusetts, Squanto lived for years in England, where he learned to speak English. He came home in 1619 and, two years later, met the Pilgrims, who were starving after their first winter. He showed them how to plant corn and where to hunt and fish. The harvest that year led to the first New England Thanksgiving, to which the Pilgrims invited their Native American friends for a three-day festival.

Activities After Read-Aloud:

1. In small groups, have the students choose one important event from the story, write a script, and prepare a readers theater presentation.

2. Compile a class list of the most important things that Squanto did to help the Pilgrims survive.

3. Have the students each create new history to reflect what would have happened to the Pilgrims if Squanto had *not* helped them during that critical year. Reinforce the importance of Squanto's role in the establishment of a successful colony in New England.

4. Squanto could speak English, just as the Pilgrims did. Let each student write how else they could have communicated if they did not speak the same language. Have the children share their solutions. _____

■ ■ ■ **(7) CONCEPT:** Cities and towns must be planned carefully to meet the needs of the people who will be living there.

Literature: *Roxaboxen* by A. McLerran (Lothrop, 1991), 32 pp.

Listed in: *Best Books for Children* (R. R. Bowker, 1998).

Synopsis: Marian, her sisters, and their friends live in the desert. They create an imaginary town on a hill with rocks and wooden boxes.

Activities After Read-Aloud:

1. Contact Rand McNally and Company (8255 N. Central Park, Skokie, IL, 60076) to say that the class is studying the community and ask if the company will

send some one-use cameras. After the cameras arrive, take the class on a walking trip and let students take pictures of the houses and buildings in the neighborhood. Then send the cameras back to the company and Rand McNally will create a map for the class.

2. Have the children, in cooperative groups, create their own imaginary town, using construction paper, markers or crayons, empty milk cartons of various sizes (clean and dry), and other art materials. Give each group a 2' × 3' piece of cardboard or tagboard on which to build their town. The Designated Writer in each group can prepare a paragraph describing the town and how it got its name.

3. Reread the story, reminding the children to focus on the illustrations. Ask "Where do you think the story takes place?" Then, share some books about the desert, e.g., Ron Hirschi's *Desert* (Bantam, 1992) and Elsa Posell's *Deserts* (Children's Press, 1982). Finally, help the class fill out a web with facts about deserts.

4. Help the class plan an ideal city on the planet Mars for the not-too-distant future. _____

■ ■ ■ **(8) CONCEPT:** Brave men on earth and the Big Dipper in the sky helped lead slaves to freedom on the Underground Railroad before the American Civil War.

Literature: *The Drinking Gourd* by F. Mongo (Harper, 1970), 64 pp.

Listed in: *Best Books for Children* (R. R. Bowker, 1998).

Synopsis: A New England white boy helps an escaping black family of runaway slaves follow the drinking gourd (Big Dipper). He becomes, for a short time, a part of the Underground Railroad that led slaves to freedom in Canada.

Activities After Read-Aloud:

1. Have the children recreate drinking gourds on dark blue construction papers, using silver stars. Remind the class that the Big Dipper is a constellation and has seven stars.

2. Let each child pretend that he or she is Tommy, and ask the students to write what they think happened the day after Tommy's adventure.

3. Reflect with the students briefly on whether or not they would have told the Marshal that they had found the runaways. Then have them each write the reason for their decision.

4. Distribute outline maps of the United States, showing only state lines. Then provide books and encyclopedias that show the Underground Railroad, and have the class indicate on their maps the routes that some runaways took to go North. _____

■ ■ ■ **(9) CONCEPT:** Benjamin Banneker was the first important African American astronomer and mathematician.

Literature: *Dear Benjamin Banneker* by A. Pinkney (Harcourt, 1994), 32 pp.

Listed in: *Best Books for Children* (R. R. Bowker, 1998).

Synopsis: Born into a family of freed slaves, Banneker taught himself mathematics and astronomy. He published annual almanacs for several years, sending a copy of the first one to Secretary of State Thomas Jefferson, who forwarded it to the Royal Academy of Sciences in Paris. He was also a surveyor.

Activities After Read-Aloud:

1. Have the children pretend that they lived back in the 1700s and have them write letters to Banneker, asking about his childhood, his work in helping to lay out the boundaries of the District of Columbia, his special wood clock, his math skills, and anything else they would like to know about him.

2. Develop with the class a story plot of the book. Include the main character(s), the setting, the problem, and the solution.

3. Check out from the library media center copies of almanacs. Have the children, in groups, peruse a copy. Let each student select one interesting fact, copy it,

and explain why he or she chose it. (In his almanac, Banneker predicted the weather and calculated the tides.)

4. Tell the class that Banneker's friend Jefferson once wrote that "all men are created equal." Then have the students each write a paragraph telling why they think that all people have equal rights in the United States. Later, discuss if all members in a family, community, or school have equal rights and ask, "Why?" or "Why not?" Stress that with equal rights come responsibilities. _____

■ ■ ■ **(10) CONCEPT:**   Neighborhoods change over the years.

Literature: *The House on Maple Street* by B. Pryor (Morrow, 1987), 32 pp.

Listed in: *Best Books for Children* (R. R. Bowker, 1998).

Synopsis: When their family moves to Maple Street, Jenny and Chris find a small china cup and begin a historic exploration of their home and the neighborhood. They learn that many people have passed by the house or lived there during the last 300 years.

Activities After Read-Aloud:

1. Develop with the class a simple timeline, starting with the plain forest and ending with the house on Maple Street. Then have the students individually make personal timelines and later label and illustrate events on their timelines.

2. Distribute to each child two sheets of unlined paper on which eight-inch circles have been drawn. One circle is to have one one-eighth section cut out. The second circle is marked with eight sections, on each of which the child must write one important event from the story. Circles are cut out, holes poked in the middle of each circle, a brad attached, and the "pie" turns. Students can read and discuss their choices.

3. Draw the Old House and make copies for each child. Then have the students each draw how they think the house will look as the years go by, next to or below the Old House. They may add windows, extra stories, sidewalks, shrubbery, and so forth.

4. Have the children each bring in a discarded shoebox. Give them construction paper, markers, glue sticks, and other materials to help them build a Remodeled House at 107 Maple Street. _____

CHILDREN'S LITERATURE CITED

Kindergarten

Brett, J. (reteller)   *Goldilocks and the Three Bears* (Dodd, 1987).
Brown, M.   *Arthur's New Puppy* (Little, Brown, 1993).
Carricks, C.   *Patrick's Dinosaurs* (Houghton Mifflin, 1983).
Crews, D.   *School Bus* (Greenwillow, 1984).
Flack, M.   *The Story about Ping* (Puffin, 1933).
Havill, J.   *Jamaica's Find* (Houghton Mifflin, 1986).
Henkes, K.   *Lilly's Purple Plastic Purse* (Greenwillow, 1996).
Lobel, A.   *Frog and Toad Are Friends* (Harper, 1970).
Robart, R.   *The Cake That Mack Ate* (Little, Brown, 1991).
Sendak, M.   *Pierre* (Harper, 1962).

Grade One

Bartone, E.   *Peppe the Lamplighter* (Lothrop, 1993).
Caudill, R.   *Did You Carry the Flag Today, Charley?* (Holt, 1966).
Cooney, B.   *Miss Rumphius* (Puffin, 1982).
Hoban, R.   *Bargain for Frances* (Harper, 1970).
Keats, E.   *The Snowy Day* (Puffin, 1962).
Levitin, S.   *Nine for California* (Orchard, 1996).
Rylant, C.   *When I Was Young in the Mountains* (Dutton, 1982).
Stevens, J.   *Tops and Bottoms* (Scholastic, 1995).
Viorst, J.   *Alexander and the Terrible, Horrible, No Good, Very Bad Day* (Macmillan, 1972).
Yashima, T.   *Umbrella* (Viking, 1958).

Grade Two

Adler, D.   *A Picture Book of Rosa Parks* (Holiday, 1993).

Aliki.   *A Weed Is a Flower: The Life of George Washington Carver* (Simon & Schuster, 1988).

Berger, M. & Berger, G.   *Where Does the Mail Go: A Book about the Postal System* (Chelsea House, 1994).

Flournoy, V.   *The Patchwork Quilt* (Dial, 1985).

Friedman, I.   *How My Parents Learned to Eat* (Houghton Mifflin, 1987).

Galbraith, K.   *Laura Charlotte* (Philomel, 1990).

Gibbons, G.   *The Milk Makers* (Macmillan, 1985).

Hoffman, M.   *Boundless Grace* (Dial, 1995).

Williams, V.   *A Chair for My Mother* (Greenwillow, 1982).

Ziefert, H.   *A New Coat for Anna* (Knopf, 1986).

Grade Three

Aardema, V. (reteller)   *Bringing the Rain to Kapiti Plain* (Dial, 1981).

Cohen, B.   *Molly's Pilgrim* (Lothrop, Lee, 1983).

Goble, P.   *Buffalo Woman* (Macmillan, 1984).

Goble, P. & Goble, D.   *The Friendly Wolf* (Bradbury, 1974).

Kent, D.   *The Lincoln Memorial* (Children's Press, 1996).

Kessel, J.   *Squanto and the First Thanksgiving* (Carolrhoda, 1983).

McLerran, A.   *Roxaboxen* (Lothrop, 1991).

Mongo, F.   *The Drinking Gourd* (Harper, 1970).

Pinkney, A.   *Dear Benjamin Banneker* (Harcourt, 1994).

Pryor, B.   *The House on Maple Street* (Morrow, 1987).

RECENT AND RECOMMENDED: RELATED BOOKS FOR ADDITIONAL READING

The Child

(Areas included are: self-concept and self-esteem, personal character traits and human values, fantast and imagination, and emotions.)

Cech, J.   *Django* (Four Winds, 1994).
> A young boy named Django learns to play a magic fiddle and is able to attract the animals from the swamps near his Florida home. He becomes a legend after he saves the animals during a storm.

Climo, S.   *The Korean Cinderella* (HarperCollins, 1993).
> In this version, a frog, an ox, and some sparrows replace the traditional godmother and successfully help Pear Blossom gain happiness.

Cooper, W.   *The Bear Under the Stairs* (Dial, 1993).
> William fears the hungry bear that he imagines living in the closet and so feeds it everyday to keep it happy. When his mother notices the terrible smell of old food coming from the closet, William tells her of his fear and so is able to overcome it.

Grimm, J. & Grimm, W.   *The Golden Goose* (Farrar, Strauss, 1995).
> Anyone who touches the golden goose gets stuck and must follow the simple-minded owner. The more people who get stuck, the sillier the parade in this famous folktale.

Hess, D.   *Wilson Sat Alone* (Simon & Schuster, 1994).
> Wilson is a lonely child who never gets involved with his classmates. One day, however, a new girl in the class shows him how to join in the fun with the other children.

Johnston, T.   *The Iguana Brothers* (Scholastic, 1995).
> Two iguanas named Dom and Tom live in Mexico and search for identify, friendship, and food. Some Spanish words are used meaningfully in the story.

Martin, J. & Marx, P.   *Now Everybody Really Hates Me!* (HarperCollins, 1993).
> Patti is sent to her room for fussing and hitting her brother during his birthday party. There she fantasizes about escaping, until her parents carry her back for cake and ice cream.

Pinkney, B.   *JoJo's Flying Side Kick* (Simon & Schuster, 1995).
> Although JoJo's Tae Kwon Do teacher says JoJo is ready to try for her yellow belt, JoJo is not so sure. Family and friends help her overcome her fears.

Pomerantz, C. *Halfway to Your House* (Greenwillow, 1993).

Whimsical times in the life of a young child are described in thirty short, appealing poems.

Rogers, J. *Best Friends Sleep Over* (Scholastic, 1993).

A fantasy about a group of large jungle animals that has a slumber party. Away from home for the first time is Gilbert Gorilla, who gets the support of his friends and so has a memorable evening.

Simard, R. *The Magic Boot* (Annick Press, 1995).

A legend about the origins of Italy, it tells how a young boy with very large feet was given a pair of magical boots that grew larger and larger every time they touched water.

Wood, A. *The Napping House Wakes Up* (Harcourt, 1994).

A sequel to *The Napping House* (1984), this cumulative story in a pop-up book describes the napping house occupants as they wake up. The illustrations move from blue to yellow as the sun rises.

The Child's Home and Family

(Areas included are family relationships, daily experiences, food, clothing, home and shelter, and family traditions/cultural traditions.)

Beard, D. *The Pumpkin Man from Piney Creek* (Simon & Schuster, 1995).

In nineteenth-century rural America, young Hattie lives on a pumpkin farm and wants very much to carve her favorite pumpkin into a jack-o'-lantern. She gets her wish and a recipe for pumpkin pie, too.

Best, C. *Taxi! Taxi!* (Little, Brown, 1994).

Tina's father (who does not live with her and her mother) drives a taxi. One Sunday, Tina and her father share an outing through the city and out into the country. Some Spanish words are included.

Calmenson, S. *Hotter than a Hot Dog* (Little, Brown, 1994).

On a very hot summer day in a large city, a little girl and her grandmother take the train to the beach for a pleasant family outing.

Ernst, L. *The Luckiest Kid on the Planet* (Bradbury, 1994).

Lucky Morgenstern thinks he is, indeed, the luckiest kid until he learns one day that his real name is Herbert. His luck seems to change until he discovers the one thing that makes him especially lucky—his grandfather, who is his best friend.

Franklin, K. *The Shepherd Boy* (Atheneum, 1994).

A Navajo boy must tend a flock of fifty sheep for the summer. When a lamb is missing one day, the boy must find it before nightfall.

Hartmann, W. *All the Magic in the World* (Dutton, 1993).

Set in South Africa, the story is about children at play, especially Lena and her friends, who learn the magic of play from an odd-job man named Joseph. The story conveys the universal message about human relationships.

Johnson, A. *Julius* (Orchard, 1993).

Maya receives an Alaskan pig as a gift from her Granddaddy. She includes Julius in her daily activities and even teaches him manners.

MacLachlan, P. *What You Know First* (HarperCollins, 1995).

Sadly, a young girl prepares to leave her prairie home for a new family home on the coast. She recollects her present life as her father reminds her that "what you know first stays with you."

Mitchell, R. *Hue Boy* (Dial, 1993).

A young Caribbean boy tries to grow taller. He is teased for being too short, but no solution works until his father returns home. Then Hue Boy learns to walk tall with the guidance of his family.

Russo, M. *Trade-in Mother* (Greenwillow, 1993).

Max is frustrated because he cannot get his way with his mother. So he outlines all the mothers who could replace her. She, however, deals with the common dilemma wisely and calmly.

Wells, R. *Lucy Comes to Stay* (Dial, 1994).

> Mary Elizabeth helps care for a newborn puppy named Lucy and learns that it is unpredictable and humorous. There are mini-chapters.

Zalben, J. *Pearl Plants a Tree* (Simon & Schuster, 1995).

> Pearl plants an apple seed, as her immigrant grandfather had done. Later, Grandpa helps her plant her small tree and they picnic nearby, thinking of future generations. The book includes a summary of tree-planting holidays worldwide.

The Child's Community

(Areas included are friendships, celebrations, outings, and new encounters.)

Bunting, E. *Cheyenne Again* (Clarion, 1995).

> Young Bull is taken to a Native American reservation school where nothing familiar is left to him. He learns to cope by retaining the Cheyenne ideals within himself while appearing to change on the outside.

Finchler, J. *Miss Malarkey Doesn't Live in Room 10* (Walker, 1995).

> A first-grader is shocked when his teacher moves into his apartment building because he had believed that teachers live at school.

Kastner, J. *Snake Hunt* (Four Winds, 1993).

> After Granddad tells of his adventures wrestling a rattlesnake and eating it in a stew, his granddaughter wants to go snake hunting also. A day in the woods develops special bonding between the two characters.

Krull, K. *Maria Molina and the Days of the Dead* (Macmillan, 1994).

> Maria and her family celebrate the Days of the Dead, which honor the family members who have died. When the family moves from Mexico to the United States, there is a comparison of their customs with U.S. Halloween customs.

Littlesugar, A. *Josiah True and the Art Maker* (Simon & Schuster, 1995).

> A woman artist travels from town to town, painting portraits. Young Josiah is inspired when she stays with his family. Later, she gives him his own paintbrush to encourage a possible career.

Lucas, B. *Snowed In* (Bradbury, 1993).

> Luke, Grace, and their parents are often snowed in on their Wyoming farm during the winter. This seasonal event requires months of preparation.

McDonald, M. *Insects Are My Life* (Orchard, 1995).

> Amanda develops a strong interest in bugs that gets her into trouble at home and at school. However, she soon finds a friend who is also fascinated by an unusual hobby—reptiles!

McPhail, D. *Santa's Book of Names* (Little, Brown, 1993).

> Edward cannot read so when Santa leaves his "Book of Names" at Edward's house, the boy must use his alphabet and phonics skills to help Santa. Edward's success in signaling Santa and then decoding the names of the children and their gifts should encourage other nonreaders to learn.

Moore, L. *I Never Did That Before* (Atheneum, 1995).

> These fourteen poems are linked to the theme of discovery—a child doing something for the very first time. Illustrations are whimsical and warm.

Pinkney, A. *Seven Candles for Kwanzaa* (Dial, 1993).

> Kwanzaa is a seven-day harvest festival celebrated by many African Americans. The simple text describes one family's daily candlelighting ritual for the seven principles of Kwanzaa.

Pinkney, G. *The Sunday Outing* (Dial, 1994).

> Every Sunday, Ernestine and her great-aunt go to the station to watch the trains. She wants to visit her birthplace in North Carolina, so her family works together to realize the girl's wish.

Rattigan, J. *Dumpling Soup* (Little, Brown, 1993).

> Marisa tries to make dumplings for her racially and culturally mixed, extended family, The story tells of the customs surrounding a New Year's celebration in Hawaii. Elements of five different languages and cultures are presented.

The Child's World

(Areas included are seasons and weather, plants and animals, environments, and patterns [colors, numbers, sizes, and shapes.])

Casey, D. *Weather Everywhere* (Macmillan, 1995).

> A simple and clear text, together with diagrams and photographs, introduces the many factors that create weather and climate everywhere.

Dugan, B. *Leaving Home with a Pickle Jar* (Greenwillow, 1993).

> A child, his mother, and sister must move from an urban neighborhood to a country home in Minnesota. He takes along a grasshopper in a pickle jar to help him adjust to the move.

Evans, D. & Williams, C. *Color and Light* (Scholastic, 1993).

> An activity book introduces the properties of color and light to young children. Color photographs give visual directions for completing experiments.

Falwell, C. *Feast for 10* (Clarion, 1993).

> In preparation for a feast, the family goes grocery shopping and the readers can count along.

Franklin, K. *When the Monkeys Came Back* (Atheneum, 1994).

> When some of the woodland in Central America is cut down, the monkeys disappear. So a mother and her children spend a lifetime restoring the forest. (Editions available in English and Spanish.)

Garland, S. *The Summer Sands* (Harcourt, 1995).

> The book tells how Christmas trees are recycled to restore sand dunes destroyed by storms. Community efforts, especially those of one family, are described.

Hansard, P. *A Field Full of Horses* (Candlewick, 1994).

> During a walk on a farm, the narrator offers interesting facts about horses. Helpful captions accompany the pictures.

Havill, J. *Sato and the Elephants* (Lothrop, 1993).

> Sato wants to become a master ivory carver until he finds a bullet lodged in a piece of ivory on which he is working. The text looks at elephants and other endangered species.

Machotka, H. *Outstanding Outsides* (Morrow, 1993).

> Each close-up photo asks the reader to guess the animal from its body covering. The following page then shows the entire animal and offers simple information about its covering (fur, feathers, scales, or shell).

Rocklin, J. *Musical Chairs and Dancing Bears* (Holt, 1993).

> The story is set at a birthday party. Ten bears dance the polka, counting backwards as they are eliminated from a game of musical chairs.

Stolz, M. *Say Something* (HarperCollins, 1993).

> A prose poem about nature, suggesting comments and queries that will encourage young children to reach their own conclusions. Illustrations are both imaginative and realistic.

Taylor, D. *Nature's Creatures of the Dark* (Dial, 1993).

> This pop-up book glows in the dark. A small, folded flap on the right of each spread gives the creature's name and some interesting facts about it, and then unfolds to more pictures.

INDEX OF
CHILDREN'S LITERATURE